An American Country Kitchen

An American Country Kitchen

Recipes and Photos
by Marion Ham

Drawings
by Carolyn Ringland

An Allen D. Bragdon Book

SMITHMARK

TO
BARBARA LYNN HAM

WITH LOVE

EDITORIAL PRODUCTION
Allen D. Bragdon Publishers, Inc
252 Great Western Road
South Yarmouth, MA 02664

Editor in Chief—Allen D. Bragdon
Recipes & Photos—Marion N. Ham
Illustrations—Carolyn Ringland
Consulting Editor—Jeanne A. Voltz
Editor—Amanda Claiborne
Designer—Conrad Warre
Layout Associate—Michael Eastman
Jacket Design—For Art Sake, Inc.
Jacket Art—Marieluise Hutchinson

ACKNOWLEDGMENTS
Marion Ham would like to thank the following individuals: Barbara Lynn Ham for testing and creating recipes, and for cooking at Quail Hill; Marion Ritter, Eleanor B. Warren and Madeline Williams for the use of antiques from their collection for photography; Fran Crampton for reviewing recipes; and Ruth J. Christoffers for custom flowers and plants. The editors would like to acknowledge contributions made by the following individuals and other sources:

Arco Publishing, Inc. for permission to reprint illustrations and text from *Mitton's Practical Modern Herbal* © 1976, 1982 by F. and V. Mitton, artwork © 1976, 1982 by W. Foulsham & Co., Ltd. in "The Identification of Herbs and Spices" in Chapter 8; The Greene County Cooperative Extension Office and Professor Raymond T. Fox, Professor of Floriculture, College of Agriculture and Life Sciences, Cornell University for collecting natural materials for dried bouquets in Chapter 13; C. M. Offray and Son, Inc. for

"Gift Bows" in Chapter 14; Mark Sherman for preparing the material on wrapping and packing for Chapter 14; Carol Winter for drawing the how-to diagrams for Chapter 14; Star Market Co., 625 Mt. Auburn Street, Cambridge, MA 02138 for permission to excerpt material from the "Nutrition Guide for Fruits and Vegetables" by Joyce A. Nettleton in "Consumer's Guide to Selecting Fresh Produce" in the Appendix; Susan Rhodes for proofreading; Bookbuilders, Ltd. for film.

First published as
"Gifts From A Country Kitchen".
This edition published in 1995 by
SMITHMARK Publishers Inc.,
16 East 32nd Street,
New York, NY 10016.

SMITHMARK books are available for bulk purchase for sales promotion and premium use. For details write or call the manager of special sales, SMITHMARK Publishers Inc., 16 East 32nd Street, New York, NY 10016 (212) 532-6600.

ISBN 0-8317-3886-3

Printed in South Korea

10 9 8 7 6 5 4 3 2 1

CONTENTS

EDITOR'S INTRODUCTION

The recipes and decorative ideas in this very personal collection have been time-tested in family homes where holidays are celebrated with exuberance and love. Marion Ham—who compiled the recipes and took the photographs—understands the warm and wonderful joy of gathering, cooking, baking, and putting a pretty touch on food for celebrating with family and friends. She has lived the part with her husband, and with her four children—now in their twenties. She knows, too, the pitfalls in tackling creative kitchen projects that are too tricky, especially during the hectic holiday times. For that reason, simplicity and reliability were important criteria when she assembled this collection. To further aid the harried cook, Marion included the yield information and preparation time for each recipe.

Many of these recipes were passed down from grandmothers and great-grandmothers. Others, tasted at friends' houses, were gifts from them. Still others evolved from ideas jotted down here and there when an idea seemed interesting; and were included in the book when they proved good enough to survive as part of the menu at Quail Hill Farm in Limerick, Maine—where Marion conducts summer workshops in hooking primitive rugs.

Our guess is that many of the old-fashioned recipes in this collection will resemble some that your own grandmother made part of her holiday traditions—treats almost forgotten. Other recipes reproduce unusual regional or old-time dishes rescued from oblivion. (You almost never see a recipe for pork cake these days, for example, but it is here—an inexpensive but festive cake for wintertime occasions.)

The marvelously creative, but inexpensive, wrappings, trappings, garnishes, and gift-presentation ideas that the Swedish-American artist, Lynn Ringland, has invented, lend a new dimension to the recipes. Lynn, like Marion, understands the practical needs and unique joy of creative activity in a family context. Her husband and two daughters don't simply stand back in awe-struck admiration of her creative energy and talent—they contribute however they can. Whether Lynn is designing, baking, and decorating the trimmings for a 100% edible Christmas tree, or creating hollow Easter eggs of gingerbread decorated inside and out like Fabergé jewels—whatever Lynn undertakes will bring a smile to the lips and a sparkle to the eyes of someone.

She and Marion can do wonders with a scrap of ribbon, a cheery, store-bought dishcloth, colorful tissue paper, dime-store baskets, and yard-sale bottles. They tell you, for example, when and how to tuck a sprig of evergreen in a gift tie, or how to make a modest gift look special with a wooden spoon stuck in the bow. And every idea is illustrated with one of Lynn's charming color drawings.

As a further boost to your own creativity, the chapter on "Wrapping and Packing" includes step-by-step instructions for tying fancy ribbon bows, and making cheery gift wraps. There are plans for making a bright-red Scandinavian wooden sled that you can stand behind and push along like a scooter. On the day before Christmas, you can pile it high with gifts for your neighbors, and then—after the children have delivered them—it can start its life as a cherished heirloom toy for a child.

Marion and Lynn are both giving people who know that life is too short not to work their hardest and give their best to those they love and trust. They have a twinkle in their hearts, too. Who else would think to give someone homey Podunk Gingerbread for a birthday celebration, and elegant, cream-filled, Lace Cookies a month later for an anniversary. When they see a beautiful old jar on a thrift shop's back shelf, or when they're putting up a traditional pumpkin pickle on a crisp fall day, they remember the neighbor who so willingly lent his new power mower, or the babysitter who came on a moment's notice. Then they can't rest until they have washed the jar clean, filled it with the spicy pickle, and quietly left it just inside a door with a note.

When it's time to celebrate, the whole house can become a holiday decoration—with a wreath, swag, or centerpiece for every door, window, mantel, and table. Even the outdoors can be decorated brightly. Hang a suet-filled grapefruit in a tree, and celebrate your feathered friends as they swoop down on their holiday treats. Their flashing color and motion engage the attention and curiosity of young children, too, encouraging them to learn more.

The chapter engagingly called "Little Hands Helping" demonstrates Marion's understanding of the very substance of the holidays. Children want to join in the busy activities of getting a house ready for important, exciting people like Santa and an "Uncle George" who brings surprises and always has projects to keep secret from the grown-ups to enliven the season. But a busy parent must assign to little fingers only the tasks that they can accomplish with minimum guidance, muss, and fuss. For example, set a couple of small children free—well, free within clearly defined limits—with an inkpad, paper, and colored pencils for thumb-printing. Their own thumbs are the ever-ready patterns to decorate stationery, cards for grandmas and other friends, or placecards to help Mom and Dad with a holiday party meal.

Party menus for grand-scale dinners, the kind of feasts that you serve proudly on Thanksgiving and Christmas, for an authentic Hanukkah meal, and for an elegant luncheon, are here to help you make decisions on menus and serving. The menus are festive, but capitalize on homey, old-fashioned dishes that everybody loves. Another chapter supplies recipes for cheery beverages for the simplest of all holiday parties—the open house.

In addition to Marion's recipes and photos, and Lynn's creative ideas and drawings, this book provides the home cook and gift-maker with a wide variety of practical resources. There is at least one in almost every chapter. For example, a chart in Chapter 1 shows how to gauge the temperature of sugar syrup for making candies when you don't have a thermometer. Chapter 2 has a table of tips for baking yeast breads that diagnoses problems and provides the solutions. Chapter 3 has a similar table for pie crust, plus step-by-step color photographs that show how to decorate cakes and cookies with icing. Another series of color photographs in Chapter 4 illustrates each step in constructing a gingerbread house. "Creative Canning," in Chapter 5, explains all you'll need to know to put up your own jams, jellies, pickles, and relishes. In the same chapter, instructions and illustrations demonstrate how to make calico "bonnets" to turn the filled jars into attractive gifts. "The Frozen Harvest," in Chapter 6, offers handy tips on using your freezer to preserve the bounty of summer.

In Chapter 14, an alphabetical table of freshness and nutrition information for over 75 fruits and vegetables helps you select the best fresh produce at its peak. If you grow your own produce, see the yield chart for vegetables in Chapter 6, to help you decide how much of which vegetables to plant. In Chapter 13, flower-fanciers will find instructions for forcing spring flowers in winter and for collecting natural materials for dried bouquets. To help you entertain elegantly, suggested table settings and layouts are illustrated for the formal dinner and buffets in Chapter 10. Intricate napkin folds are also shown there in step-by-step drawings. Directions for spectacular ice containers for wines and spirits to put the finishing touch on your holiday table are given in Chapter 11. Chapter 8 includes a five-page chart illustrating 40 herbs in full color, including all the ones mentioned in the recipes. Just for fun, the herb chart also offers bits of lore and folk beliefs about the medicinal and other non-culinary properties of each herb. In the last pages of the book, Lynn has provided designs for over a dozen different personalized tags, labels, etc. for you to reproduce and color yourself.

Reading this book and studying the pictures can put you "in the spirit," as children sometimes call that very special feeling that comes on as the holidays approach. The spirit hits suddenly, like a fever, but it's a delicious, happy aura of anticipation that grabs your heart and speeds up your feet. It makes a small child want to squeal with joy, and an adult want to race around prettying up the house, baking cookies, and hiding surprise packages for this or that member of the family.

We hope this book will become a helpful partner in your planning for the holidays, and will join you in your effort to bring a treat to someone from your kitchen on any day of the year.

CANDIES AND COMFITS

Arranged on an antique tablecloth of Cluny lace is a tempting assortment of homemade candies. Clockwise from lower left, they are: Rainbow Crystals, Chocolate-dipped Cherries, Salted Oven Pecans, Cherry Chocolate Morsels, Spiced Nuts, Peanut Butter Buckeyes, Chocolate-dipped Dried Apricots, Chocolate-dipped Strawberries, and Candied Fruit Peel (in green Depression glass).

1

Homemade candies are interesting to prepare and pure magic in the way a few simple ingredients are transformed into professional-looking delicacies. Only the best commercial candies can duplicate the authentic richness and flavor of homemade creations made with real butter, cream, fruits, and nuts. Home-salted and candied nuts, too, are so very different from commercial snack foods that they will become prized gifts.

For all their beauty, candies are relatively simple to make. For best results use a candy thermometer to gauge temperature accurately. You can also use the cold-water test described in this chapter, but it is not as precise. If your thermometer's been jangling around in a kitchen drawer for a year or two, it's probably best to test it before making a batch of candy. Immerse it in a pan of water and gradually bring the water to a boil. Allow it to boil for 10 minutes—temperature should read 212°F at sea level, and one degree less for every 500 feet in altitude.

Before plunging your thermometer in hot syrup, warm it gradually.

One time-honored caution: candy is best made in dry weather. So if the humidity is high, heat the syrup two degrees higher than called for to compensate for increased moisture in the air.

Candies should be cooked in heavy saucepans of the capacity called for in each recipe. Thick metal distributes heat from the flame or coil so the syrup is less likely to burn on the hot-spot. The liquid will expand as it boils and bubble up to two or three times its original volume when cold. Use a long-handled wooden spoon because the liquid is likely to spatter.

A clean pastry brush and a cup of cold water also come in handy to wash sugar crystals off the sides of the pan. Crystals, while not the end of the world, are a problem to the home candy-maker. To prevent them from forming in candy, dissolve sugar in liquid *before* heating. As the mixture cooks, stir slowly and in one direction only, being careful not to pick up crystals as they form on the sides of the pan.

Candy making is a science—changing a liquid (sugar syrup) into a solid—so be sure to follow heating, working, and shaping instructions carefully. With the recipes here, and attention to the details of making candies, your holiday creations can be cheerfully impressive, and will give you a well-earned sense of accomplishment.

Fruit and Nut Divinity

Makes 1 pound
Preparation time: 1 hour

3 cups sugar
1 cup light corn syrup
1 cup water
3 egg whites, beaten stiff
1 teaspoon vanilla
½ cup chopped nuts
¾ cup candied fruit

In a 2-quart saucepan combine sugar, corn syrup, and water. Cook, stirring, until sugar dissolves. Then cook to hard-ball stage (260°F). Pour syrup in a thin stream into beaten egg whites, beating at medium speed until mixture begins to thicken. Add vanilla, candied fruit, and nuts. Then beat with wooden spoon, lifting high to incorporate air until candy is very stiff. Pour into buttered square pan to cool. Cut into squares. Let dry until firm and wrap individually in waxed paper or store in a tightly covered tin.

The fruits and nuts in a snowy white base make a most festive looking Christmas candy. Place in small covered apothecary jars for giving or arrange on a dish and cover with plastic film. For a party, serve in small petit-four paper cups on a cut glass dish topped with a sprig of holly leaves.

Candied Fruit Peel

Makes ¼ pound
Preparation time: 30 minutes
Drying time: 8 hours or overnight

    1 grapefruit peel or 2 orange peels
      Water
      Sugar

Candied Fruit Peel is a delightful garnish to use on cakes, pies, puddings, etc. It is also a refreshing candy after a meal.

Remove white pith from rinds and cut peel into thin strips about ¼-inch wide. Place in saucepan and cover with cold water. Bring to boiling point, drain, and repeat process three times.

Dissolve ½ cup sugar in ½ cup water; add peel and boil until all syrup has been absorbed. Cool, roll in granulated sugar, and spread to dry.

Wrap candy—firecracker-fashion—in yellow cellophane and tie both ends with lime-colored ribbon. For a truly elegant wrapping use a salvaged pale blue Tiffany box (or your local best). Line the box with foil and pile in the candied peel. A small, white fork might be placed in with the peel.

Candied Nuts

Makes ½ pound
Preparation time: 20 minutes
Baking time: 30 minutes
Drying time: 1 hour

    1 egg white
    ½ cup sugar
    1 teaspoon salt
    ½ pound (2 cups) pecan or walnut
      meats
    ⅔ cup butter

Preheat oven to 300°F. Beat egg white until very stiff; add sugar and salt. Fold in nuts. Melt butter in shallow baking dish or pie plate; add nut mixture and bake 30 minutes, stirring several times. Remove nuts from oven and spread on brown paper to dry. Store in airtight container.

Make small packets of nuts, using colorful nylon net, and tie with contrasting ribbon. Tie on a honey dipper, pie dough cutter, or salt/nut spoon and hang on your tree for a visiting friend.

Spiced Nuts

Makes 4 cups nuts
Preparation time: 30 minutes

    1 pound (4 cups) walnut or pecan
      halves (or mixed)
    1 cup butter
    3 cups confectioners sugar
    2 tablespoons nutmeg
    2 tablespoons cloves
    2 tablespoons cinnamon

In heavy skillet toast nuts and butter over low heat for 20 minutes, stirring frequently until lightly browned. Mix together the remaining ingredients in a paper bag. Remove nuts from pan and drain on paper towels. Toss nuts with other ingredients in paper bag until generously coated. Turn into a sieve or colander to shake off excess coating. Cool and store in a covered container.

Pile these nuts into a small wooden box (available from craft supply stores); then tie a deep rust-colored ribbon around the box and tuck in a few green sprigs.

Southern Penuche

Makes thirty 1-inch pieces
Preparation time: 1 hour

    2 cups sugar
    2 cups light brown sugar, firmly
      packed
    2 cups light cream
    1 teaspoon soft butter
    ¾ teaspoon vanilla
    ½ cup walnuts, chopped (optional)

Combine sugars and cream in a 2-quart saucepan, stirring until sugars are dissolved. Boil uncovered without stirring until syrup reaches soft-ball stage (235°F to 240°F). Cool for 10 minutes. Spread out on flat baking dish and beat with a wooden spoon until mixture becomes thick and holds its shape. Add vanilla and nuts. Pour into flat dish, cool thoroughly, and cut into squares. Store in a covered container.

For gift giving, stack penuche on an inexpensive crystal dish or plate. Cover with light-colored cellophane and top with a ribbon bow. Penuche squares can also be wrapped individually and packed in a decorative box, the candy cushioned with shredded green paper.

CANDIES AND COMFITS

Candy/Cookie Brittle

Makes 1 pound
Preparation time: 30 minutes
Baking time: 20 minutes

- 1 cup margarine
- 1 teaspoon salt
- 1½ teaspoons vanilla
- 1 cup sugar
- 2 cups flour
- 1½ cups semisweet chocolate pieces
- ½ cup finely chopped nuts—macadamia, pecan, walnut, etc.

Preheat oven to 350°F. Blend together margarine, salt, and vanilla. Beat in sugar using an electric mixer at medium speed. Stir in flour and chocolate pieces. Spread dough evenly in ungreased 10 x 15-inch pan. Sprinkle with nuts. Bake 20 minutes. Turn onto wire rack to cool and break into irregular pieces. Store lightly covered.

Wash out tomato or other vegetable cans and cover with gift wrap. Stack brittle in clean cans. Seal cans with foil or plastic film, and tie with bright gift ribbon.

Orange Poppy Seed Candies

Makes 80 pieces
Preparation time: 1 hour

- ¾ cup sugar
- 3 cups honey
- 1½ pounds poppy seeds
- 1 cup candied orange peel, diced
- 2 cups walnuts, finely chopped
- Confectioners sugar

In 2-quart saucepan cook honey and sugar over moderate heat until sugar dissolves. Add poppy seeds and boil until mixture reaches hard-crack stage (300°F), about 30 minutes. Add orange peel and nuts and stir until mixture boils. Turn out onto a large platter that has been moistened with cold water. Flatten with a spatula dipped in hot water. Sprinkle with confectioners sugar. Allow to cool 8 to 10 minutes. Cut into small squares.

This is a pretty candy and makes a nice gift packed into a glass or plastic goblet. Cover with plastic film and tie a pretty ribbon around stem of goblet.

Christmas Party Walnut Crunchies

Makes 2 cups
Preparation time: 30 minutes
Baking time: 50 minutes

- 2 cups walnuts, coarsely chopped
- 4 tablespoons butter
- 1 egg white
- ½ cup sugar
- ⅛ teaspoon salt
- ¼ teaspoon cinnamon

Serve these as after dinner nuts. The subtle sweet spicy flavor complements any meal. Preheat oven to 300°F. Spread nuts over bottom of 13 x 9-inch baking dish. Dot with 2 tablespoons butter. Bake 20 minutes, stirring frequently. Add remaining 2 tablespoons butter and mix well. Beat egg white stiff; add sugar, salt, and cinnamon and beat well. Stir into nuts, mix well. Bake at 325°F for 30 minutes. Cool. Break into pieces. Store in covered container.

Plastic sandwich bags filled with Walnut Crunchies and decorated with a Christmas seal and ribbon make a thoughtful gift from your country kitchen. Or pack in a gift highball glass—the perfect holder for these walnuts. Pack the walnuts loosely; cover with plastic wrap and your gift is ready to serve the moment you present it.

Salted Oven Pecans

Makes 1 pound
Preparation time: 10 minutes
Baking time: 1 hour

- 1 pound (4 cups) pecan halves
- ¼ pound butter
- Salt

In large heavy skillet bake nuts with butter at 250°F for 1 hour, stirring occasionally. Cool and sprinkle with salt. Store in a covered container.

Fill a small crock or coffee mug with nuts. Seal with plastic wrap and tie a ribbon around the handle. An inexpensive cereal bowl also makes a fine container. Wrap in plastic film and the nuts are ready to serve when you hand this gift to your host or hostess.

Cream Caramels

Makes 3 pounds
or about one hundred 1-inch pieces
Preparation time: 1 hour

    4 cups sugar
 1½ cups light corn syrup
    6 cups heavy cream
    1 teaspoon vanilla
       Vegetable oil

In a 3-quart heavy saucepan combine sugar, corn syrup, and 2 cups of cream. Stir constantly until soft-ball stage (240°F). Slowly add 2 more cups of cream and cook, stirring, until temperature reaches 240°F again. Add last 2 cups of cream and cook until mixture reaches hard-crack stage (300°F). Stir in vanilla and pour immediately into large oiled pan ¾ to 1 inch in depth. When cold, cut into 1-inch squares. Wrap each square in waxed paper.

For gifts, save little boxes throughout the year (square, oval, round, etc.) and cover them using doll house wallpaper or small patterned gift wrap. A small saucer picked up at a tag sale also makes a pretty container for these rich little confections. Arrange the caramels one layer deep on the saucer and overwrap them with plastic film. Or wrap it in waxed paper and glue on a paper doily for a pretty topper.

Peanut Butter Buckeyes

Makes 100 pieces
Preparation time: 1 hour
Chilling time: 8 hours or overnight

 1¾ cups peanut butter
    1 cup butter or margarine, softened

 4¼ cups confectioners sugar
    2 cups semisweet chocolate pieces
    1 tablespoon vegetable oil
       Toothpicks

In large bowl cream together peanut butter and butter or margarine until light and creamy. Add sugar and mix well. Roll into small balls about ¾-inch in diameter. Place on waxed paper and chill for 8 hours or overnight. Melt chocolate pieces and oil in top of double boiler over hot, not boiling, water until completely melted. Using toothpicks spear each ball, dip lower half into melted chocolate, and return to waxed paper. Refrigerate to harden. Store between layers of waxed paper in airtight containers. Keep in a cool place.

To make Cherry Chocolate Morsels, follow procedure for making peanut butter cream. Instead of rolling into balls, wrap it around stemmed maraschino cherries. Proceed as for Buckeyes, rolling candies in finely ground pistachio nuts after dipping in chocolate. Refrigerate to harden.

These chocolate tasties look pretty wrapped three to a square of colored cellophane. Or fit several Buckeyes snugly into a deep yellow cereal bowl or saucer so the Buckeye shows its tawny heart. Overwrap in plastic film and tie the package with green yarn.

Rainbow Crystals

Makes about 1½ pounds
Preparation time: 2 hours

    2 cups sugar
  ¾ cup light corn syrup
    1 cup water
  ¾ teaspoon oil flavoring*
       Food coloring
    1 cup confectioners sugar

Combine in a heavy 4-quart saucepan sugar, corn syrup, and water. Cook over medium heat, stirring constantly with wooden spoon until sugar is completely dissolved and mixture boils. Allow to boil *without* stirring until syrup reaches hard-crack stage (300°F). Stir in oil flavoring. Pour out onto well-greased and chilled platter, pan, or marble slab. Fold taffy-like candy over itself using spatula as you add 5 to 6 drops of desired coloring. Keep folding and working candy until cool enough to touch and stiff; cut into ½-inch strips with scissors. Twist strips for novelty effects. Place candy onto a cookie sheet. When completely cool dust heavily with confectioners sugar. Store in tightly covered container. Make as many different batches as you have flavorings.

Suggestions for colors and flavorings: red-cinnamon; blue-peppermint; white-licorice; green-spearmint; orange-orange; yellow-lemon; purple (use equal amounts of red and blue color)-clove; brown (use equal amounts of red and green)-sassafras.

*Oil flavors are available at some drug stores.

CANDIES AND COMFITS

Pack these "jewels" in glass or clear plastic boxes and tape securely before mailing or giving. For the finale to an elegant dinner party, present each guest with a crystal saucer of these glowing candies.

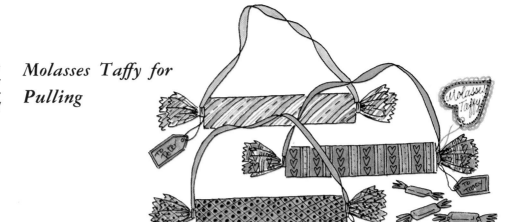

Chocolate Creams

Makes 100 pieces
Preparation time: 1 hour
Chilling time: 8 hours or overnight

4¼ cups confectioners sugar
1 cup butter or margarine, softened
2 cups semisweet chocolate pieces
1 tablespoon vegetable oil
Toothpicks
¾ cup crème de menthe, crème de cacao, or 3 tablespoons coconut extract or liqueur
½ cup finely ground nuts or ¾ cup sweetened shredded coconut

Pecans or walnuts, finely chopped for garnish
Shredded coconut for garnish

Cream together butter or margarine and sugar. Add flavorings and nuts or coconut. Proceed as for Peanut Butter Buckeyes. Roll in finely chopped nuts or shredded coconut after dipping in chocolate. Refrigerate to harden.

These candies are perfect for a "sampler." Place in individual paper candy cups and pack into a gift-wrap covered box. Tie a silk rose on top for a Valentine's Day present. Be sure to keep candy refrigerated until giving.

Molasses Taffy for Pulling

Makes 1½ pounds or about fifty 2-inch pieces
Preparation time: 45 minutes

1 cup sugar
½ cup dark brown sugar, firmly packed
2 cups dark molasses
¾ cup water
2 teaspoons white vinegar
⅛ teaspoon baking soda
¼ teaspoon salt
Butter
Oil of peppermint, spearmint, or cinnamon (optional)

This candy is best made with a friend or two, to help with the pulling.

In 2-quart saucepan cook sugars, molasses, and water together, stirring only until sugars are dissolved. Boil uncovered without stirring until syrup reaches soft-crack stage (270°F). Remove from heat; add vinegar, baking soda, salt, and 3 drops oil flavoring (if desired). Stir only until all ingredients are incorporated, then pour onto a large buttered platter. Allow to cool for 10 minutes or until candy can be handled but is still warm. With buttered fingers pinch off about ¼ of candy and pull and twist until firm and light, forming a 1-inch rope-like strand. Using buttered scissors, cut off pieces and wrap each in waxed paper twisting ends to seal. Store in covered containers.

If you make more than one batch, color code each flavor by wrapping in a different color cellophane. Or tie small pieces of yarn to ends of wrapped candies: green for peppermint, blue for molasses, red for cinnamon, yellow for spearmint, etc. After wrapping fill salvaged glass jars with taffy; screw on the caps and decorate with gummed gift-wrap tape in bright colors.

Chocolate-dipped Fruits

Makes 4 cups
Preparation time: 45 minutes

2 cups semisweet chocolate pieces
1 tablespoons vegetable oil
Toothpicks
4 cups whole strawberries, large maraschino cherries, dried whole apricots, etc.

Melt chocolate pieces and oil in top of double boiler over hot, not boiling, water until completely melted. Using toothpicks dip fruit half-way into chocolate and allow to cool on waxed paper.

These candies are the priciest things at New York's posh chocolate shops. Serve on stemmed crystal plates or in individual foil candy cups. Or add these to a dried fruit and nut platter, include a cocktail fork, and wrap in plastic film for a special gift to your host or hostess.

COLD-WATER TEST

The cold-water test can be used to judge stages of the candy syrup, although it is not as reliable as a thermometer. Remove the pan of syrup from the heat for each test. Spoon out one-half teaspoon of syrup and drop into a glass of very cold water. Note behavior of syrup and refer to chart below.

Stage	Temperature	Behavior	Examples
Soft ball	234°–240°F	Syrup forms a soft ball that flattens on removal from water.	Cream caramels Penuche
Firm ball	244°–248°F	Syrup forms a firm ball that holds its shape.	Caramels
Hard ball	250°–265°F	Syrup forms a hard ball that holds its shape but is still pliable.	Divinity
Soft crack	270°–290°F	Syrup separates into threads that are hard but not brittle.	Taffy
Hard crack	300°–310°F	Syrup separates into threads that are hard and brittle.	Rainbow Crystals Poppy Seed Candies

BREADS
AND
MUFFINS

A quartet of breads with old-fashioned appeal cools in front of the brick fireplace of this restored Colonial home of 1747. On top of the early-19th-century iron spatula is a crusty loaf of Health Bread, and, next to it, nutritious Bran/Corn Bread. Favorite Buttermilk Bread and Country White Bread (center) round out the group.

2

Home-baked bread is ooh! and aah! food any-time, but especially appreciated by people who don't bake or don't have time to bake during the holidays. Besides that, bread is fun to make and smells so welcoming in the baking. Almost no task is more soul-satisfying than kneading a batch of bread dough on a wintry morning, and it is all the more fun knowing that one of the fragrant loaves will go to somebody very special as a surprise. Even the simplest loaves make heart-warming gifts. See an older neighbor's eyes sparkle when he or she unwraps half a loaf of buttermilk bread, say, on Christmas morning. It will be a tea-time treat for several days ahead because this recipe keeps well. Or give a loaf of health bread to a robust young family, or the co-riander-spiced bread to a gourmet friend who packs the classiest lunch in the office brown-bagger brigade.

The muffins here are made to celebrate. Give batches of them to suit the size of the family. For that picture-perfect mushroom shape, be sure to grease the top of the muffin tin whether or not you use paper liners. And do provide reheating instructions so those who want them hot can serve them that way with plenty of butter.

Breads help welcome holiday guests, too. The houseful of young folk home from college will go through several loaves of bread in a day or two. You'll find yourself slicing bread to go with soups, and simple meals, for toast at breakfasts, and for your own family tea.

Technology can lend a hand with heavy baking chores. A food processor handles mixing and kneading in a couple of minutes (and one bowl) and rising takes only five to fifteen minutes in a microwave oven at its lowest setting. If you use a gallon-size plastic bag for a rising bowl you can cut down on your wash-up time. It's almost impossible to gauge volume in a plastic bag so use the two-finger test to tell whether bread has doubled. (Stick two fingers into ball of dough. If indentations remain, then dough has doubled.)

All of these breads can be baked long before the hectic holidays and frozen, then reheated in a microwave or conventional oven (in a moistened paper bag) until warm and crusty. So bake anytime and make yours the household always prepared with reheatable bread in the freezer.

English Muffin Loaves

Makes 2 loaves, 16 slices per loaf
Preparation time: 30 minutes
Rising time: 45 minutes
Baking time: 25 minutes

- 2 cups milk
- ½ cup water
- 6 cups flour
- 1 tablespoon sugar
- 1½ teaspoons salt
- ¼ teaspoon baking soda
- 2 envelopes active dry yeast
- Cornmeal

Combine milk and water in large saucepan and heat until tiny bubbles form at edge of pan. Cool to lukewarm.

Combine 3 cups flour, sugar, salt, baking soda, and yeast. Add lukewarm milk mixture, beat well, and stir in remaining 3 cups flour.

Grease 2 loaf pans and sprinkle with cornmeal. Spoon batter into pans and sprinkle batter with cornmeal. Allow to rise in warm place for 45 minutes. Bake in preheated 400°F oven for 25 minutes. Remove from pans and cool on wire racks. Slice and toast to serve.

Wrap thick slices of bread and arrange in a long bread basket with a jar of your favorite jam or jelly for gift giving. Fold an inexpensive bandana into a skinny strip and use as a tie for the bread and basket.

Bran/Corn Bread

Makes 1 loaf
Preparation time: 30 minutes
Baking time: 30 minutes

½ cup vegetable oil
¼ cup sugar
2 eggs
¼ cup wheat germ
½ cup 100% bran cereal
1 cup milk
1 cup flour
½ cup yellow cornmeal
1 tablespoon baking powder
½ teaspoon salt
½ cup nonfat dry milk
½ cup raisins (optional)

Without the raisins, this loaf makes a great accompaniment to soup. Add a salad and a special dessert for a lovely lunch during the holiday season.

Preheat oven to 400°F. Beat together oil, sugar, and eggs until creamy. Add wheat germ, bran, and milk; allow to stand for 5 minutes. Mix together flour, cornmeal, baking powder, salt, and dry milk. Add to bran mixture. Fold in raisins and spoon into a greased loaf pan. Bake 30 minutes. Remove from pan and cool on wire rack.

Wrap in a plastic bag and tie on a new wooden spoon with red or green yarn. Or place bread on a small, inexpensive bread board and stretch plastic film over it. Tie with a big green ribbon and bow.

Yeast Pumpkin Bread

Makes 1 loaf
Preparation time: 30 minutes
Rising time: 2 hours
Baking time: 35 minutes

2 envelopes active dry yeast
½ cup warm water
½ teaspoon sugar
3½ cups plus 1 tablespoon flour
½ teaspoon ginger
¼ teaspoon nutmeg
¼ teaspoon cloves
1 teaspoon salt
½ cup cooked, mashed pumpkin (fresh or canned)
3 tablespoons butter, melted
½ cup dark brown sugar, firmly packed
¾ cup milk

Dissolve yeast in warm water and stir in ½ teaspoon sugar and 1 tablespoon flour. Let stand until bubbly.

Combine 3½ cups flour, spices, and salt, and mix together pumpkin, butter, brown sugar, and milk. Add pumpkin mixture and yeast mixture alternately to flour and spices, adding more flour to make a kneadable dough. Knead until smooth and elastic. Cover and let rise until doubled, about 1 hour.

Punch down dough and knead again. On lightly floured surface shape dough into a loaf or flatten into a rectangle and roll up and place in a greased loaf pan Allow to rise in a warm place until doubled in bulk, about 45 minutes. Bake in a preheated oven at 325°F for 35 to 40 minutes. Remove from pan and cool on a wire rack.

Wrap a loaf in waxed paper and place in a deep green napkin, folded envelope-style over the bread. Tie with red yarn.

Spiced Zucchini Bread

Makes 2 loaves
Preparation time: 30 minutes
Baking time: 1 hour

2 cups coarsely shredded zucchini
1 can (8 ounces) crushed pineapple, drained
3 eggs, lightly beaten
1½ cups sugar
1 cup vegetable oil
2 teaspoons vanilla
3 cups flour
½ teaspoon baking powder
2 teaspoons baking soda
¾ teaspoon salt
¾ cup chopped nuts

When your garden is overloaded with zucchini, this is the recipe to make. It freezes well and is easily packaged to send to a friend for the holidays.

Preheat oven to 350°F. Combine zucchini and pineapple in a large bowl. Add sugar, oil, and vanilla to beaten eggs and beat until creamy. Mix together flour, baking powder, baking soda, and salt. Add egg mixture to zucchini mixture. Then add dry ingredients. Stir in nuts and mix just until moistened. Spoon into 2 greased and floured loaf pans and bake 1 hour or until a toothpick inserted in center comes out clean. Turn out and cool on wire rack.

Having several loaves of this in the freezer makes impromptu gift-giving a pleasure. Keep a package of plastic bags and a spool of bright green or red ribbon handy for wrapping a surprise gift on a moment's notice. Small Christmas ball decorations can be twisted onto pipe cleaners and then attached to the bow.

Southern Corn Bread or Muffins

Makes 12 muffins or one 8-inch square
Preparation time: 30 minutes
Baking time: 20 to 25 minutes

1 cup flour
2 cups yellow cornmeal
⅓ cup sugar
4 teaspoons baking powder
1 teaspoon salt
1 egg
1 cup milk
⅓ cup shortening, melted

This recipe of southern cornmeal muffins served with pea soup is a favorite supper for holidays and all year long. For "cracklin bread" add 1 cup pork fat cracklings to this recipe.

Preheat oven to 400°F. In a large bowl combine flour, cornmeal, sugar, baking powder, and salt. Mix together egg, milk, and shortening and add to dry mixture. *Stir only until moistened.* Pour into greased tin or pan and bake 20 to 25 minutes. Serve hot with butter.

Note: When using an 8 x 8-inch square pan, precook 2 strips of bacon and lay criss-cross on bottom of greased pan; pour in batter, then bake.

Wrap in plastic wrap and tie a brown bow on top. Or fit four or five of these muffins into a 6-inch black iron skillet and tie a checked blue gift tie on the handle. Wrap the skillet with plastic film to cover the golden muffins—a nice homey kitchen gift.

Berry Corn Bread

Makes 1 loaf or 12 muffins
Preparation time: 30 minutes
Baking time: 30 to 40 minutes

3 tablespoons butter, melted
2 tablespoons sugar
1 egg
1 cup milk
½ cup berries
1 cup flour
1 cup yellow cornmeal
4 teaspoons baking powder
1 teaspoon salt
3 tablespoons nonfat dry milk

A very quick and easy bread. You may use fresh chopped cranberries, fresh or frozen blueberries, strawberries, or raspberries.

Preheat oven to 375°F. Combine butter, sugar, egg, and milk; set aside. Stir berries into flour; set aside. Mix together corn meal, baking powder, salt, and dry milk. Add to butter mixture. Stir in berry mixture and pour into greased loaf pan or muffin tin. Bake 40 minutes or until a toothpick inserted in center comes out clean. Remove from pan and cool on wire rack. When cool, wrap bread airtight and allow to ripen at least 24 hours before serving.

Wrap in a plastic bag. Tie tightly with red and green gift ribbon and attach a card that says, "Refrigerate, slice thin, and serve with cream cheese and jam or sliced bananas."

Favorite Buttermilk Bread

Makes 2 loaves
Preparation time: 30 minutes
Rising time: 2 hours
Baking time: 30 minutes

1 cup buttermilk
3 tablespoons sugar
2 teaspoons salt
6 tablespoons shortening
1 cup warm water
1 envelope active dry yeast
½ teaspoon baking soda
6 cups flour

Heat buttermilk, but don't allow to boil. Stir in sugar, salt, and 6 tablespoons shortening. Cool to lukewarm. In large mixing bowl, dissolve yeast in water and add lukewarm buttermilk mixture. Combine baking soda and 3 cups flour. Add to yeast mixture and beat until smooth. Stir in remaining flour. Turn dough out onto lightly floured board and knead until smooth and elastic. If dough is too sticky, add more flour. Place dough in greased bowl. Brush top with shortening and allow to rise in warm place until doubled in bulk, about 1 hour.

Punch down and turn out onto lightly floured surface. Knead briefly and shape into 2 loaves. Place in greased loaf pans and dust tops with flour. Allow to rise until center of loaf is slightly higher than edge of pan, about 1 hour. Dust tops with flour and bake in preheated 325°F oven for 30 to 40 minutes. Remove from pans and cool on wire racks. Wrap well and freeze if desired.

This homey loaf looks good packed on a bread tray (rattan, earthenware, or good-looking plastic). Wrap the tray and bread in plastic film and finish off the package with red ribbon and a big bow.

Country White Bread

Makes 2 loaves
Preparation time: 40 minutes
Rising time: 1 hour and 45 minutes
Baking time: 30 minutes

  2 envelopes active dry yeast
½ cup warm water
  1 tablespoon sugar
5-6 cups plus 1 tablespoon flour
1¼ cups milk
1½ teaspoons salt
¼ cup butter
½ cup water
¼ cup honey
  1 egg

Dissolve yeast in ½ cup warm water and stir in sugar and 1 tablespoon of flour. Let stand until bubbly.

Place milk, salt, butter, ½ cup water, and honey in a saucepan and heat until butter melts. Cool to lukewarm. Pour mixture into a large bowl; add yeast mixture, egg, and 4 cups flour. Mix thoroughly, adding remaining flour to make a kneadable dough. Turn dough out onto a floured board and knead until smooth and elastic. If dough is too sticky, add more flour. Let rise in a warm place until doubled in bulk, about 1 hour. Punch down, and knead lightly. Divide in half and roll each half to fit into a greased loaf pan. Allow to rise in a warm place until dough rises to top of pan, about 45 minutes. Bake in preheated 350°F oven for 30 minutes. Remove from pans and cool on wire racks.

Wrap a loaf in plastic film and wrapping paper and tie it to a new wire bread rack with a wide ribbon. Or, place loaf in a new loaf pan. Overwrap with plastic film and seal with colorful wrapping tape.

Breakfast Bran/Oatmeal Muffins

Makes 4 dozen muffins
Preparation time: 30 minutes
Baking time: 20 minutes

  2 cups 100% bran cereal
  2 cups boiling water
  2 cups sugar
  1 cup shortening
  4 eggs
  1 quart buttermilk
  5 cups flour
½ teaspoon salt
  5 teaspoons baking soda
  4 cups rolled oats
  1 cup raisins or currants (optional)

Preheat oven to 400°F. Pour boiling water over bran, set aside. Cream sugar and shortening. Add eggs and milk to creamed mixture. Combine flour, salt, and soda and add to creamed mixture. Add oats and raisins or currants, if you're using them. Stir just until moistened and spoon into greased muffin tins. Bake 20 minutes or until done and nicely brown.

Tie a pretty colored ribbon around a muffin tin containing muffins and tie on this recipe. A miniature tray of these muffins and a jar of special jam would make a glorious gift for a singleton or couple. Wrap tray, muffins, and jar of jam in plastic wrap; then wrap in red tissue paper. Add a white ribbon and tuck a couple of shiny Christmas balls into the ribbon tie.

Blueberry Muffins

Makes 12 muffins or one 9 x 9-inch square
Preparation time: 30 minutes
Baking time: 30 minutes

½ cup shortening
¾ cup sugar
  2 eggs
½ cup milk
  2 cups flour
½ teaspoon salt
  2 teaspoons baking powder
2½ cups fresh blueberries, preferably wild
    Sugar cubes
    Juice of 1 lemon

Preheat oven to 375°F. Cream shortening and sugar. Add eggs one at a time, blending thoroughly. Mix dry ingredients together in large bowl and add ½ cup blueberries. Alternately add milk and creamed mixture to flour mixture. Stir in remaining berries. Pile high in paper-lined muffin tins or greased 9-inch square pan. Bake 25 to 30 minutes.

For an easy and delightful topping: mash half a cube of sugar, saturate with lemon juice, and place on top of each muffin while still warm.

Note: This recipe is excellent with other berries as well.

Muffins are best fresh, so give these generously in the neighborhood. Overwrap a filled plate with clear cellophane and tie with a silver or gold gift cord.

Brushed with an eggy glaze and sprinkled with poppy seeds, this glossy Challah is an example of the best traditional Jewish cooking.

Challah

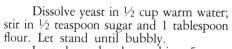

Makes 2 loaves
Preparation time: 1 hour
Rising time: 2 hours
Baking time: 30 to 45 minutes

  2 envelopes active dry yeast
2¾ cups warm water
  ½ cup plus ½ teaspoon sugar
7½ cups plus 1 tablespoon flour
  ½ cup vegetable oil
1½ tablespoons salt
  3 eggs
    Poppy seeds or sesame seeds

Dissolve yeast in ½ cup warm water; stir in ½ teaspoon sugar and 1 tablespoon flour. Let stand until bubbly.

In a large bowl, combine 5 cups flour with 2¼ cups warm water, ½ cup oil, ½ cup sugar, salt, and 2 eggs; mix thoroughly. Add yeast mixture and gradually add 2–2½ cups flour. Knead dough until smooth and elastic. Cover and let rise about 45 minutes to 1 hour or until doubled in bulk. Punch down dough and knead, working in more flour so dough is not sticky.

To shape loaves, divide dough into six pieces. Make each piece into a strand about 10 inches long by rolling dough gently on floured surface with palms of hands. For each loaf, take 3 strands and fold under ends on one side. Braid loosely, and tuck other ends under. Place diagonally on a greased cookie sheet, and allow to rise until doubled in bulk, about 1 hour.

To make glaze, beat one egg and add 1 tablespoon sugar. Brush carefullly over top of braids, and sprinkle with poppy or sesame seeds. Bake in preheated 350°F oven for 30 to 45 minutes or until done. Place on wire rack to cool.

Wrap this braid in plastic film and criss-cross with deep blue ribbon—an impressive gift indeed. A jar of homemade or purchased jam is a thoughtful extra.

Health Bread

Makes 2 loaves
Preparation time: 40 minutes
Rising time: 2½ hours
Baking time: 1 hour

    2 envelopes active dry yeast
    3 cups warm water
    3 tablespoons honey
 4½ cups unbleached flour
    3 cups whole wheat flour
  ½ cup soy flour
    6 tablespoons wheat germ
  ¾ cup nonfat dry milk
    1 tablespoon salt
    3 tablespoons vegetable oil

Dissolve yeast in warm water. Then mix in honey and ½ cup flour, and let stand until bubbly.

In large bowl, combine flours, wheat germ, dry milk, and oil. Add yeast mixture to flour mixture, and knead until smooth and elastic, adding more flour if necessary. Set in warm place to rise until doubled in bulk (about 2 hours).

Punch down dough, knead, and shape into 2 round loaves. Place on greased cookie sheets. Allow to rise about 30 minutes, and make a cross on top of each loaf using a sharp knife. Bake in a preheated oven at 350°F for 45–50 minutes. (If bread is browning too quickly, reduce heat to 325°F.) Cool on wire racks.

This robust bread looks the part in a square of burlap in a deep earth color such as rust or deep gold. Tie the fabric around the bread with dark green or lighter gold yarn and tuck a mini-sheaf of wheat (available where dried flowers are sold) in the knot of the gift tie. Or wrap it in plastic film overwrapped with a blue checkered towel and tied with a red ribbon.

Cranberry Anadama Bread

Makes 2 loaves
Preparation time: 45 minutes
Rising time: 2 hours
Baking time: 45 minutes

 1½ cups fresh cranberries, washed and chopped coarsely
  ¼ cup sugar
    1 orange peel, grated
    2 envelopes active dry yeast
  ½ cup warm water
  ½ teaspoon sugar

  7-8 cups plus 1 tablespoon flour
  ⅔ cup yellow cornmeal
 2½ cups boiling water
  ¼ cup margarine
  ½ cup dark molasses
 2½ teaspoons salt

When cranberry season arrives, this is one of my first recipes to add to the freezer for the holidays. If you have a food processor, it saves time to peel the orange, discarding white pith, and process with sugar for 30 seconds using steel blade. Then add whole berries and process 30 seconds longer.

Dissolve yeast in ½ cup warm water and stir in ½ teaspoon sugar and 1 tablespoon flour. Let stand until bubbly.

Stir cornmeal slowly into boiling water and cook until thickened. Add margarine, molasses, and salt. Cool to lukewarm. Stir in yeast mixture, berries, and orange peel. Knead in flour to form a smooth, elastic dough, and allow to rise in a warm place until doubled in bulk, about 45 minutes.

Turn out onto a lightly floured surface and knead again. Divide dough in half and place each half in a greased loaf pan. Allow to rise to top of pan, 45 minutes to 1 hour. Bake in a preheated oven at 350°F for 45 minutes. Remove from pans and cool on wire racks.

Wrap in colored cellophane and tie on a piece of yew or evergreen with a big red bow. Alternatively, slip the loaf into a plastic bag, and then into a bright red shopping bag. Add a small pot of one of the fruit butters in Chapter 5.

French Loaves

comes out clean. Remove from pan and cool on wire rack. When cool, remove paper and wrap in foil to store or ship.

Makes 2 small loaves
Preparation time: 40 minutes
Rising time: 1½ hours
Baking time: 30 minutes

    1 envelope active dry yeast
    1¼ cups warm water
    1 teaspoon salt
    1 tablespoon shortening
    1 tablespoon sugar
    3½ cups flour
      Cornmeal

Dissolve yeast in water. Add salt, shortening, and sugar. Stir in flour and knead by hand 8 minutes or 2 minutes in food processor until elastic and not sticky. Place in greased bowl and let rise in warm place about 30 minutes, until almost doubled.

Punch down, knead slightly, and cut dough into 2 equal portions. Roll each into a rectangle 8 x 10 inches. Beginning with the wide side, roll up tightly. Seal edges by pinching together. With hands on each edge, roll gently to taper ends. Place on greased baking sheet sprinkled with cornmeal, and allow to rise for 1 hour. Make ¼-inch slashes at 3-inch intervals using a sharp knife. Bake in preheated 375°F oven for 30–35 minutes until golden brown. Cool on wire racks.

Use up old holiday wrapping paper by making long bags with yarn handles (see Chapter 14) and placing a loaf in each for giving. Add a jar of homemade jelly or jam covered with a calico top (see Chapter 5) for a perfect holiday gift. Another

suggestion: build a shallow nest of crushed red or green tissue paper on a rectangle of cardboard. Wrap a loaf in plastic film and lay it gently in the bright paper nest. Tie bread and packaging together with contrasting gift wrap yarn, or use tag ends of knitting and coarse crochet yarn.

Travelers' Date Nut Bread

Makes 1 loaf
Preparation time: 30 minutes
Baking time: 1½ hours

    1 pound pitted dates, chopped
    1½ cups boiling water
    2 teaspoons baking soda
    2¼ cups flour
    ½ teaspoon baking powder
    1½ cups sugar
    ½ teaspoon salt
    1 egg, beaten
    1 tablespoon butter, melted
    1 teaspoon vanilla
    1 cup chopped walnuts or pecans

This recipe is called "travelers' bread" because it's been mailed all over the country, sometimes in the pan in which it was baked.

Preheat oven to 350°F. Combine dates, boiling water, and baking soda. Stir and set aside. In a large bowl, mix flour, baking powder, sugar, and salt together.

Combine egg, butter, and vanilla. Alternately add egg mixture and date mixture to dry ingredients. Stir in nuts and pour into loaf pan that has been lined with greased brown paper. Bake 1½ hours or until a toothpick inserted in center

Since this bread travels so well, wrap it in aluminum foil, folding and sealing it neatly and securely. Red ribbon against the silver foil is bright. To ship, find a box in which the wrapped bread fits snugly. Or fill the box with popped corn, just as good a cushion as plastic packing materials.

Wheat Germ Muffins

Makes 16 muffins
Preparation time: 20 minutes
Baking time: 20 minutes

    1 egg, well beaten
    ⅓ cup raw or light brown sugar
    1¼ cups milk
    ⅓ cup butter, melted
    1 cup unbleached flour
    ½ teaspoon salt
    4 teaspoons baking powder
    1 cup wheat germ

Preheat oven to 425°F. In large bowl beat together egg, sugar, milk, and butter. Mix together flour, salt, baking powder, and wheat germ. Add dry ingredients to egg mixture and stir lightly to mix. Fill greased muffin pans ⅔ full and bake 20 minutes. Serve hot or cold.

Bake these in individual custard cups. After baking, wash and dry the cups, return the muffins to them, and wrap individually in foil or plastic film. Place a medallion sticker on the side of each cup. Give one, two, three, or more cup-and-muffin gifts to singletons or small families.

Lemon Bread

Makes 1 loaf
Preparation time: 30 minutes
Baking time: 1 hour

    1 cup sugar
    5 tablespoons butter
    2 eggs
      Grated peel and juice of 1 lemon
    ½ cup milk
    ½ teaspoon salt
    1½ cups flour
    1 teaspoon baking powder
    ½ cup finely chopped nuts (optional)

Lemon bread freezes well and is a great accompaniment to a cup of afternoon tea.

Preheat oven to 325°F. Cream butter and sugar and beat in eggs. Add milk and mix well. Combine flour, salt, and baking powder. Add to butter mixture and stir until smooth. Stir in lemon peel and nuts. Pour into greased loaf pan and bake 1 hour.

Make a glaze by mixing together lemon juice and ½ cup sugar. Spoon over hot bread when just taken from the oven.

A loaf of lemon bread on a small bread tray can be wrapped in shiny green gift wrap and decorated with fresh lemon leaves (from the florist) and a small spray of baby's breath.

Coriander Gingerbread

Makes 1 large loaf or 2 small loaves
Preparation time: 30 minutes
Baking time: 1 hour

    ½ cup butter
    ½ cup dark brown sugar, firmly packed
    1 cup molasses
    1 tablespoon ginger
    1 tablespoon coriander
    ½ teaspoon nutmeg, freshly grated
    ½ teaspoon cinnamon
    3 eggs
    3 cups flour
    ½ cup orange juice
    2 tablespoons grated orange peel
    1 teaspoon baking soda
    2 tablespoons water
    1 cup raisins

This bread is an excellent keeper; it freezes well and is a delight served with a fresh fruit butter.

Preheat oven to 375°F. Cream butter and sugar. Add molasses and spices; beat in eggs. Add flour and orange juice, alternately to creamed mixture. Add orange peel. Dissolve baking soda in water and stir into mixture. Add raisins and pour batter into a greased loaf pan or pans.

Bake 1 hour. Cool on wire rack.

Note: if top is browning too quickly, place foil around the sides and top of pan; do not cover loaf completely.

Loaves of this bread look pretty wrapped in a flower-printed cotton napkin or a square of sprigged cotton fabric cut with pinking shears. Put wrapped bread in a basket of appropriate size. Tie it with bright knitting yarn or ribbon and put a gift tag on it.

Molasses and Apple Muffins

Makes 12 muffins
Preparation time: 20 minutes
Baking time: 25 minutes

    2 cups flour
    1 teaspoon cinnamon
    ¼ teaspoon ginger
    ¼ teaspoon nutmeg
    ½ teaspoon salt
    1 teaspoon baking soda
    3 tablespoons dark brown sugar
    ¼ cup butter, melted
    ¾ cup dark molasses
    1 tablespoon milk
    1 egg, well beaten
    ¼ cup currants
    2 apples or pears—peeled, cored, and thickly sliced

Preheat oven to 350°F. Combine flour, spices, salt, and baking soda in a large bowl. Mix together sugar, molasses, and then butter, milk, and egg; mix well. Add to dry ingredients and stir in currants. Arrange apple or pear slices on bottom of greased muffin tin and spoon muffin mixture over them. Bake 25 minutes. Serve hot.

These fruity muffins—wrapped in a napkin-lined basket with a fresh apple or pear nestling among them makes a pretty gift.

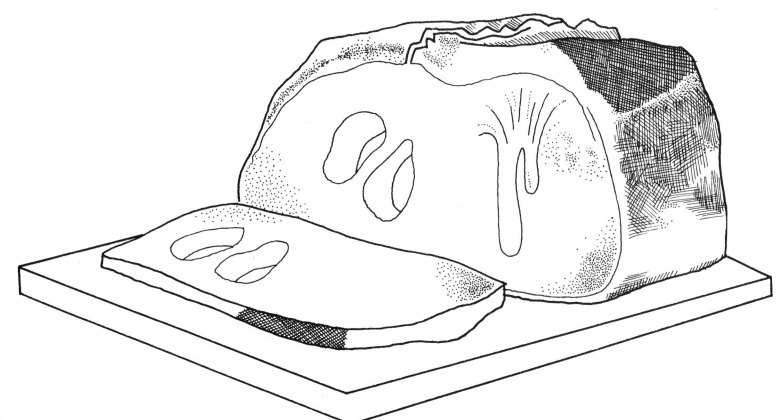

WHAT WENT WRONG HERE?

Making perfect yeast breads

It's impossible for your yeast bread to have as many problems as the one pictured above, and even imperfect loaves usually make good eating. But if you're dissatisfied with the look, taste, or texture of your bread, look below for the solution.

Burned: If the top is overly brown, but the inside just done, try covering the top loosely with foil for the last 10 to 15 minutes of baking.

Cracked: It tastes good anyway, doesn't it? This is something that happens to even the most experienced bakers and no one has yet devised a way to prevent it.

Dry: You either added too little liquid or too much flour, or you baked the loaf too long. Be cautious when adding flour during kneading; some of the stickiness will go away as you knead.

Flat: If your dough didn't rise, the water you dissolved the yeast in was either too hot or too cold. It should be between

105°F and 115°F. Try testing the water with a yeast or dairy thermometer until you learn to know by feel how hot the water should be. Alternatively, the yeast could have been too old. If yeast doesn't foam when dissolved in water, discard it and start over again.

Gooey: If bread has gooey streaks, the second rising was probably too long and the dough collapsed in the hot oven.

Holey: Dough was overkneaded or was allowed to rise for too long. However, if you like your bread this way, there is nothing really wrong with it.

Lumpy: If bread has hard or gooey lumps, it was probably not mixed sufficiently before kneading.

Moldy: If bread molds in less than five days, you must have done the unthinkable and wrapped still warm bread in plastic. Always allow bread to cool completely on wire racks, and if it won't be used within two to three days, freeze it.

Pale: If the top is nicely browned, but the sides and bottom pale and soft, try taking the bread out of the pan and placing it directly on the oven rack for the last 10 to 15 minutes of baking.

Saggy: If top is sunken rather than nicely rounded, and crumb tastes soggy, then bread was not kneaded sufficiently

and/or too much liquid was added. Ten minutes of kneading is not too much for some breads.

Shapeless: Breads that are baked on cookie sheets instead of loaf pans must have a fairly dense dough. Check recipes to see which breads are suited to being baked in this way. You can also use the ring from a springform pan to contain the dough during the second rising and baking.

Slow: If the dough took an unusually long time to rise, the rising place was probably not warm enough. If your oven doesn't have a pilot light, try placing a baking pan of boiling water on the bottom of the oven with the dough in a bowl on the rack above. Alternatively, put oven on lowest setting for eight to ten minutes. Turn oven off, and when racks are cool enough to touch with your bare hand, place rising bowl in oven.

Soggy: Bread was not baked long enough. Resist the temptation to take the bread out of the oven as soon as it starts smelling wonderful. Cutting into a hot loaf can also cause it to deflate, but who cares when the bread is hot and fragrant and dripping with butter!

Uneven: Oven may not be level. Experiment with different ways of placing bread during baking.

CAKES AND PIES

Shown on an antique indigo-dyed apron, the sunny yellow tartness of Limington Pie is hidden under its delicate meringue topping. The wire egg basket dates from 1870, and its traditional form remains popular today. The mysterious gadget on the right is a still functional wooden lemon squeezer from 1890.

3

Even the names of some of these cakes and pies make your mouth water and dreams of sugarplums pop into your head. Dark Fruitcake, Brazil Nut Cake, Apple Cider Cake, and Rum-Raisin Carrot Cake, read like they were taken from a page in a good cook's diary; and they taste like it too.

These cakes come in every shape, size, and many styles. Some are light and airy. Some are so rich and dense you will want to slice them very thinly as miniature sweets to nibble with a cup of eggnog or holiday tea.

To succeed at cake baking, equip yourself with a variety of baking pans and a mixer that can handle both heavy batters and light-as-air sponge and angel cakes. You need wooden spoons, scrapers, and a set of mixing bowls, too. If you go in for elaborate frostings, though most of these cakes don't require them, you'll need at least two pastry bags (one for each color frosting) and a variety of metal decorator's tips to make different shapes (see "Tip Tips"

in this chapter). And, although natural is prettiest for most foods, you may indulge your fancy for bright colors at holiday time by purchasing a good grade of food colors to tint icings and frostings. (They're available in cake decorating supply shops and supermarkets.)

For pies, make sure you have pie plates in several sizes. Oven-proof glass is ideal, since the crust browns well in the glass, which holds and spreads the heat. Dark metal pans are good too. See "Perfecting the Imperfect Crust" in this chapter.

The pies and light cakes are designed for your parties and treats at home, or to be taken carefully to a friend for a party. Serve them with coffee or one of the hot mulled drinks from "Nogs and Toddies." If you do take a pie or holiday cake to a neighboring family as a gift, take along a jar of cold toddy or mulled drink so that they can heat it up when they eat the pie.

Great-grandmother's Strawberry Cake

Serves 8 to 10
Preparation time: 40 minutes
Baking time: 30 minutes

- ½ cup butter
- 1½ cups sugar
- 3 eggs, separated
- 2¼ cups flour
- 1 tablespoon baking powder
- ¾ cup milk
  Strawberry Filling (recipe follows)
  Extra large berries or toasted coconut for garnish

Preheat oven to 325°F. In large bowl cream butter and sugar; beat in egg yolks. Combine flour and baking powder and add alternately with milk to creamed mixture. Beat egg whites until stiff; fold into batter. Grease and flour two 8-inch layer cake pans. Pour batter in pans and bake 30 minutes or until top springs back when touched. Cool in pan 5 minutes

before turning out onto rack to cool completely. When cool, spread Strawberry Filling between layers and over top. Garnish with large plump berries.

Strawberry Filling

- 1 cup strawberries, crushed
- 1 cup sugar
- 1 egg white, beaten

Beat all together until mixture thickens. Variation: proceed as above but bake in 10-inch tube pan instead of layer cake pans. Bake for 40 minutes or until top springs back when touched. Cool in pan 5 minutes before turning out onto rack to cool completely. When cool, frost top and sides with Strawberries and Cream Frosting, and garnish with toasted coconut.

Strawberries and Cream Frosting

- 1 cup heavy cream
- 1 tablespoon sugar
- ½ cup strawberries, crushed

Whip cream until stiff and fold in sugar and strawberries.

An inexpensive milk glass plate is ideal for this cake. Cover cake and berries with plastic film and make sure your host or hostess serves this cake soon, or berries will soak in.

Rum Raisin Carrot Cake

Serves 12
Preparation time: 20 minutes
Baking time: 1 hour

- 1 cup raisins
- ½ cup dark rum
- ¾ cup vegetable oil
- 1 cup sugar
- 4 eggs, beaten
- 2 cups shredded carrots
- 2 cups flour
- 2 teaspoons baking soda
- ¼ teaspoon salt
- 1 tablespoon cinnamon
- 1 teaspoon freshly grated nutmeg
  Confectioners sugar

Preheat oven to 350°F. Combine raisins and rum; let stand while mixing batter. In large bowl mix together oil, sugar, and eggs; add grated carrots. Combine flour, baking soda, salt, and spices and blend into egg mixture. Stir in raisins and rum. Turn batter into greased 10-inch Bundt pan. Bake 1 hour. Cool in pan 5 minutes before turning out onto rack. If you do not have an old sugar shaker, place 2 tablespoons confectioners sugar in a wire strainer and stir the sugar with a spoon over the cake.

Serve with a sprig of holly leaves in center, or wrap in foil and tie with red yarn— a lavish gift indeed for a holiday host or hostess.

Old-fashioned Oatmeal Cake

Serves 8 to 10
Preparation time: 20 minutes, plus 30 minutes to soak oats
Baking time: 30 to 45 minutes

- 1 cup quick rolled oats
- 1½ cups boiling water
- ½ cup butter
- 1 cup dark brown sugar, firmly packed
- ½ cup sugar
- 2 eggs
- 1 teaspoon vanilla
- 1½ cups flour
- 1 teaspoon baking soda
- 1 teaspoon cinnamon
- ½ teaspoon salt
  Coconut Topping (recipe follows)

Preheat oven to 350°F. Add oats to boiling water; stir and allow to stand for 30 minutes. Cream butter and sugars; beat in eggs and vanilla. In large bowl mix together flour, baking soda, cinnamon, and salt. Alternately add soaked oatmeal and butter mixture to dry ingredients. Grease 9-inch square pan. Pour in batter and bake 30 to 45 minutes or until toothpick inserted in center comes out clean. Spread topping on cake while still warm.

Coconut Topping

- ½ stick butter or margarine
- 1 cup dark brown sugar, firmly packed
- ¼ cup evaporated milk
- 1 teaspoon vanilla
- 1 cup unsweetened coconut

In saucepan combine all ingredients except coconut and bring to a boil. Remove from heat and stir in coconut.

Squares of this cake can be packed snugly in a small disposable foil pan to give to a favorite singleton or couple for a holiday breakfast. Wrap the foil pan in plastic film, tie with green or red ribbon, and tuck in artificial holly berries (real holly berries are poisonous, so should not be used with food). The topping can also be packaged separately in its own pretty jar. Tie the recipe around the neck of the jar with ribbon or gift yarn.

Cranberry Nut Loaf

Makes 1 loaf
Preparation time: 30 minutes
Baking time: 1 hour

- 2 cups flour
- ¾ teaspoon salt
- 1½ teaspoons baking powder
- ½ teaspoon baking soda
- 1 cup chopped walnuts
- 1 cup cranberries, chopped coarsely
  Juice and grated peel of 1 orange
- ¼ cup butter
  Boiling water
- 1 egg, beaten
- ¾ cup sugar

This loaf freezes well (up to 3 months), and one is grateful to have it on hand as a last-minute gift for a friend.

Preheat oven to 350°F. Combine flour, salt, baking powder, and baking soda in a large bowl. Add nuts and cranberries to flour mixture. Place orange juice, peel, and butter in a measuring cup; add boiling water to make ¾ cup liquid. Add to flour mixture. Combine beaten egg and sugar; add to batter. Stir well. Pour batter into greased loaf pan and bake 1 hour. Cool in pan 10 minutes, turn out on wire rack and cool thoroughly.

Tie this fragrant loaf in a plastic bag and give the twist tie a collar of evergreens or a dried flower wreath.

Poppy Seed Special and Holiday Nut Spiral

Makes 2 poppy seed loaves and 2 nut loaves
Preparation time: 1 hour
Rising time: 1½ hours
Baking time: 30 minutes

    2 envelopes active dry yeast
    ½ cup warm water
    1 cup butter or margarine
    5 cups flour
    2 eggs, plus 4 egg yolks
    ¼ cup sugar
    1 teaspoon salt
    1 cup sour cream
    ½ cup milk, scalded
      Poppy Seed Filling (recipe follows)
      Walnut Filling (recipe follows)

Dissolve yeast in water. Cut butter into flour with pastry blender. Beat together egg yolks, 1 egg, sugar, and salt until thick; add to flour mixture. Add sour cream, milk, and yeast mixture. Beat until well blended. Turn out on floured board and knead until satiny. Divide dough into 4 equal portions. Roll each portion into an 8x10-inch rectangle, ½-inch thick. Spread 2 with Poppy Seed Filling and 2 with Walnut Filling. Roll up jelly roll fashion, leaving seams on top, and place on greased baking sheets. Brush surfaces with remaining egg, beaten. Allow to rise until almost doubled in bulk, about 1½ hours. Bake in preheated 375°F oven for 30 minutes. Cool on wire racks.

Poppy Seed Filling

    1 pound (6 cups) poppy seeds, ground
    1 cup honey
    1½ cups milk
    1 teaspoon cinnamon
    2 teaspoons grated lemon peel

Combine all ingredients and cook and stir over low heat until mixture holds together.

Walnut Filling

    1 pound (4 cups) finely ground walnuts
    2 cups sugar
    1 teaspoon grated lemon peel
    ½ cup milk
    1½ teaspoons cinnamon

Combine all ingredients together, mixing well.

These rich holiday breads are made for giving. Wrap loaves singly, one to a family, in plastic film or cellophane and tie with bright narrow ribbons.

Poppy Seed Swirls

Serves 8 to 10
Preparation time: 45 minutes
Rising time: 1½ hours
Baking time: 30 minutes

    1 envelope active dry yeast
    ½ cup plus 1 tablespoon sugar
    ¼ cup water
    3½-4 cups plus 1 teaspoon flour
    1 cup milk
    ¼ cup butter or margarine
    1½ teaspoons salt
      Poppy Seed Filling, ½ recipe
    1 egg, beaten

Mix together yeast, 1 tablespoon sugar, water, and 1 teaspoon flour in a warm bowl. Let stand until bubbly. Scald milk; add butter, salt, and ½ cup sugar. Cool to lukewarm. Add to yeast mixture. In large bowl add liquid to flour forming a soft dough. Use more flour if necessary in order to knead. Knead until smooth and elastic. Roll out into an 8x12-inch rectangle, ¼-inch thick. Spread with Poppy Seed Filling and roll up jelly roll fashion. Slice into 8 to 10 even portions (see note below) and place in a greased oblong pan or greased cookie sheet overlapping slices

slightly. Allow to rise about 1½ hours; brush with milk or beaten egg. Bake in preheated 375°F oven for 30 minutes.

Note: to cut a yeast dough jelly roll, pull a 12-inch piece of string under dough and cross string over itself to slice through dough.

Cut cardboard to fit this loaf, wrap the cardboard in foil, place the bread on it and stretch-wrap it in clear plastic. Seal it with colorful holiday stickers or tie it with yarn.

Ginger Crumb Cheesecake

Serves 8 to 10
Preparation time: 30 minutes
Baking time: 1 hour

    1½ cups crushed graham crackers
    ½ cup confectioners' sugar
    ¼ cup finely chopped crystallized ginger
    ¼ cup butter or margarine, melted
    24 ounces cream cheese, softened
    5 eggs
    ¾ cup sugar
    ¼ teaspoon salt
    ¾ teaspoon almond extract
    1½ cups sour cream
    2 tablespoons sugar
    ¾ teaspoon vanilla
      Fruit Topping (recipe follows)

Preheat oven to 325°F. Mix together cracker crumbs, sugar, and ginger. Add melted butter or margarine and mix well. Press into bottom of 9-inch spring-form pan. Bake 10 minutes, cool.

When crust has cooled, beat cream cheese until fluffy; beat in eggs one at a time. Add ¾ cup sugar, salt, and almond extract. Pour onto baked ginger graham crust in the cake pan. Bake at 325°F for

45 to 50 minutes until set, remove from oven. Cool 15 minutes. Combine sour cream, 2 tablespoons sugar, and vanilla; mix well. Pour on cake—still in the pan. Bake 10 minutes and allow to cool thoroughly. Remove from pan and refrigerate. This cake may be served plain or with Fruit Topping.

Fruit Topping

  2 cups fresh berries or cherries
  ¾ cup sugar
  ¼ cup water
  1½ tablespoons cornstarch
  ⅛ teaspoon salt
  1 teaspoon butter

    Wash berries or wash and pit cherries. Drain, and crush 1 cupful of fruit; add sugar, water, cornstarch, and salt. Cook over medium heat, until clear and thickened. Stir in butter. Strain through a wire strainer. Cool. Stir in second cup of fruit just before serving.

With or without the fruit topping, this sumptuous cheesecake makes a marvelous gift. Place cake and pan on a sturdy round of cardboard, wrapped in aluminum foil to make it look good. Cover it loosely with red or green cellophane. When you arrive at your destination, unmold the cake carefully, and take your pan home in the shopping bag that you thoughtfully brought along.

The Ginger Crumb Cheesecake, displayed on a pressed glass "Westward Ho" pattern cake stand, is made from an unusual recipe that includes crystallized ginger in the buttery crumb crust. It is shown here with a cherry topping, but strawberries or raspberries would work just as well.

Chocolate Cream Layers

Serves 8 to 10
Preparation time: 45 minutes
Baking time: 45 minutes

½ cup butter
1 cup brewed strong coffee
½ cup buttermilk
2 eggs, beaten
1 teaspoon vanilla
2 cups flour
5 tablespoons cocoa
1½ cups sugar
1½ teaspoons baking soda
   Coffee Butter Icing (recipe follows)
   Chocolate for garnish

Preheat oven to 325°F. Melt butter; add coffee, buttermilk, eggs, and vanilla. Mix well. In large bowl combine flour, cocoa, sugar, and baking soda. Mix liquid ingredients into dry ingredients and beat at medium speed until well blended. Grease two 8-inch round cake pans well. Pour batter into pans and bake 45 minutes until toothpick inserted in center comes out clean. Cool in pan 5 minutes before turning out onto racks. Create four layers by cutting each layer horizontally into two layers. Fill and frost with Coffee Butter Icing. Garnish with curls of chocolate, scraped from a solid chocolate bar using a potato peeler; or melt chocolate chips in a double boiler and freeze on a baking sheet—scrape off thick curls using a cheese plane.

Coffee Butter Icing

½ cup butter
2½ cups confectioners sugar (sifted)

1 teaspoon cocoa
1½ teaspoons hot coffee
1 egg white

Combine butter, sugar, cocoa, and coffee and mix well. Add egg white and beat until smooth and of spreading consistency.

A layer cake deserves a cake box. For chocolate, line the box with pink or deep magenta tissue paper, crushing the tissue so that it does not mar the elegant cake. Tie the box with ribbon to match the lining paper.

Party Ice Cream Sponge Cake

Serves 20 to 24
Preparation time: 45 minutes
Baking time: 1 hour

4 eggs, separated
3 tablespoons cold water
1½ cups sugar
½ cup boiling water
1½ cups flour
1 teaspoon baking powder
¼ teaspoon salt
½ teaspoon lemon extract
½ teaspoon cream of tartar
2 pints ice cream—strawberry, pistachio, or lemon
1 pint heavy cream
1 tablespoon vanilla
2 tablespoons confectioners sugar
   Crystallized flowers for garnish

Preheat oven to 350°F. In large bowl beat egg yolks until light colored. Add 3 tablespoons cold water and sugar. Beat while adding boiling water. Combine flour, baking powder, and salt. Mix well. Add to yolk mixture; add lemon extract and beat again. Beat egg whites with cream of tartar until stiff. Fold egg whites into batter. Bake in an ungreased 10-inch tube pan 1 hour or until top springs back when touched. Invert pan on rack and allow cake to cool; remove pan.

Split cake horizontally into 2 layers; spoon ice cream between layers and stack. Whip cream and fold in vanilla and confectioners sugar. Spread whipped cream over top and sides of cake. Decorate with crystallized flowers (see Chapter 13) and freeze until ready to serve.

This opulent cake is a stay-at-home, since it is frozen. Show it on a footed cake stand—your finest.

Apple Duffle

Serves 6 to 8
Preparation time: 40 minutes
Baking time: 30 minutes

3 apples—peeled, cored, and sliced (1½ cups)
1 cup sugar
2 teaspoons cinnamon
¼ teaspoon nutmeg
1¾ cups flour
½ cup butter
1 egg
½ cup milk
2 teaspoons baking powder
¼ teaspoon salt

Preheat oven to 375°F. Mix together apples, ¼ cup sugar, 1½ teaspoons cinnamon, and nutmeg. Set aside.

For crumb mixture: mix together ¼ cup flour, ¼ cup sugar, ½ teaspoon cinnamon, and ¼ cup butter. Set aside.

Cream ½ cup sugar and ¼ cup butter; beat in egg. Stir in milk. Add flour, baking powder, and salt. Mix well. Spread half of batter in a greased 8- or 9-inch square pan. Top with apple mixture and then remaining batter. Spread crumb mixture on top. Bake 25 to 30 minutes and serve warm or cold.

Bake half this recipe in a chicken pot-pie dish or other small baking dish for a couple or live-aloner. Cover with waxed paper, then wrap in a red bandana and tie with white gift-wrap yarn.

Podunk Gingerbread

Serves 10
Preparation time: 30 minutes
Baking time: 1 hour

- 2 cups flour
- 2 teaspoons baking powder
- 1 teaspoon baking soda
- ¼ teaspoon salt
- 1½ teaspoons ginger
- 1 teaspoon cinnamon
- ½ cup shortening
- ½ cup dark brown sugar, firmly packed
- 2 eggs, beaten
- 1 cup sour cream or buttermilk
- ¼ cup dark molasses

Preheat oven to 350°F. In large bowl combine flour, baking powder, baking soda, salt, and spices. Cream together shortening and sugar; beat in eggs. Add sour cream and molasses. Gradually add sour cream mixture to dry ingredients, beating well. Bake in greased 9-inch square pan 1 hour. Cool in pan 5 minutes before turning out onto rack.

A few slices of this old-fashioned gingerbread will delight an elderly friend. Overlap the slices in a small box and tie it jauntily with red satin ribbon.

Chocolate-chip Apple Cake

Serves 12 to 16
Preparation time: 40 minutes
Baking time: 40 minutes

- 2 eggs
- ¾ cup dark brown sugar, firmly packed
- ¾ cup sugar
- 2¼ cups plus 1 tablespoon flour
- 2 teaspoons baking soda
- ½ teaspoon salt
- 1 teaspoon cinnamon
- 1 cup buttermilk
- 2 cups apples—peeled, cored, and chopped
- ½ cup semisweet chocolate pieces

Preheat oven to 350°F. Beat eggs, then beat in ½ cup of each sugar. In large bowl, combine flour, baking soda, salt, and cinnamon. Add egg mixture and milk alternately to dry ingredients, stir thoroughly. Pour into greased 10-inch tube pan or 9 x 13-inch loaf pan. For topping mix together and sprinkle over cake: ¼ cup of each sugar, 1 tablespoon flour, ½ cup semisweet chocolate pieces. Bake 40 minutes.

This giant-sized cake in a cake box, is welcomed by a family with kids home for the holidays. The cake box can be purchased at a bakery or cake-baking supply shop and made festive by gluing on gilt paper doilies in decorative patterns.

Brazil Nut Cake

Serves 12 generously or 24 modestly
Preparation time: 25 minutes
Baking time: 1½ hours

- ¾ cup flour
- ¾ cup sugar
- ½ teaspoon baking powder
- ½ teaspoon salt
- 2 cups whole Brazil nuts (not chopped)
- 1 8-ounce package pitted dates (not chopped)
- 1 cup maraschino cherries, drained (not chopped)
- 3 eggs, beaten
- 1 teaspoon vanilla

This Christmas Special needs no icing or decorating. When sliced, whole nuts and fruits show off beautifully—a delight to serve.

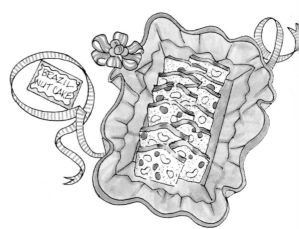

Preheat oven to 300°F. Mix together dry ingredients in large bowl; add nuts, dates, and cherries; mix lightly. Stir in beaten eggs and vanilla, mix together using a wooden spoon. Pour into a greased 9x5-inch glass loaf pan lined with brown paper that has been greased. Bake 1½ hours. Cool in pan for 15 minutes. Cool thoroughly on rack.

Note: wrap tightly in aluminum foil and refrigerate. Keeps indefinitely—always ready to serve to unexpected guests.

Give this cake like a precious jewel—in slices, wrapped in plastic film and nestled in bright tissue paper in a tiny box.

Breakfast Stollen

Makes 3 large stollen
Preparation time: 45 minutes
Rising time: 2 hours
Baking time: 20 to 25 minutes

  2 envelopes active dry yeast
  1 tablespoon sugar
  ½ cup warm water
  ¾ cup butter
  ½ cup sugar
  1 cup milk, scalded
  1½ teaspoons salt
  2 eggs, beaten
  2 teaspoons grated lemon peel
  6 cups flour
  1½ cups raisins
  1 cup mixed candied fruit
  1 cup candied cherries
  1 cup walnuts, chopped
  ¼ cup dark brown sugar, firmly packed
  2 teaspoons cinnamon
  2 cups confectioners sugar
  2 tablespoons light corn syrup
  Milk

Mix together yeast, sugar, and water; set in warm place until bubbly. Cream butter and sugar; add to hot milk with salt. Cool. Add eggs and lemon peel. In large bowl add 3 cups of flour to fruits and nuts. Add milk mixture alternately with yeast mixture to flour mixture. Add remaining flour and knead. Let rise until double in bulk, about 1 hour. Punch down. Divide dough into thirds; roll each into an 8x10-inch rectangle, ½-inch thick. Combine brown sugar, cinnamon, and ½ cup butter and sprinkle on dough. Roll up jelly roll fashion with seams on top. Allow to rise in warm place until almost doubled, about 1 hour. Bake in preheated 375°F oven for 20 minutes. Cool on wire racks.

While stollen are cooling, make the icing by blending confectioners sugar and corn syrup with enough milk to make a smooth, spreadable icing. When stollen are completely cool, spread with icing.

Note: these loaves can be frozen up to 3 months. Make icing and spread on just before serving. Garnish with holly leaves.

One of these plump loaves wrapped in plastic film and tied with a red ribbon is the ultimate in Christmas gifts to many people. This bread reheats beautifully for Christmas morning breakfast, but omit the frosting if you plan to heat it.

Fresh Plum Kuchen

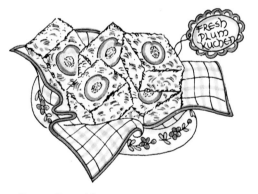

Serves 8 to 10
Preparation time: 30 minutes
Baking time: 45 minutes

  1 cup flour
  ½ cup, plus 1 tablespoon sugar
  ⅛ teaspoon salt
  ½ cup butter
  2 eggs beaten, plus 1 egg yolk
  1 tablespoon milk
  2 pounds plums, pitted and cut in half
  Cinnamon

Preheat oven to 350°F. Combine flour, ½ cup sugar, and salt; work in butter using a fork. Gradually add egg yolk and milk to form a pastry dough. Pat dough on bottom of 8-inch square pan. Arrange plums cut side up on dough, forming rows. Beat 2 eggs and 1 tablespoon sugar, pour over all. Sprinkle cinnamon on top and bake 45 minutes. Cut into squares for serving.

Give a few squares of this cake on rustic-looking pottery plates, overwrapped first with plastic film, then a checkered napkin.

Applesauce Cake

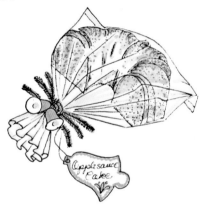

Serves 10 to 12
Preparation time: 30 minutes
Baking time: 1 hour

  1 cup dark brown sugar, firmly packed
  ½ cup butter
  1 egg
  1 teaspoon vanilla
  2 cups flour
  2 teaspoons baking soda
  ½ teaspoon cinnamon
  ¼ teaspoon cloves
  1 cup raisins, chopped
  1 cup chopped dates
  ½ cup chopped nuts
  1½ cups applesauce
  ¼ cup dark brown sugar, firmly packed (optional)
  ½ cup brandy (optional)

This cake is excellent for mailing to faraway friends and family.

Preheat oven to 350°F. Cream butter and sugar; add egg and vanilla and beat well. In large bowl combine flour, baking soda, and spices; add raisins dates, and nuts. Add applesauce and butter mixture alternately to dry ingredients. Pour into a buttered and floured 9-inch tube pan and bake 1 hour. Cool in pan 5 minutes before turning out onto rack.

For an optional topping, heat ¼ cup brown sugar in ½ cup brandy until sugar is melted. Pour over cake while still warm from oven.

A large wedge of this cake, a half or a quarter, makes a thoughtful gift for a young career couple who don't have time to bake. Pack the cake in a plastic bag and twist-tie it closed with a green pipe cleaner. A novelty gift-wrap ball can be twisted into the closing.

Black Fruitcake

Makes 2 loaf cakes, 3 pounds each
Serves 24
Preparation time: 1 hour
Baking time: 2½ hours

1¼ cups sliced dry figs
1 cup cooked whole prunes, drained
2 cups seeded raisins, chopped
2 cups seedless raisins
3 cups currants
1½ cups blanched almonds, toasted and sliced
1 cup (6 ounce package) pitted dates, chopped
1 cup whole candied cherries
½ cup diced candied orange peel
3 cups dark rum
1 cup soft butter or margarine
2 cups dark brown sugar, firmly packed
1½ teaspoons cinnamon
1½ teaspoons freshly grated nutmeg
5 eggs
2 cups flour
2 teaspoons baking powder
½ teaspoon salt

A delicious cake made the old-time way and it keeps forever! Make at least one month before the holidays to improve flavor.

A few days before making cake, combine all fruits, peel, and almonds. Mix well and stir in rum. Cover tightly and store unrefrigerated. On baking day, preheat oven to 275°F. In large bowl

cream butter and sugar; add spices; beat in 2 eggs. Combine flour, baking powder, and salt. Add 1 cup flour mixture to butter mixture, beat in remaining eggs. Stir in rum-soaked fruit, add remaining flour mixture, and mix well. Line 2 greased 9 x 5 x 3-inch loaf pans with brown paper and grease lightly. Divide batter equally between pans. Bake 2½ hours or until toothpick inserted in center comes out clean. Cool in pan 1 hour.

Note: keep a shallow pan of hot water on bottom oven rack during baking to prevent cakes from becoming too dry (make sure that the water does not all cook away, checking after 1 hour and again after 2 hours). Wrap tightly and store in covered tins.

This rich cake should be cut for giving. A half a loaf will please most families. Wrap it tightly in foil or plastic film, and pack in gilt boxes with bright tissue inside to make the cake look as special as it is.

Golden Jonquil Cake

Serves 10 to 12
Preparation time: 45 minutes
Baking time: 25 minutes

2⅓ cups cake flour (not self rising)
2½ teaspoons baking powder
½ teaspoon salt
¾ cup butter
1½ cups sugar
3 eggs
⅔ cup milk
1 teaspoon vanilla
Lemon Filling (recipe follows)
1 pint heavy cream, whipped
Lemon peel for garnish

Preheat oven to 375°F. In large bowl sift together cake flour, baking powder,

and salt. Cream butter, add sugar gradually, beat until light and fluffy. Beat eggs into butter mixture one at a time; add vanilla. Add butter mixture and milk alternately to flour mixture.

Line two 9-inch round cake pans with waxed paper and grease. Pour batter into pans. Bake 25 minutes. Cool in pans 5 minutes before turning out onto racks.

With long sharp knife, split cakes horizontally to form 4 layers. Spread lemon filling between layers and frost with whipped cream. Garnish with long thin strips of lemon peel.

Lemon Filling

1½ cups water
1 cup sugar
⅛ teaspoon salt
1½ tablespoons cornstarch
Grated peel and juice of 1 lemon
½ tablespoon butter
2 egg yolks

Bring water to boil in large saucepan. Blend sugar, salt, and cornstarch. Stir into boiling water. Cook and stir until clear and slightly thickened. Stir in grated lemon peel, juice, and butter. Lightly beat egg yolks; add 2 or 3 tablespoons hot mixture and stir well. Pour egg yolk mixture into saucepan and cook, stirring, over medium heat until slightly thickened. Cool.

This cake travels only a few blocks, but it will be welcomed wherever it goes. Take the cake on its own elegant cake plate, to be retrieved if it is your own or to be given to the host or hostess if you wish. A few lemon leaves, clustered at a corner of the cake, add a festive air.

Pork Cake

Serves 12
Preparation time: 40 minutes
Baking time: 45 minutes

2 cups boiling water
¾ cup finely diced salt pork
1 cup sugar
2 teaspoons baking soda
2 cups molasses
3½ cups flour
2 teaspoons cinnamon
2 teaspoons freshly grated nutmeg
2 teaspoons cloves
1 cup raisins
½ cup citron
½ cup currants (optional)

Preheat oven to 350°F. Pour boiling water over chopped salt port in large bowl, stir, add sugar, and allow to stand until cool. Dissolve baking soda in molasses. Combine flour, spices, raisins, citron, and currants (if desired). Add molasses and dry ingredients alternately to pork mixture. Spoon into greased 10-inch ring mold or large loaf pan. Bake 45 minutes. Cool in pan 5 minutes before turning out onto rack.

This cake is a slice of yesteryear. Show it off appropriately, in a basket lined with foil or waxed paper and a wrap of calico figured dimity or a sweet pastel ribbon tie.

Apple Cider Cake

Serves 10 to 12
Preparation time: 30 minutes
Baking time: 50 minutes

2½ cups flour
2 teaspoons baking soda
½ teaspoon salt
1 cup dark raisins
½ cup butter or margarine
1 cup dark brown sugar, firmly packed
1 egg
1 cup apple cider

A quick and easy cake! Bake in a Bundt pan or large or small loaf pans.

Preheat oven to 375°F. Combine dry ingredients in large bowl; stir in raisins. Cream together butter and sugar; beat in egg. Add cider alternately with butter mixture to dry ingredients. Turn into greased pan(s), filling no more than ⅔ full. Bake 50 minutes for large cake, 40 minutes for smaller cakes, or until toothpick inserted in center comes out clean. Cool in pan(s) 5 minutes before turning out onto rack.

Small loaves of this festive cake are darling gifts. Wrap individually in plastic film or foil and tie with red gift ribbon and a shiny Christmas ball.

Minnesota Apple Upside-down Cake

Serves 12
Preparation time: 30 minutes
Baking time: 40 minutes

8 cups peeled, cored, and sliced apples
1¼ cups sugar
¾ teaspoon cinnamon
½ cup plus 3 tablespoons butter
2 eggs
1 cup milk
1 teaspoon vanilla
2 cups flour
2½ teaspoons baking powder
1 teaspoon salt
Toasted almonds for garnish

Preheat oven to 350°F. Combine apples, ¾ cup sugar, cinnamon, and 3 tablespoons butter in a large saucepan. Cook over low heat, stirring now and then, until apples are tender. Pour into greased 13 x 9-inch pan. Cream ½ cup

butter and ½ cup sugar; beat in eggs. Combine milk and vanilla. In large bowl combine flour, baking powder, and salt. Add milk and butter mixture alternately to dry ingredients. Spread batter over apples in pan. Bake 40 minutes. Cool slightly. Turn upside down over large platter and let stand 10 minutes. Remove pan. Sprinkle with toasted almonds and serve warm or cold.

To share this lavish cake with friends, turn it out on a large disposable foil tray. Decorate with a few lady apples and a sprig of food-safe greens and cover the cake and decoration with plastic film.

Pie Crusts

Basic Recipe

Makes one 8- or 9-inch pie shell

1 cup flour
½ teaspoon salt
⅓ cup plus 1 tablespoon vegetable shortening
⅜ tablespoons cold water

Makes one 8- or 9-inch 2-crust pie

1½ cups flour
¾ teaspoon salt
½ cup plus 1½ tablespoons vegetable shortening
3 tablespoons cold water

Makes two 8- or 9-inch 2 crust pies or one 8- or 9-inch pie shell and 20 tart shells

3 cups flour
2 teaspoons salt
1 cup shortening
½ cup cold water

Mixing method I: In large bowl, mix flour and salt together. Work in shortening using pastry blender or fork until mixture resembles cornmeal. Sprinkle in water and mix just until dough holds together.

Mixing method II: Using food processor, mix chilled shortening and liquid first; then add flour and process *only* until dough begins to mass together.

Divide dough into portions, wrap in wax paper, and chill ½ hour. On lightly floured surface roll out dough 2 inches larger than pans. For 2-crust pie, roll top crust 2 inches smaller than bottom crust.

For unbaked pie shell, fit loosely into pans and crimp edges. For baked pie shells, fit loosely into pans, prick bottom all over with fork, crimp edges, and bake in preheated 400°F oven for 12 to 15 minutes.

Quantity Recipe

Makes two 10-inch 2-crust pies or one 8- or 9-inch pie shell and 20 tart shells

4 cups flour
1 tablespoon sugar
2 teaspoons salt
1¾ cups solid vegetable shortening
½ cup water
1 tablespoon white or cider vinegar
1 large egg

Combine flour, sugar, and salt and mix well. Work in shortening using a pastry blender or fork until mixture resembles cornmeal. Mix together water, vinegar, and egg; add to flour mixture. Chill, roll out, and bake following instructions in Basic Recipe.

No-roll Pie Crust

Makes one 8- or 9-inch pie shell

1 cup plus 3 tablespoons flour
½ cup butter or margarine

Mix ingredients together with pastry blender or form until mixture resembles cornmeal. Press into bottom and sides of pan. Bake shell at 375°F for 10 to 12 minutes. For a double crust, double recipe and spoon second half on top of pie filling before baking filled pie.

PERFECTING THE IMPERFECT CRUST

Did your last crust taste like cardboard, or was it so crumbly that you couldn't get it out of the pan? Do your pie shells buckle, and your meringue pies weep? Did your last apple pie look more like a mountain range than something to eat? Take heart, these things happen to everyone, but with the tips below they may stop happening to you!

Solid white shortening makes a flakier, more reliable, crust than margarine, butter, or oil alone. A 50–50 combination of solid white shortening mixed with margarine, butter or oil works well too. Cut in shortening with a pastry blender or two knives, forming particles that range in size from that of a small pea to cornmeal. These particles are what makes crust flaky.

Mix in only enough water to make dry ingredients clump together. The amount of water required will vary according to the amount of humidity in the air and in the flour, so add water slowly and observe carefully. Too much water will make your crust tough.

Chill pastry before rolling it out and handle it as little as possible. Heat will melt the shortening and cause the crust to be crumbly or tough.

Roll out pastry on a lightly floured pastry cloth with a rolling pin in a knitted sleeve. The cloth and rolling pin cover allow you to use a minimum of flour, preventing a floury, tough crust.

When fitting pastry into the pie plate, take care not to stretch it, or it will surely tear or buckle. Prick the bottom in several places to allow air to escape. To prevent shrinkage, crimp edges tightly to the rim of the pie plate with fork or fingers. Chill crust for a few minutes before baking.

When making meringue pies, be sure to bring the meringue out over the crimped edges. This will keep the meringue from shrinking while cooking.

When making pie shells that will be filled after they are baked, brush the inside of the shells with unbeaten egg white and fill with dry beans or pastry weights before baking.

For evenly golden-brown, crisp crusts, bake pies and pie shells in ovenproof glass, dull metal, or dark enamelware pie plates. Shiny metal reflects heat and tends to bake pastry with dark and light spots or soggy bottom crusts. Position pies or pie shells low in the oven. Pies set on a middle or top rack may have soggy, underbaked crusts. If the top edge of the pie begins to brown before the filling and bottom of the pastry are done, shield rim from heat with a ring of foil.

Serve fruit and meringue pies within a few hours of baking. Fruit pies held longer tend to soak fruit juices into the crust, making a previously crispy crust soggy and unappealing. Meringue pies tend to weep and seep down into the crust. Leftover fruit pie can be somewhat freshened by heating in a moderate oven. Heating in a microwave oven will only accentuate the sogginess.

If you're upset by an apple pie with a crust that looks too mountainous, blame the apples. Hard green apples will not cook down as well as softer varieties like Rome Beauty, McIntosh, and Cortland, and are responsible for those hills and valleys. However many people feel that harder apples make tastier pies and don't mind the bumps.

When you've perfected your technique, make crusts in quantity and freeze them. There's nothing like a freezer full of perfect crusts to make an imperfect cook feel smug.

Sugar Cookie Pie Crust

Makes one 16-inch tart crust or two 8- or 9-inch pie shells

- ¾ cup butter
- ½ cup sugar
- 1 egg yolk
- 2 cups cake flour
- ½ teaspoon vanilla
- 2 tablespoons heavy cream

Cream butter and sugar until light and fluffy; add egg yolk, vanilla, and cream. Mix well. Beat in flour. Chill, roll out, and bake following instructions in Basic Recipe.

Southern Pecan Pie

Serves 10
Preparation time: 25 minutes
Baking time: 40 minutes

- 3 eggs, well beaten
- ¾ cup sugar
- 1 cup light corn syrup
- 1 cup pecans, chopped coarsely
- 2 teaspoons butter, melted
- ⅛ teaspoon salt
- 1 unbaked 9-inch pie shell
  Whole pecans for garnish

Preheat oven to 400°F. In large bowl combine eggs, sugar, and corn syrup. Add pecans, butter, and salt. Pour into pie shell. Garnish with whole pecans. Bake 10 minutes then reduce temperature to 350°F. Bake 30 minutes until toothpick inserted in center comes out clean.

Treat yourself to a pie-carrying basket that has a rack (basket holds 2 pies). Tie bells on the handle with a large, wide ribbon.

Carry one pie to your neighbor and continue on your way with one for another friend. You can bake this pie in a disposable foil pan for easy carrying. Cover it with plastic film and wrap gummed holiday tape over and under to form six or eight spoke-like decorations.

Orange Liqueur Pumpkin Pie

Makes 2 pies
Serves 12
Preparation time: 30 minutes
Baking time: 40 minutes

- 2 unbaked 8-inch pie shells
- 3 eggs, separated
- 2 cups cooked, mashed pumpkin (fresh or canned)
- ½ cup sugar
- ¼ cup dark molasses
- ¾ teaspoon salt
- ¾ teaspoon cinnamon
- ¾ teaspoon nutmeg
- 2 cups heavy cream
- 3 ounces orange-flavored liqueur
  Chopped pistachio or macadamia nuts for garnish

A surprise when you cut into this pie—layers appear, making it most attractive!

Chill pie shells while preparing filling.

Preheat oven to 450°F. Beat egg yolks slightly; stir in pumpkin, sugar, molasses, salt, and spices. Stir in heavy cream, mixing thoroughly. Beat egg whites until stiff. Fold in egg whites and liqueur. Pour into unbaked pie shells and sprinkle with nuts. Bake 10 minutes then reduce heat to 325°F. Bake 30 minutes until filling is set.

This golden pie is a treat to take along to a Thanksgiving dinner. The nuts and small jar of cream can go along with it.

Pumpkin Chiffon Pie

Serves 6
Preparation time: 30 minutes
Chilling time: 30 minutes

- 2 teaspoons unflavored gelatin
- ½ cup dark brown sugar, firmly packed
- ¼ teaspoon salt
- ¼ teaspoon cinnamon
- ¼ teaspoon nutmeg
- ¼ teaspoon ginger
- ¾ cup cooked, mashed pumpkin (fresh or canned)
- 2 eggs, separated
- ⅓ cup milk
- ¼ teaspoon cream of tartar
- ⅓ cup sugar
- 1 baked 8-inch pie shell
  Heavy cream, whipped for garnish
  Green grapes for garnish

Combine gelatin, brown sugar, salt, and spices in saucepan. Stir in pumpkin, slightly beaten egg yolks, and milk. Cook over medium heat stirring constantly until gelatin is dissolved. Set saucepan in pan of cold water to cool. Beat egg whites with cream of tartar and sugar until stiff. Fold into cooled pumpkin mixture. Pour into pie shell. Chill until firm. Serve with whipped cream or garnish with green grapes.

Wrap in plastic film to show off this pie's pretty color. If you like, attach a colorful ribbon bow with a wooden toothpick.

Rhubarb Pie

Serves 6
Preparation time: 20 minutes
Baking time: 45 minutes

  Pastry for 2-crust 8-inch pie
3 tablespoons flour
1 cup sugar
1 egg, beaten
2 cups cut rhubarb
  Milk (optional)

Line 8-inch pie plate with half the pastry; crimp edges. Chill while preparing filling.

Preheat oven to 425°F. In large bowl combine flour and sugar. Beat in egg; stir in rhubarb. Pour filling into pie shell. Cover with top crust; crimp edges and cut slits in crust to let steam escape. If a brown crust is desired, brush with milk. Bake 10 minutes then reduce heat to 350°F. Bake 35 minutes until crust is golden and filling bubbles.

Bake this pie fresh to take along for a springtime supper. Wrap foil loosely over the top and loop a folded kitchen towel around the base of the pie plate to help hold in the heat.

Fresh Berry Pie

Serves 6
Preparation time: 25 minutes

1 quart berries (raspberries, strawberries, or blueberries)
1 baked 9-inch pie shell
3 tablespoons cornstarch
¾ cup sugar
2 tablespoons water
¼ teaspoon salt
1 teaspoon butter
  Whole berries for garnish
1 cup heavy cream, whipped, for garnish

Place ⅔ of fresh berries in pie shell. In saucepan combine cornstarch, sugar, water, salt, butter, and remaining berries. Cook and stir until smooth and slightly thickened. Cool. Pour sauce over berries. Top with more fresh berries and whipped cream.

This berry pie in its pie plate looks very special on a crystal plate with lemon leaves or other fresh greenery for decoration. Cover all with foil or waxed paper and tie it with a strip cut from pastel nylon net.

Fresh Gooseberry Pie

Serves 6
Preparation time: 20 minutes
Baking time: 45 minutes

  Pastry for 2-crust 8-inch pie
3½ cups gooseberries
1 cup sugar
2 tablespoons cornstarch
1 tablespoon butter
  Milk (optional)

Line an 8-inch pie plate with half the pastry; crimp edges. Chill while preparing the filling.

Preheat oven to 350°F. Spread berries evenly in pie shell. Combine sugar and cornstarch and sprinkle over berries. Dot with butter. Cut remaining pastry in strips and weave in lattice pattern over berries. For brown crust, brush top with milk.

Bake about 45 minutes until crust is golden and filling bubbles.

Yum! Slip the gooseberry pie into a basket that fits it, cover the pie with waxed paper, then a fresh cotton napkin. Take along a carton of cream to whip or to pour onto wedges of pie, British-style.

Shaker Lemon Pie

Serves 6
Preparation time: 20 minutes
Setting time: several hours
Baking time: 40 minutes

  Pastry for 2-crust 8-inch pie
2 lemons, seeded and sliced very thin
2 cups sugar
4 eggs, well beaten

Line an 8-inch pie plate with half the pastry; crimp edges. Chill while preparing the filling.

Combine lemon slices and sugar; allow to set for several hours or overnight.

Preheat oven to 400°F. Stir well-beaten eggs into lemon mixture and pour into pie plate. Arrange lemon slices around pie. Cover with top crust; crimp edges and cut slits in crust to allow steam to escape.

Bake 10 minutes then reduce heat to 350°F. Bake 30 minutes until crust is golden and filling bubbles.

This old-fashioned, homey pie looks as good as it tastes set on a figured cotton doily on a tray. Cover the pie and tray with plastic film.

Limington Pie

Serves 8
Preparation time: 1 hour
Baking time: 12 minutes

   1 baked 9-inch deep pie shell
   1 cup sugar
  ¼ cup plus 2 tablespoons cornstarch
  ¼ teaspoon salt
  ½ cup water
  ½ cup lemon juice
   3 egg yolks, well beaten
   2 tablespoons butter
   1 tablespoon grated lemon peel
 1½ cups hot water
    Meringue Topping (recipe follows)

Preheat oven to 350°F. In large saucepan mix together sugar, cornstarch, and salt. Add ½ cup water and lemon juice and stir until smooth. Add egg yolks, butter, and lemon peel. Stir in hot water gradually, bring the mixture to a boil. Reduce heat and boil 1 minute. Remove from heat; cool slightly and pour into baked pie shell.

Spread Meringue Topping on pie, sealing to pie shell all around. Bake 12 minutes, until golden brown. Use a sharp knife dipped in hot water to cut Limington Pie.

Meringue Topping

   3 egg whites
  ¼ teaspoon cream of tartar
  ¼ cup sugar

Beat egg whites until frothy, add cream of tartar, and beat until they hold peaks. Add sugar slowly, then beat until stiff.

Note: if you prefer a meringue that stands high on the pie, substitute 1 teaspoon baking powder for cream of tartar. Combine baking powder with sugar and add mixture to egg whites. Beat well.

Show the Limington Pie in a pie server, a lemon curl and lemon leaves tucked into the meringue at one edge. This provides no protection, so clearly this is a gift to take next door to a friend's dinner party. (Make sure the leaves are lemon leaves—some other leaves look similar but are poisonous.)

Ten-minute Custard Pie

Serves 8
Preparation time: 10 minutes
Baking time: 45 to 60 minutes

   4 eggs
   2 cups milk
   1 cup sugar
  ½ teaspoon salt
  ½ cup flour
   1 stick margarine, softened
   1 teaspoon vanilla
   1 cup flaked sweetened coconut
  ¼ teaspoon fresh grated nutmeg

A quick-baking pie that bakes its own crust!

Preheat oven to 350°F. Grease 10-inch pie pan well. Put all ingredients in blender in order given. Blend until smooth and well mixed. Pour into greased pan. Bake 45 to 60 minutes until bottom crust is nicely brown. Cool and serve.

This last-minute dessert can be your contribution to an impromptu dinner party. Set the pie plate in a box cover that fits it and pad the cover with colorful tissue or cellophane. Cover lightly with plastic film and wrap with a yarn tie.

Holiday Angel Pie

Serves 8
Preparation time: 30 minutes
Baking time: 1 hour

   4 eggs, separated
  ¼ teaspoon cream of tartar
 1¼ cups sugar
   3 tablespoons lemon juice
   1 tablespoon grated lemon peel
  ⅛ teaspoon salt
   1 cup heavy cream, whipped
    Candied lemon rind for garnish
    (optional)

Preheat oven to 275°F. For pie shell, beat egg whites with cream of tartar and ¾ cup sugar until stiff. Spread in greased pie pan. Bake 1 hour. Cool.

In saucepan, beat yolks; add ½ cup sugar, lemon juice and peel, and salt. Stir over medium heat until thick. Cool. Fold in whipped cream and pour into cooled pie shell. Garnish with more whipped cream, if desired, and thin coiled strips of candied lemon rind.

Look for the right box for this high-standing confection in a bakery supply shop, set the pie in it, close the box and seal with gummed gift wrap tape. Green and pastel yellow are pretty for spring, red and dark green for the holidays.

Glazed Fresh Fruit Tart

Serves 12
Preparation time: 35 minutes
Baking time: 8 minutes

    Sugar Cookie Pie Crust or refrigerated cookie dough
   8 ounces cream cheese, softened
  ½ cup sugar
   1 teaspoon vanilla
   1 pint strawberries, sliced or whole
   2 kiwi fruits, peeled and sliced

CAKES AND PIES

6 ounces red currant or apple jelly
1 tablespoon unflavored gelatin
¼ cup water

Line a 16-inch pizza pan or two 8-inch pie pans with dough; crimp edges. Bake 8 minutes and allow to cool.

Combine cream cheese, sugar, and vanilla. Mix well and spread over bottom of crust. Arrange slices of fruit over cheese mixture. Heat jelly to liquid state, add gelatin and stir to dissolve. Remove from heat; add water and mix well. Pour mixture over fruit tart. Cool in refrigerator until serving time.

Note: other fruits such as pineapple, green grapes, peaches, and bananas may be used.

This tart is most splendid in the pizza-size and should remain in the pan for taking along as a gift. The pie itself is a marvel of color. Wrap it in plastic film so the fruits show. A spray of greenery and small red bow might be attached at the edge, but the tart is smashing as is.

The luscious Glazed Fresh Fruit Tart is made here in holiday colors: strawberry red and kiwi green. To cool the eye as well as the palate in summer, make the tart with pale green grapes, blueberries, and bananas.

39

TIP TIPS

The point of this picture is to show what different cake decorating tips look like, and what each of them can do. Manufacturers in the U.S. give each one a number. Lower numbers have smaller holes. Working from top left to lower right, the tips are: #20, #18, #30, and #191—all "star" tips; #67—a "leaf" tip; #3 and #8—both "writing" tips; and #47 and #101—two more "leaf" tips. "Leaf" and "star" tips can make many different designs, especially if you turn the bag as you squeeze. The "writing" tips are used not only for writing, but for piping lines of icing when joining pieces of the Gingerbread House (Chapter 4).

A pastry bag is used for applying decorative icing. These are made of plastic-lined cloth. Disposable bags made of plastic or paper can also be used. A good size is about 10 inches long. A threaded plastic adapter nozzle fits part way through the hole at the tip of the bag. This allows you to change tips without emptying the icing from the bag. The metal tip fits onto the protruding nozzle and is held in place with a plastic coupling ring threaded to match the nozzle.

Icing will stay moist and workable if no air gets to it to dry it out. You can buy a tip cover to seal off the small end of a bag full of icing. Tightly fold the large end of the bag to seal it off, then you can leave that bag for a while, perhaps to work with another bag filled with icing of a different color. For this reason, it is a good idea to have two or three bags, adapter nozzles with coupling rings, and tip covers.

After you buy a pastry bag, the tip must be snipped off with scissors so the hole is just big enough for half of the threaded rings of the coupler to be exposed when you push it through. After attaching the metal tip, fill the bag only half full of icing. Work it down to the tip end and flatten the large end. Fold the two corners inward so they overlap each other; then role the empty end down toward the full end, like a tube of toothpaste. Hold it there with one hand and squeeze the icing out through the tip with the other hand. Practice on waxed paper or plastic film until you get the hang of it.

Soft Boiled Icing

*Makes enough to frost a 2-layer
cake or a 9 x 13-inch sheet cake
Preparation time: 20 minutes*

> 5 tablespoons flour
> 1 cup milk
> 1 cup butter
> 1 cup sugar
> 1 tablespoon vanilla (or ½ teaspoon
>   vanilla and ½ teaspoon almond
>   extract)

Combine flour and milk; cook in double
boiler until thick, cool. In large bowl
cream butter and sugar until light and
fluffy. Add vanilla and flour mixture and
beat for 5 to 10 minutes with an electric
mixer at high speed.

Variation: instead of vanilla, try 4 to
6 raspberries or strawberries, or juice and
grated peel of 1 lemon.

Royal Icing

*Makes 2 cups
Preparation time: 15 minutes*

> 4 cups confectioners sugar
> 3 egg whites
> ½ teaspoon cream of tartar

Combine all ingredients in large bowl
and beat with electric mixer at low speed
until blended. Then beat at high speed
7 to 10 minutes. Icing is ready to use
when knife drawn through it leaves a clear
path which holds its shape.

Note: do not double this recipe. If you
need more, make 2 or more separate
batches.

Coloring Icing

Hint: if you are using two frosting colors
in one area, work with only one color at
a time, and allow it to dry at least an
hour before applying another, so the two
will not bleed into each other.

1. To tint icing, divide batch and put
into small bowls (disposable plastic bowls
are good for this because you need a
separate dish for each color icing). Dip
tip of toothpick in food coloring and dot
on icing.

Icing dries out very quickly, so keep bowls
covered with damp cloths, damp paper
towels, or plastic film even while you are
working with them. Do not refrigerate.

2. Use rubber spatula to mix food coloring
into icing, stirring to blend thoroughly.
Add more food coloring a bit at a time
with a toothpick until you get desired
intensity.

It's a good idea to mix all the colors you
will need before you start decorating.

1. Icing is "piped" through metal tips attached to parchment cones or cloth or plastic-lined pastry bags. Disposable parchment paper triangles come in packages of 100 and are inexpensive. They are especially practical if you are using several icing colors, since each color must be applied in a separate container.

To fold a parchment triangle into a cone shape, first hold it in your hands so the point of the triangle is on top.

2. Now bring the other two points together and draw them around to meet the first point, Staple or glue points together. Cut ½ inch off cone tip and fit a metal tip inside.

If you are using a pastry bag, fit it with an adapter and tip following above instructions. See photograph for different tips and what they do.

3. Using spatula, scoop icing from bowl into parchment cone. Fill cone about ½ full, working icing towards tip as you proceed.

4. Fold three sides of cone down and into cone, leaving a point. Press icing down firmly in tip before you start rolling the top down.

5. Fold point over and over several times (like rolling up a toothpaste tube) to seal icing in cone. Squeeze a little icing through tip to be sure all the air is out before starting to pipe on the design outlines.

6. The flow of icing from the cone tip is controlled by the pressure of your hand and fingers. You may want to practice on aluminum foil or waxed paper before starting to decorate.

CAKES AND PIES

Flow Frosting

1. Use Flow Frosting to cover surfaces within icing outlines. Stir small amounts of water into bowl of tinted or white Royal Icing until it flows slowly in an even stream, like heavy cream.

2. Roll a parchment cone and cut ¼ inch off the tip. Fill with frosting and gently squeeze a puddle into center of design outlined in icing. Keep bowl of frosting covered with damp cloth or paper towels.

3. The icing acts like a dike around the frosting. Be sure the piped outline of icing has dried hard before filling in with frosting.

Poke frosting into corners with toothpick so area inside icing is completely and evenly filled.

COLOR BLENDING CHART				To produce these additional colors, mix the proportions shown
Green	Yellow	Red	Blue	
—	2	1	—	Orange
—	—	3	1	Purple
1	—	—	3	Turquoise
1	12	—	—	Chartreuse
1	4	3	—	Toast
—	—	1	2	Violet

4. Another technique is simply to dip a knife into the bowl of frosting and let it run down blade into area to be frosted, then work it into corners with point of blade.

5. Some people like to use an artist's paintbrush to paint frosting directly from bowl onto cookie or to coax it into corners from a puddle in center of design area.

COOKIES

Spicy, buttery, Walnut Speculaas are displayed in a pine grain scoop from the 1800s. The cookies were formed in hand-carved, wooden butter molds. The print served to identify the butter maker, or just added a loving, personal touch to the family table.

4

Cookies are the very soul of a happy holiday, the food of which magic and tradition are made. The recipes here are updated versions of fine cookies that have been baked for centuries to delight children and grown-ups. If you don't have time to bake all the varieties you want, why not organize a cookie swap? Each person bakes two or three recipes, then swaps a dozen or so of the best with the other barter-bakers. Each cookie-maker will have a glittering assortment of cookies to serve during the holidays.

Cookies are simple to make, but remember that on a cold day, when the thermostat is low, the dough performs better if butter or other shortening is brought to room temperature and if flour and other ingredients are warmed slightly before mixing. (Set them on top of the oven while something is baking, or in a warm spot in the kitchen for a few hours before you mix cookies.) If dough is too firm to manage easily, add water—a few drops at a time—and work it in just until the dough is manageable.

Cookies are the perfect gift, the delicacy that you can give by the half dozen or dozen to a young couple or a singleton friend or neighbor. Cookies are also grand to have around for your convivial holiday doings. Bring out a plateful of cookies to serve with hot cocoa or mulled fruit juice to offer to friends and relatives who drop by with a holiday wish. Cookies and a glass of milk are the perfect quiet-time snack for a tired child and a tired Mom or Dad.

If you're ambitious, a gingerbread house using Heart Molasses dough is a holiday tradition worth reviving. The grown-ups do the baking and building, but the whole family can lend a hand with the decorating. Mix up the Royal Icing and let the gumdrops fall where they may.

Heart Molasses Cookies

Makes 2½ dozen
Preparation time: 30 minutes
Chilling time: 8 hours or overnight
Baking time: 30 minutes

1 teaspoon baking soda
1 cup dark molasses
¾ cup sugar
⅓ cup butter
⅓ cup vegetable shortening
¼ cup water or orange juice
3 cups flour
1 cup whole wheat flour
2 teaspoons ginger
½ teaspoon cloves
½ teaspoon freshly grated nutmeg
½ teaspoon allspice
1 teaspoon salt
1 egg yolk
1 teaspoon water

Add soda to molasses and allow to foam for 5 minutes. Cream butter, shortening, and sugar; add water or orange juice. Mix flours with spices and salt in large bowl. Add molasses mixture alternately with butter mixture to flour mixture. Chill dough, preferably overnight.

Preheat oven to 350°F. Roll out dough on floured board to ¼-inch thickness. Cut out hearts with 3-inch cutter. Make a hole in the top of each heart using the tip of an apple corer and place on greased cookie sheets. Beat egg yolk with water and paint mixture on cookies. Bake 10 to 12 minutes until lightly browned. Cool on sheets for 5 minutes before removing to wire racks.

Variation: you can use the Heart Molasses dough to make cookies that are reminiscent of old-time slipware pottery. Roll out dough and cut into rounds with a pie crimping wheel. Brush tops with egg yolk/water mixture and bake and cool as above. When cool use a pastry bag and decorator's tips to pipe on designs in yellow Royal Icing (Chapter 3). For an authentic slipware look, pipe on names of foods: "apples," "nuts," "clams," etc.

To share this specialty, string cookies on a ribbon and stack gently in salvaged plastic container. Wrap container in holiday paper and glue a big sticker on the cover. For a tree trimming party, arrange smallest cookies and shiny balls in the compartments of an ornament box. Be sure to pack extra cookies so that all the ornaments don't get eaten.

Grandmother's Date and Nut Bars

Makes 2 dozen
Preparation time: 30 minutes
Baking time: 25 minutes

      1 cup butter
  2⅓ cups light brown sugar, firmly packed
      3 eggs
      3 cups flour
      1 teaspoon baking powder
    ½ teaspoon baking soda
  2½ cups pitted dates, coarsely chopped
      1 cup nuts, chopped

Preheat oven to 375°F. In large bowl cream butter and sugar until light; beat in eggs one at a time. Combine flour, baking powder, and baking soda. Add to butter mixture. Stir in dates and nuts. Spread batter ½-inch thick on greased cookie sheet. Bake 20 to 25 minutes. Cool in the pan and cut into bars. Store in a tightly covered tin.

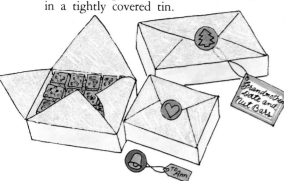

Pack these rich brown bars in foil-lined boxes. Fold the foil over envelope-style, and seal with a colorful sticker.

Party Date Bars

Makes 2 dozen
Preparation time: 30 minutes
Baking time: 30 minutes

  2½ cups pitted dates
      1 cup dark brown sugar, firmly packed
          Juice of ½ lemon
    ¾ cup water
    ¾ teaspoon salt
  1½ cups rolled oats
  1½ cups flour
    ¼ cup butter
    ¼ cup shortening
      1 tablespoon sugar

In small saucepan mix together dates, brown sugar, lemon juice, water, and ¼ teaspoon salt. Cook, stirring occasionally, until mixture is smooth.

Preheat oven to 325°F. Combine oats, flour, butter, shortening, sugar, and ½ teaspoon salt. Work until crumbly. Place half of oats mixture on bottom of greased 9 x 11-inch pan. Spread date mixture evenly over oats and top with reserved oats. Bake 30 minutes, or until lightly browned. Cool and cut into bars.

Wrap twin bars back to back in aluminum foil or a flexible gift wrap. Tie with red or green ribbon and make a ribbon loop. Hang on the Christmas tree for shiny little ornaments and as surprise gifts for drop-in guests.

Printed Spice Cookies

Makes 4 dozen
Preparation time: 30 minutes
Chilling time: 1 hour
Baking time: 10 minutes

    ¾ cup butter or margarine, softened
      1 cup dark brown sugar, firmly packed
      1 egg
    ¼ cup dark molasses
  2½ cups flour
      2 teaspoons baking soda
      1 teaspoon cinnamon
      2 teaspoons ginger
    ¾ teaspoon cloves
    ¼ teaspoon salt
          Sugar

Cream butter and sugar, beat in egg and molasses. Combine flour, baking soda, spices, and salt. Stir into creamed mixture. Chill 1 hour.

Preheat oven to 375°F. Roll dough into 1½-inch balls. Dip tops in sugar. Place balls, sugar side up, about 3 inches apart on greased cookie sheet. Bake 10 to 12 minutes, until set but not hard. Firmly press top of each cookie as soon as it comes from oven with homemade clay stamp (Chapter 9) or wooden butter mold. Cool on wire racks.

These decorated cookies are ornaments in themselves. To dramatize their good looks, cut cardboard (discarded shirt cardboard or other stiff cardboard) in a strip that will hold three to five cookies. Cover the cardboard neatly with colored holiday wrap, then place cookies in a row on it. Wrap tightly in plastic film to give as a gift or show as a table decoration. For a more spring-y centerpiece, place a small crock of blooming narcissus bulbs in the center of a pretty dish and surround with print cookies.

Lemon Spritz Cookies

Makes 4 dozen
Preparation time: 45 minutes
Chilling time: 1 hour
Baking time: 10 to 12 minutes

      1 cup butter, softened
      6 tablespoons cream cheese, softened
      1 cup sugar
      1 egg, slightly beaten
      3 tablespoons lemon juice
      1 teaspoon grated lemon peel
  2½ cups flour
      1 teaspoon baking powder
      1 cup confectioners sugar
    ½ cup nuts, coarsely chopped

In large bowl cream butter, cheese, and sugar until light and fluffy. Add egg, 1 tablespoon lemon juice, and lemon peel. Mix well. Combine flour and baking powder. Add to butter mixture, mix until smooth. Chill dough 1 hour.

Preheat oven to 375°F. Using a star plate on a cookie press, make 3-inch strips in an "S" or "?" shape. Bake on greased cookie sheets 10 to 12 minutes, or just until edges brown. Remove carefully from cookie sheets and cool on wire racks. To make glaze, combine confectioners sugar and 2 tablespoons lemon juice. Mix until smooth. Dip ends of cookies in lemon glaze, then in chopped nuts.

These festive lemon cookies are too fragile for packing and shipping so save them for good friends close by. Offer them on a plastic plate with a poinsettia design, or an heirloom cake plate.

Pfefferneusse

Makes 9 dozen
Preparation time: 45 minutes
Baking time: 12 minutes

5 eggs
2 cups sugar
1 tablespoon butter
1 tablespoon water
4 cups flour
½ teaspoon salt
4 teaspoons baking powder
1 tablespoon cinnamon
½ teaspoon cloves
1 teaspoon nutmeg, freshly grated
1 tablespoon ground anise
3 ounces citron, chopped
2 teaspoons light corn syrup

¼ teaspoon ground cardamom
1½ cups confectioners sugar

Preheat oven to 350°F. Beat 4 eggs until light; add sugar, butter, and water, and mix well. Combine flour, salt, baking powder, and all spices; add citron. Add to egg mixture. Shape into 1-inch balls and place on greased cookie sheets. Bake 12 to 15 minutes. Cool on wire racks.

In 1-quart mixing bowl, mix together remaining egg, corn syrup, and cardamom; gradually beat in confectioners sugar. In separate bowl, place 12 to 14 pfefferneusse and 2 tablespoons of frosting. Stir, using a fork, until cookies are lightly covered. Remove and place on wax paper until frosting hardens.

A salvaged mayonnaise or peanut butter jar makes a showy container for mailing these cookies. Carefully pack the cookies in the jar, cushioning them with crumpled colored cellophane. Screw the lid on tight and seal with printed Christmas sealing tape. Another strip around the base of the jar finishes off the package nicely. If you don't plan to mail these, they look stunning packed in antique apothecary jars. Tie with ribbon and tuck in a sprig of evergreen.

Lace Cookies

Makes 2 dozen
Preparation time: 30 minutes
Baking time: 6 to 8 minutes

1 cup nuts, chopped
1 cup flour
½ cup dark brown sugar, firmly packed
½ cup light corn syrup
½ cup butter
1 teaspoon vanilla

Preheat oven to 350°F. Mix together nuts and flour, set aside. In a 2-quart saucepan, combine sugar, corn syrup, and butter. Bring to a boil. Remove from heat and stir in vanilla and flour mixture. Drop by ½ teaspoonfuls 3 inches apart onto greased or non-stick cookie sheet. Bake for 6 to 8 minutes. Cool in pan for 5 minutes before removing to wire racks.

Variation: for an elegant dessert, roll the still warm cookies around a cone or cylinder. Allow to cool, remove the cone, and fill the cone-shaped cookie with flavored whipped cream, fresh berries, or ice cream.

Line a tin with bright pink cellophane or tissue paper. Pack cookies snugly and cushion with crumpled cellophane or tissue paper to prevent crumbling.

Anise Drops

Makes 4 to 5 dozen
Preparation time: 25 minutes
Resting time: overnight
Baking time: 10 minutes

6 eggs
1 cup sugar
2 cups confectioners sugar
½ teaspoon anise extract
3½ cups flour

In large bowl beat eggs until light colored, add sugars and anise extract. Add flour, mix thoroughly. Drop by teaspoonfuls onto lightly buttered cookie sheet or use a pastry bag and large decorator's tip to press dough onto cookie sheet. Allow to stand overnight at room temperature. Preheat oven to 350°F. Bake 10 minutes. Remove to wire rack and cool. Store in tightly covered tin.

These cookies have an Old World flavor, so give them an old-fashioned wrapping—a small basket lined with a figured cloth napkin and tied with yarn to match one of the colors in the print.

Teatime Tassies

Makes 2 dozen
Preparation time: 30 minutes
Chilling time: 1 hour
Baking time: 25 minutes

- 6 tablespoons cream cheese, softened
- ½ cup plus 1 tablespoon butter or margarine, softened
- 1 cup flour
- ¾ cup dark brown sugar, firmly packed
- 1 egg
- ½ teaspoon salt
- 1 teaspoon vanilla
- ⅔ cup pecans, coarsely chopped

Blend cream cheese and ½ cup butter or margarine. Work in flour and chill about 1 hour.

Preheat oven to 325°F. Shape dough into 2 dozen 1-inch balls and place in paper-lined miniature muffin tins. Press dough on bottom and sides and set aside. Cream sugar, 1 tablespoon butter, and egg. Add salt and beat until smooth. Divide half of the pecans among pastry-lined cups. Spoon sugar mixture on top of pecans and sprinkle with remaining pecans. Bake 25 minutes or until filling sets. Cool and remove from pans.

A half-dozen tassies on a porcelain dessert plate make an enchanting personal gift for a live-aloner. For a couple or small family, buy a miniature muffin pan that holds a dozen cakes. Place a tassie in each cup. Wrap with see-through paper and tie on the recipe with a festive bow.

Chocolate Cherry Bars

Makes 3 dozen
Preparation time: 30 minutes
Baking time: 20 minutes

- 1 cup butter or margarine
- 1¼ cups sugar
- 1 egg, beaten
- 1 teaspoon vanilla
- 2¼ cups flour
- 1¼ teaspoons baking powder
- ¼ teaspoon salt
- ¼ cup nuts, chopped
- ¼ cup flaked sweetened coconut
- 1 cup semisweet chocolate pieces
- ¼ cup maraschino cherries, drained and with stems removed

Preheat oven to 375°F. In large bowl cream butter and sugar; add egg and vanilla. Combine flour, baking powder, and salt. Stir in nuts, coconut, chocolate pieces, and cherries. Add to butter mixture. Mix well. Pour into greased 11 x 16-inch pan and bake 20 minutes, or use a 9 x 13-inch glass pan and bake 35 minutes at 350°F. Cool in pan and cut into bars.

A tiny lacquered tray makes a perfect base for a half-dozen of these cookie bars. The tray and cookies can be wrapped in a plastic bag, pulled taut over cookies and tray, and tied with ribbon and a carnation or spray of baby's breath.

Apricot Crunch Bars

Makes 2 dozen
Preparation time: 30 minutes
Baking time: 35 minutes

- 1½ cups flour
- 1 teaspoon baking powder
- ¼ teaspoon salt
- 1½ cups rolled oats
- 1 cup light brown sugar, firmly packed
- ¾ cup butter or margarine
- 1½ cups apricot jam
- 2 teaspoons grated lemon peel

Preheat oven to 375°F. In large bowl combine flour, baking powder, and salt; stir in oats and sugar. Cut in butter and stir until mixed and crumbly. Pack ⅔ of pastry into bottom of a 7 x 11-inch pan. Combine jam and peel and spread over pastry. Sprinkle remaining pastry evenly over top. Bake 35 minutes. Cool in pan and cut in squares.

Stack these cookies 4 or 5 to a skinny glass, or 6 or 7 to a champagne flute so you can see the jewel-like filling through the glass. Wrap the whole gift in plastic film tied with gilt ribbon.

Pantry Gingersnaps

Makes 3 dozen
Preparation time: 25 minutes
Baking time: 6 minutes

- ¾ cup shortening
- 1 cup sugar
- ⅓ cup dark molasses
- 1 egg, beaten
- 2 cups flour
- 2 teaspoons baking soda
- 1 teaspoon cinnamon
- ½ teaspoon ginger
- ¼ teaspoon cloves
- Sugar

Preheat oven to 375°F. In large bowl cream shortening and sugar until fluffy; add molasses and egg. Mix well. Combine flour, baking soda, and spices. Stir into creamed mixture. Mix well. Mold into 1-inch balls. Roll in sugar. Place on greased cookie sheets. Bake about 6 minutes. Cool on wire racks.

To send by mail, pack cookies snugly in a paper towel tube. Make a cushion of bright green cellophane or colored foil at the bottom and another at the top and finish with a spiral of gift-wrap tape.

Green Apple Squares

Makes 2 dozen
Preparation time: 30 minutes
Baking time: 45 minutes

  ¼ cup shortening
  1 cup sugar
  1 egg, beaten
  3 cups apples—peeled, cored, and finely diced
  ¼ cup nuts, chopped
  1 teaspoon vanilla
  1 cup flour
  ½ teaspoon baking powder
  ½ teaspoon baking soda
  ½ teaspoon salt

Preheat oven to 350°F. In large bowl cream shortening and sugar, add egg. Stir in apples, nuts, and vanilla. Combine flour, baking powder, baking soda, and salt. Add to shortening mixture. Pour into 8-inch square pan. Bake 45 minutes. Cool in pan and cut into squares.

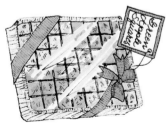

Stack bars in a pair of wide soup mugs. Cover with plastic film and tie with a ribbon. Or pack bars in shallow foil pan checkerboard-fashion with a darker bar such as Grandmother's Date and Nut Bars for contrast. Overwrap with clear plastic film and crisscross tape over the center.

Walnut Speculaas

Makes seven 10-inch figures or fifteen 5-inch cookies
Preparation time: 45 minutes
Baking time: 20 to 30 minutes

  1 cup dark brown sugar, firmly packed
  3 tablespoons milk
  3 cups flour
  1½ teaspoons cloves
  1½ teaspoons cinnamon
  ¾ teaspoon ginger
  ¾ teaspoon freshly grated nutmeg
  ⅛ teaspoon baking powder
  ⅛ teaspoon salt
  1¼ cups butter or margarine
  ¼ cup walnuts, ground

Preheat oven to 350°F. Mix together sugar and milk until smooth. In large bowl combine flour, spices, baking powder, and salt. Cut in butter until mixture resembles cornmeal. Add sugar and walnuts. To use wooden molds, brush carvings with small brush and dust thoroughly with flour. Lightly grease cookie sheet. Roll out dough and press into molds to fill completely. Remove excess dough with small knife. Invert molds on cookie sheet and tap until dough slips out onto sheet. Bake 20 to 30 minutes.

Note: you may also roll out the dough and cut it into 5-inch scalloped rounds.

Place each figure on a foil-covered piece of cardboard. Wrap with plastic film and tie a ribbon around it. Or give a plate of these to a family with a milk pitcher as a companion gift.

Pecan Bars

Makes 3 dozen
Preparation time: 45 minutes
Baking time: 40 minutes

  ½ cup butter
  ¼ cup sugar
  3 eggs
  1½ teaspoons vanilla
  1¼ cups plus 2 tablespoons flour
  ¾ teaspoon salt
  1½ cups dark brown sugar, firmly packed
  ½ cup flaked sweetened coconut
  1 cup pecans, chopped
  ½ teaspoon baking powder
  1½ cups confectioners sugar
     Juice of one lemon

Preheat oven to 350°F. In large bowl cream butter and sugar until fluffy. Beat in 1 egg and ½ teaspoon vanilla. Combine 1¼ cups flour and ¼ teaspoon salt and add gradually to butter mixture, blending well. Spread dough evenly in 9 x 12-inch pan. Bake 15 minutes.

Combine 2 eggs and brown sugar, beat well. Add coconut, pecans, 2 tablespoons flour, baking powder, ½ teaspoon salt, and 1 teaspoon vanilla. Mix well and spread evenly over cooked pastry base; bake 25 minutes. Cool in pan and cut into squares. For icing, thin confectioners sugar to spreading consistency with lemon juice. Spread cooled bars with icing.

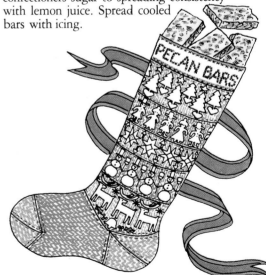

Wrap pecan bars back to back in plastic film and pack into a pair of new socks. Tie with bright ribbons and hang "by the chimney with care."

Brandy Wreaths

Makes 7 to 8 dozen
Preparation time: 30 minutes
Chilling time: 1 hour
Baking time: 10 minutes

1⅓ cups butter, softened
¾ cup sugar
1 egg yolk
¼ cup brandy
3¼ cups flour
Cinnamon candies (optional)
Royal Icing (Chapter 3, optional)

Cream butter and sugar until fluffy; beat in egg yolk and brandy. Gradually blend in flour, mixing well. Chill dough 1 hour.

Preheat oven to 350° F. Pinch off small pieces of dough and roll on lightly floured surface into thin fingers about 5 inches long. Twist 2 pieces together to make ropes and shape into wreaths. Place on greased cookie sheets and bake 10 minutes. Cool on wire racks. Decorate with cinnamon candies and Royal Icing (Chapter 3) if desired.

These wreaths make fun cookies for children. Box, wrap in colorful newspaper "funnies," and tie with bright yarns. For an imaginative centerpiece for a holiday party, stack wreaths on a candy cane anchored in florist's foam. Cover foam with greens and decorate with wrapped peppermint candies.

Wine Cookies

Makes 4 dozen
Preparation time: 30 minutes
Baking time: 10 to 12 minutes

1 cup butter, softened
1 cup sugar
6 tablespoons white wine (not cooking wine)
2 teaspoons cinnamon
2 cups flour
1 egg white, slightly beaten
Colored sugars or chopped nuts (optional)

Preheat oven to 350°F. Cream butter and sugar until fluffy. Add wine and cinnamon. Stir in flour, mixing well. Roll out on lightly floured board. Cut into shapes with cookie cutters. Transfer to greased cookie sheets. Brush with egg white and sprinkle with sugars or nuts. Bake 10 to 12 minutes or until lightly brown.

Bake these cookies with a piece of string pressed into each one. Hang in the windows or on the tree.

Chocolate Fruitcake Cookies

Makes 8 dozen
Preparation time: 40 minutes
Chilling time: 1 hour
Baking time: 45 minutes

1 cup pitted dates, chopped
1 cup candied fruit
¼ cup brandy
1 cup light brown sugar, firmly packed
½ cup butter or margarine
2 squares (2 ounces) unsweetened chocolate, melted
1 egg
1 teaspoon vanilla
1½ cups flour
¼ teaspoon baking soda
¼ teaspoon salt
½ cup milk
Walnuts or candied cherries (optional)

Soak dates and fruit in ¼ cup brandy while preparing batter. In large bowl cream sugar and butter or margarine until light and fluffy. Add chocolate, egg, and vanilla; mix well. Combine flour, baking soda, and salt. Stir into batter mixture alternately with milk. Blend in fruits and nuts. Chill dough for 1 hour.

Preheat oven to 375°F. Drop dough by teaspoonfuls 2 inches apart onto greased cookie sheets. Press cherry or walnut half into each. Bake 15 minutes and cool on wire racks.

Pile a half dozen or so of these into a large glass dessert bowl and cover the bowl with a clear plastic bag or plastic wrap. Affix a sprig of artificial holly and a cheery red gift tag.

Crystal Cookies

Makes about 5 dozen
Preparation time: 35 minutes
Chilling time: 1 hour
Baking time: 8 minutes

1 cup butter
1 cup sugar
3 eggs, well beaten

COOKIES

⅓ cup milk
1 teaspoon mace
4 cups flour
   Assorted hard candies
   Heavy duty thread for hanging

These are a fine and festive cookie to make with children.

Preheat oven to 350°F. Cream butter and sugar, add eggs and milk. Combine mace and flour and mix gradually into butter mixture. Chill dough 1 hour. Meanwhile crush each color of hard candy individually using a mortar and pestle. Set aside. Preheat oven to 350°F. Roll out dough into ropes ¼-inch thick and about 10 inches long. Twist each rope into a shape and place on greased non-stick or foil-lined cookie sheets. Suggested shapes: hearts, bells, trees, diamonds, mittens, stars, etc. Fill centers with crushed candies and press in a piece of thread for hanging. Or use cookie cutters, cut out insides, and fill with finely crushed candies. Bake for 6 to 8 minutes, or until candy has melted. Cool in pan for 5 minutes before carefully removing to wire racks.

Oat Cakes

Makes 7½ dozen
Preparation time: 30 minutes
Baking time: 10 to 15 minutes

1 cup butter or margarine, softened
1 cup dark brown sugar, firmly packed
1 cup sugar
1 teaspoon vanilla
1 egg, slightly beaten
1 cup vegetable oil
3½ cups flour
1 teaspoon salt
1 teaspoon baking soda
1 cup rolled oats
1 cup nuts, chopped

In large bowl cream butter or margarine and sugars; add vanilla, egg, and oil and mix well. Combine flour, salt, and baking soda and add to butter mixture. Stir in oats and nuts. Mix well. Chill 1 hour.

Preheat oven to 350°F. Drop dough by teaspoonfuls onto ungreased cookie sheets. Bake 10 to 15 minutes. Cool on wire racks. Store in tightly covered tin or crock.

Cookie Greeting Cards

Makes 2 dozen
Preparation time: 30 minutes
Chilling time: 1 hour
Baking time: 8 to 10 minutes

¼ cup sugar
½ cup butter or margarine
2 eggs, slightly beaten
½ teaspoon almond extract
½ teaspoon vanilla
2¼ cups flour
1½ teaspoons baking powder
⅛ teaspoon salt
   Royal Icing (Chapter 3)

In large bowl cream sugar and butter or margarine until light and fluffy; beat in eggs, almond extract, and vanilla. Combine flour, baking powder, and salt and add gradually to butter mixture. Chill dough 1 hour.

Preheat oven to 350°F. Roll out dough and cut into rectangles. Use a straw to make a hole in each cookie. Bake 8 to 10 minutes on greased cookie sheets until lightly browned. Decorate with Royal Icing (Chapter 3), using pastry bag and decorator's tips

Note: if you don't have a pastry bag you can use a small plastic bag. Just spoon icing into bag, squeeze into a corner, and poke a hole in the plastic with a toothpick.

These cookies are meant to be seen, not wrapped. Hang them in a window or place them upright on a table in a saucer holder or placecard holder, positioned so that they will catch the candlelight.

These sturdy old-fashioned cookies taste marvelous anywhere, and they look like Christmas packed in a rustic basket lined with crushed red cellophane and overwrapped in more cellophane. Use a gold or silver tie.

These personalized edible messages should be placed against a sturdy cardboard square wrapped in foil. Take next door or to the teacher, butcher, baker, or candlestick maker. They're fun to hang on the tree too, one for each guest who'll come for tree trimming or present opening.

51

GINGERBREAD HOUSE

Materials

2 batches Heart Molasses Dough (recipe in this chapter)
1 batch Royal Icing; Flow Frosting.
Food coloring for following tints: red, green, yellow, blue, and brown.

Edibles: 1 (1.45 ounce) milk chocolate bar, red licorice whips; multicolored nonpareil seeds; 1 chocolate-covered cherry; 1 silver dragee.

In addition, have on hand: dull knife or spatula; masking tape; ¼-inch artist's paintbrush; full food cans; corn syrup; and a stiff, flat base of ¼-inch plywood or heavy cardboard.

Patterns

The patterns for house front/back and side are illustrated in reduced dimensions accompanied by full-sized measurements.

1. Follow insructions in "Basic Skills" for tracing and enlarging patterns, and for making cardboard patterns.

2. Cut out all window openings and reserve.

Note: be sure to make 2 cardboard house side patterns and 1 cardboard pattern each for house front and back. On the house back pattern, mark and cut out a 6-inch centered square opening instead of the windows shown on the reduced illustration. The thinly rolled dough will be iced to the corresponding cardboard pattern pieces before house is assembled and decorated.

3. Measure and cut the following cardboard patterns: one 10 x 8-inch rectangle for base; two 8-inch squares for roof pieces; and one 2-inch circle for roof tiles. (If you have a 2-inch round cookie cutter, use that to cut out the 40 tiles.)

Cutting and Baking the Pieces

Roll out and cut only ½ a batch of dough (enough for 1 cookie sheet) at a time to prevent thinly rolled dough from drying out. Wrap reserve in plastic wrap and refrigerate.

1. Roll out dough ⅛-inch thick on oiled, foil-lined cookie sheets.

2. Cut out cookie pieces for house following instructions in "Basic Skills." Cut 4 of the roof tiles in half.

Do not cut a base piece out of dough, but reserve this as well as all cardboard pattern pieces to use in assembling the house.

3. Shutters for house front and side windows are made from dough cutouts. Remove cutouts carefully with spatula and chill for a few minutes if dough is too soft. To make shutters for house side and lower front windows, divide cutouts in half lengthwise. With a dull knife or spatula, score designs as shown in color photograph. Then moisten backs of cutouts with water and attach to house.

Note: do not attach shutters for upper front window. Cut these in half lengthwise, score, and place at edge of cookie sheet for baking.

4. Bake at 350°F for 6 to 8 minutes or until cookie pieces are firm and lightly browned. Place cookie sheets on racks and cool completely before removing cookie pieces from foil.

COOKIES

Assembling the Cardboard Frame

1. Lay front on flat surface. Place 1 house side on each side of front and secure with masking tape.

2. Cut a 3 x 2-inch rectangle of cardboard. Fold in half lengthwise and tape to inside of front several inches below upper window as a platform on which to place a cookie-cutter figure.

3. Tape house back to 1 house side, tape roof pieces to tops of side pieces, and tape base at bottom of house front.

4. Lift sides and back up and tape together to form a box, then lift base and tape to sides and back.

5. Set house on cardboard base. Fold roof pieces over and tape securely into place.

Attaching the Cookie Pieces

1. Prepare 1 batch of Royal Icing following instructions in "Tip Tips" (Chapter 3). Reserve half of icing before it becomes stiff. You will use it later for Flow Frosting. Beat remaining icing until stiff, then cover tightly. Make a second batch of icing if you need it.

2. Spread a thin layer of white icing over cardboard house back and press cookie back piece into place. Allow to set. See "Tip Tips" (Chapter 3) for instructions on applying Royal Icing.

3. Lay house on its back and repeat procedure with cookie side and front pieces. Allow to set. Prop with full food cans if necessary.

4. Spread a line of icing about ¼-inch thick along both sides of upper front window, and another line, slightly thicker, about ½ inch from first line. Press reserved shutter cutouts in position, leaning slightly away from house and resting on thicker line of frosting. Prop shutters, using pencils for support until they are dry.

5. Carefully trim 3 rows of chocolate from chocolate bar, spread thin layer of icing on 1 side, and position on center of house front to make door. Allow to dry completely.

Decorating

1. Using a pastry bag or parchment cone fitted with a small star tip, pipe white icing borders around and inside windows. Allow to dry completely.

2. Lay house on its back, change to a large star tip, and pipe a row of white icing down each front corner and under each front window. Cut strips of red licorice to fit and press into icing for trimming and to make window boxes. Allow to dry.

3. Set house upright. With larger star tip, pipe a row of icing under each side window and press licorice in place to make more window boxes. Let dry completely.

4. Brush bottoms of roof tile pieces with corn syrup, then dip gently into multicolored nonpareil seeds. Allow to dry completely. Spread white icing on 1 side of roof, then press tiles in place, using color photograph as a guide. Repeat for other side of roof. Allow to dry completely.

5. Using large star tip, pipe white icing around front edge of roof, making a series of stars or a shell border. Pipe border along roof ridge, adding a large puff of icing at back. Press chocolate-covered cherry into puff for chimney. Let dry completely.

6. Pipe white icing border around front door and sprinkle with multicolored nonpareil seeds. Pipe a dot for door knob and press silver dragee into it. Let dry completely.

7. Using leaf tip, frost leaves onto window boxes, then sprinkle with multicolored nonpareil seeds.

8. Let house dry at least 4 hours or overnight before moving.

House sides (cut 2)

House front, back

Spread out in front of this Majolica
cookie jar from 1850, is an assortment
of gaily decorated Cookie Greeting Cards,
Crystal Cookies (hang them in a window
to catch the light), and Pfefferneusse.
More of the icing-dipped Pfefferneusse are
in the cookie tin at right, cushioned
with colored cellophane and ready for
mailing.

GINGERBREAD CONSTRUCTION SKILLS

Patterns

1. Tape tracing paper (or any paper you can see through) over pattern printed on page of book, and, using sharp pencil, carefully copy outline and design details inside outline. Here, one pattern has been traced and another is half done. Tape prevents paper from moving as you trace.

2. Transfer pattern outline from tracing paper to lightweight cardboard using dull pencil and carbon paper. Lay cardboard on flat surface, place carbon paper, shiny side down, on top. Position tracing over carbon paper and tape to cardboard before tracing over lines.

3. Cut out cardboard patterns with matte knife or sharp scissors. For most projects, you will need to use tracing paper patterns later to mark design details (see Cutting and Baking, step 6). You can cut out each individual tracing paper pattern or leave the sheet whole.

Patterns for rectangular construction pieces may be illustrated in reduced size, with the full-sized dimensions given. To rule full-sized patterns, use T-square, triangle, and ruler if you have them, to make exact right angles. Otherwise, use a ruler and graph paper (with a grid printed on it), or a straight-edge ruler and anything with a right angle, like a book cover.

1. Roll out dough on foil-lined cookie sheet with lightly floured rolling pin. Place damp cloth on paper towels on work surface under sheet to prevent sliding.

2. After dough is rolled to correct thickness, trim with sharp knife to within 1 inch of edge of cookie sheet.

3. Dust underside of cardboard patterns very lightly with flour and arrange on dough, leaving about ¼ inch between each. Don't crowd the patterns, but angle them when possible to make the best use of the dough.

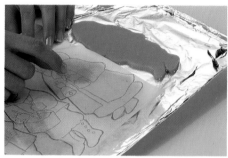

4. Carefully cut around each cardboard pattern with sharp knife.

5. Gently cut away excess dough from around cut-out shapes, using knife to lift edges as you proceed. Knead excess dough together into ball and reserve. Wrap in plastic wrap and refrigerate if you are not going to use it right away.

You may need to reroll excess dough to have enough to cut out all the project pieces.

6. If tracing paper patterns have designs inside outline, position patterns on cut-out cookie pieces. (First cut out pattern around outline if it will be easier to handle that way.) Following the lines of the interior design details, prick holes through patterns into dough with a needle or pin. Then remove the patterns. The pinpricks will show faintly after you bake the pieces and serve as a guide for decorating.

7. All ready to pop in the oven! The cookie pieces are baked in a 350°F oven for 12 to 15 minutes, or until firm and lightly browned. To check pieces for size, you can lay the cardboard patterns on them while pieces are still warm (5 minutes out of oven). Trim away parts that have expanded, or gently mold pieces into shape with your fingers.

8. After removing cookie sheets from oven, place on wire rack and cool cookie pieces completely before removing them from sheets. If they need to be cut, shaped, or have holes put through them, do that while they are still warm. They will be cool enough to handle in less than 5 minutes.

9. Remove cookie pieces from foil, lifting them firmly but with care should they stick a bit. Be sure to peel off any foil.

Put the cookie pieces in an airtight, protected container until you are ready to decorate and assemble them. (Pieces can soften and sag if they absorb moisture from air.) Low-sided, medium-sized cardboard boxes with lids work well for storage. Separate the layers of pieces with waxed paper or paper towels.

COOKIES

Construction of Gingerbread House

To make Royal Icing, combine 1 pound confectioners sugar, 3 egg whites, and ½ teaspoon cream of tartar in bowl and beat with electric mixer at low speed until blended. Then beat at high speed 7 to 10 minutes. Icing is ready to use when knife drawn through it leaves a clear path which holds its shape.

1. First join one side wall to one end piece by piping icing along one edge and pressing end of other piece into it. Or pipe icing onto both surfaces to be joined and pipe a reinforcing strip along inside of corner.

Use Royal Icing and a #2 or #3 writing tip to pipe icing onto areas to be "cemented" together (see "Tip Tips," in Chapter 3).

2. The icing must dry hard before joined pieces can be handled. Since this takes 30 minutes to 4 hours, depending on thickness, humidity, stress, etc., prop pieces so they stay together and dry at right angles to each other.

3. When first two pieces have hardened together, attach other end piece or wall. Another technique is to keep setting each new piece inside the next rather than sandwiching the two walls between the two end pieces as shown.

In the instruction text, the words "right" and "left" assume that you are facing the project.

4. When all 4 sides have hardened, pipe icing along one roof-angle of each end piece. You can also pipe icing on underside of roof piece as well. If too much icing squeezes out, scrape off with blade and wipe with moist towel before dry. To chip it off later is more risky, but less likely to leave a smudge.

5. Press roof piece into position and hold by hand briefly so icing begins to set. Prop in position with full food cans and paper towels. Apply frosting, press other roof piece into place, and prop it until dry. Use little dabs of icing to attach doors, shutters, any other cookie trim, and confections.

JAMS, JELLIES, AND BUTTERS

Cranberry Butter couldn't be simpler to make, but it adds a festive touch to any breakfast table. It's shown here surrounded by antique butter-making equipment including a covered yellow-ware butter crock, wooden butter paddles, and hand-carved butter molds. The tall wooden salt box is made of pine, which absorbs moisture and keeps the salt dry.

5

Homemade jams, jellies, and fruit butters can be as brilliant as baubles, with the jewel-like tones of the fruit delicacies shining gaily through the glass jars. Some of the recipes here, quince marmalade and gooseberry jam, are revivals from yesteryear. The butters are simple, last-minute preparations that will grace a spring brunch or a Christmas pudding.

Don't view jam and jelly-making as a tedious job. If you're rushed for time when the fruit is in season, prepare the juice or cook the fruit, strain or prepare it as needed, and freeze or refrigerate until you have time to finish the fruit spread—when you have the energy and extra moments to prepare jars, paraffin, and other paraphernalia.

Jams, jellies, and fruit butters packed in tiny jars make charming companion gifts to breads or to fresh fruits. Assemble a fruit basket of the finest apples, pears, seasonal citrus, grapes, stem raisins, and nuts, and tuck in a few of your jars of jam. This is a lavish gift indeed for a family, and the nicest surprise is the glasses of your homemade specialties nestled among the fruits.

Jam and jelly making is as precise as candy-making, in fact the principle is the same—evaporating enough water from a sugar and fruit mixture so that it sets up to a shimmery spread. This chapter includes pectin-added recipes that guarantee success for first-time jelly makers, as well as the traditional recipes that require constant watching, stirring, and testing (see "Creative Canning" at the end of this chapter) but whose cooked-down, essence-of-fruit flavor cannot be matched. Follow recipes carefully so that you and your friends can enjoy the fruits of your labor for months to come.

Raspberry Currant Jam

Makes 10 to 12 cups
Preparation time: 45 minutes

   2 cups currants
   ¾ cup water
   2½ cups raspberries, crushed
   7 cups sugar
   ½ bottle (3 fluid ounces) liquid pectin

Crush currants, add ¾ cup water, and simmer for 8 to 10 minutes. Sieve

to remove seeds. Measure pulp, adding water to make 2 cups. Place in kettle, add raspberries and sugar, and stir. Bring to a boil, stirring constantly. Boil hard 1 minute, remove from heat, and stir in pectin. Skim off foam. Pour into hot, sterilized jars and seal

A package of tea biscuits, not too sweet, is a perfect companion to this jam. Or give a special friend a small loaf of Health Bread (Chapter 2) for toasting to go with the jam. Match the gift-tie ribbon to the color of the jam—a rich claret red.

Strawberry Jam

Makes about 8 cups
Preparation time: 45 minutes

  4 cups strawberries, hulled and crushed
  7 cups sugar
    Juice of 1 lemon
  ½ bottle (3 fluid ounces) liquid pectin

Place fruit in kettle and bring to a boil, stirring to prevent sticking. Add sugar and stir, add lemon juice. Bring to a rapid boil, add pectin, and boil 1 minute. Remove from heat. Cool 5 minutes and skim off foam. Pour into hot, sterilized jars and seal.

Give a jar of this fruity jam with a jam jar to the young couple starting their household accumulation of pretty things. For the older couple whose table appointments are collected, give special coffee or tea.

Pear Harlequin

Makes about 10 cups
Preparation time: 45 minutes

  6 pounds pears
  1 can (20 ounces) crushed pineapple
    Juice and grated peel of 2 oranges
    Sugar
  1 cup maraschino cherries, cut in quarters, plus ¼ cup of the preserving syrup
  ¾ cup blanched, slivered almonds

Core and cut pears in thin slices; add pineapple, orange juice, and peel. Measure fruit, and add sugar measured to ¾ volume of the fruit. Allow to stand overnight. Simmer until syrupy and fruit is clear. Add cherries, cherry syrup, and almonds. Stir well. Pour into hot, sterilized jars and seal.

This deserves a red bow around the neck of the jar. Tuck a sprig of holly leaves into the bow and add a kitchen magnet in a fruit design.

Cranberry Jelly

Makes 10 cups
Preparation time: 45 minutes

  5 cups water
  8 cups cranberries
  5 cups sugar
  ½ bottle (3 fluid ounces) liquid pectin

Add water to cranberries and simmer, covered, for 15 minutes. Strain through a sieve. Measure 6 cups of juice and pulp. Place juice and pulp in kettle. Add sugar, stir, and bring to a boil. Add pectin and boil 1 minute. Remove from heat and skim off foam. Pour into hot, sterilized jars and seal.

Mold this in old-fashioned flared jelly glasses so you can turn it out to serve with the turkey or ham. The flared glasses are available in hardware stores or on order from manufacturers of canning jars, or maybe you're lucky enough to have saved those you had years ago or to have inherited them from your family

Quince Marmalade

Makes about 8 cups
Preparation time: 1 hour

  1½ pounds quinces
  2¾ cups sugar
  1 cup water

Peel, core, and slice quinces. Combine fruit, sugar, and water. Boil until thick and test for jellying point. Pour into hot, sterilized jars and seal.

Affix bright foil medallion stickers to jars of this clear and pretty marmalade for a festive gift.

Whole Cranberry Conserve

Makes 5 cups
Preparation time: 45 minutes

  2 cups water
  2 cups sugar
  1 quart cranberries
    Grated peel of 1 orange
    Juice of 1 lemon

Combine water and sugar; simmer for 10 minutes. Add cranberries, orange peel, and lemon juice. Cook over high heat for 20 minutes until syrup thickens. Ladle into hot, sterilized jars and seal.

Pack this in table-ready glasses for hosts and hostesses who like special foods on the ready for instant entertaining. A good shape is fat and squat. A pretty relish spoon can be given with it, if you feel extravagant, though this is a lavish gift alone.

Apricot Pineapple Conserve

Makes 8 to 10 cups
Preparation time: 45 minutes

1 pound dried apricots
2-3 oranges, including peel, chopped or ground
1 can (20 ounces) sliced pineapple
1 cup blanched, slivered almonds
Sugar

Soak apricots overnight in water to cover. Drain apricots. Combine fruits and nuts and measure them. Bring to a boil in large kettle. Add sugar equal to volume of fruit and nuts. Boil, stirring constantly, until mixture reaches jellying point. Ladle into hot, sterilized jars and seal.

A strip of lace tied around the neck of the jar gives this bright conserve a look of luxury. A scrap of hem-binding lace works well or any little snip of lace from a by-gone project.

Rhubarb Marmalade

Makes 10 cups
Preparation time: 45 minutes

4 cups diced red rhubarb, not peeled
Juice and grated peel of 1 orange
Juice and grated peel of 1 lemon
7 cups sugar
½ cup water
1 bottle (6 fluid ounces) liquid pectin

Combine rhubarb and citrus juices and peels in a kettle; add sugar. Bring to a boil, stirring frequently, and boil for 3 minutes. Remove from heat and stir in pectin. Stir for 5 minutes to cool slightly and pour into hot, sterilized jars and seal.

This marmalade and toast can make an event of Christmas morning breakfast, so give a jar of this with your best loaf of bread to a deserving family. Tie it all up in a red-checked linen towel.

Gooseberry Jam

Makes 8 cups
Preparation time: 45 minutes

4 cups gooseberries
½ cup water
4 cups sugar

Grind gooseberries, add water and sugar. Place over high heat, bring to a boil. Boil until thick. Ladle into hot, sterilized jars and seal.

A sprig of fresh greenery tucked in a tie of rick-rack braid gives these jars old-fashioned appeal. The greenery might be yew or juniper snipped from the garden, or a twig of the Christmas tree that fell off as you brought it home.

Sour Red Cherry Jam

Makes about 8 cups
Preparation time: 1 hour

4 cups cherries, pitted and coarsely ground
1 tablespoon butter
7 cups sugar
1 bottle (6 fluid ounces) liquid pectin
6 drops red food coloring (optional)
2 tablespoons kirsch

Place fruit in kettle. Add butter and sugar. Bring to a boil, stirring constantly. Boil hard for 1 minute, remove from heat, and stir in pectin, food coloring, and kirsch. Stir occasionally for 5 minutes to cool slightly and to prevent fruit from floating. Pour into hot, sterilized jars and seal.

Tiny jars of this and two or three other jams might be arranged side by side on a small tray and wrapped hobo-pack style in a square of plastic film or a plastic bag. Wrap it firmly to prevent the jam jars from slipping and use a bright tie—red and white checks or green and white stripes.

Blackberry Jam

Makes 8 cups
Preparation time: 1 hour

    10 cups blackberries
     6 cups sugar
    ¼ cup lemon juice

Crush berries and heat until soft. Press through a food mill to remove seeds. Place in kettle, add sugar and juice, and bring to a boil, stirring until sugar dissolves. Cook rapidly until mixture reaches 220°F on a candy thermometer. Pour into hot, sterilized jars and seal.

This full-flavored jam looks best in small jars, with the neck tied in a pale pink ribbon—cotton velvet or polyester. Just for fun, stick a teddy bear decal on the side of the glass. Bears love blackberries.

Fruit Compote

Serves 4 to 6
Soaking time: overnight
Preparation time: 30 minutes

    ½ cup sweet vermouth
    ½ cup orange juice
    ¼ cup lemon juice
    ¼ cup thin strips orange peel
     1 tablespoon grated lemon peel
     1 cup water
    ¾ cup sugar
     2 cinnamon sticks, 3 inches long
    2½ pounds mixed dry fruits—prunes, apricots, raisins, pears, apples—soaked overnight in cold water and drained

In 2-quart saucepan, combine vermouth, juices, peels, water, sugar, and cinnamon. Bring to a boil. Add soaked dry fruits and simmer gently for 20 minutes, until fruit is soft. Remove fruit and place in a glass dish; strain juices and pour over fruits.

A spray of lemon leaves and dark green or orange velvet ribbon bow make a lavish looking gift of this compote, packed in a jar or compote dish.

Crab Apple Jelly

Makes 4 to 5 cups
Preparation time: 45 minutes
Straining time: overnight

    4 pounds crab apples, cored and quartered
    5 cups water
       Juice and peel of 1 lemon
       Sugar

Cover apples with water, add lemon juice and peel, bring to a boil. Simmer about 45 minutes until fruit is tender. Pour pulp in jelly bag and allow to drip overnight. Measure juice and place in kettle. For every 2 cups of juice add 1¾ cups sugar. Bring to a boil, stirring often. Boil about 10 minutes until mixture reaches jelling point. Pour into hot, sterilized jars and seal.

Lady apples, the tiny sweet apples with rosy-red cheeks, are in season when it comes time to pack Christmas gifts. Affix a lady apple to the top of each jar, using florist's clay, and tie a leaf-green ribbon around the neck of the jar.

Rose Hip Jelly

Makes 10 to 12 cups
Preparation time: 1 hour
Straining time: about 1 hour

    4 pounds ripe rose hips, coarsely chopped
    2½ cups water
       Sugar

Place rose hips and water in kettle and cook 45 minutes until fruit is soft. Mash well and pour into a jelly bag. Allow to drip 1 hour or more. Measure juice and place in kettle. For every 2 cups of juice add 1¾ cups sugar. Bring to a boil and boil 10 minutes, until mixture reaches jellying point. Pour into hot, sterilized glasses and seal.

Give rose hip jelly with a small package of tea to the tea drinkers on your list, or miniature loaves of bread to toast fans.

Rose Hip Syrup

Makes 2½ cups
Preparation time: 30 minutes
Straining time: about 1 hour

    4½ quarts water
     4 pounds ripe rose hips, coarsely chopped
    2½ cups sugar

Rose hip syrup can be served on pancakes and fruit crepes. Combine water and rose hips; bring to a boil. Pour into a jelly bag and allow to drip for 1 hour or more. Bring to a boil 7½ cups juice and add sugar and simmer without stirring until dissolved. Boil for 5 minutes. Pour into hot, sterilized bottles, leaving 2-inch headspace, and seal with a cork that has been boiled for 3 minutes in water or use a screw cap; dip cork in hot paraffin to seal tightly.

Tie a bright red or green bow around the neck of the syrup bottle, or catch together thin ribbons in red, green, and white and tie all three at once to form a tri-color decoration. With a china marker, write "Rose Hip Syrup—for pancakes or crêpes" on the side of the bottle.

Cranberry Claret Jelly

Makes 6 cups
Preparation time: 20 minutes

    1 cup cranberry juice
    1 cup claret or fruity red wine
       Juice of 1 lemon
  3½ cups sugar
  ½ bottle (3 fluid ounces) liquid pectin

In double boiler combine juice, claret, and sugar. Heat until sugar is dissolved, stirring constantly. Stir in pectin and pour into jelly glasses or goblets. Seal.

Variation: substitute grape juice for the cranberry juice and Burgundy for the claret.

Give this in small, clear glasses. Glue silver stars scatter-dash on the glass and cut a round of foil to fit over the top. Press it in place on the paraffin before it is completely set. The gift should be protected from dust in a plastic bag. Tie with silver cord, if you wish.

Fresh Cranberry Butter

Makes about 1½ cups
Preparation time: 10 minutes

  1 cup butter, softened
  2 tablespoons confectioners' sugar
6-8 tablespoons coarsely ground cranberries

Serve as a spread for hot biscuits or other breads. Cream butter and sugar. Stir in berries. Refrigerate or freeze.

Note: you may use any leftover cranberry relish instead of fresh cranberries and sugar.

Pack this rosy-colored butter in tiny French earthenware pots. Top with whole cranberries and wrap securely in plastic. Tie on wooden butter spreaders with colorful yarn.

Rum Butter

Makes 1 cup
Preparation time: 10 minutes

  1 cup butter, softened
  ½ cup light brown sugar, rubbed through a sieve
  ¼ cup light rum
  ⅛ teaspoon freshly grated nutmeg

This is excellent served with plum pudding.

Cream butter, sugar, rum, and nutmeg. Beat until smooth and well blended. Spoon into a pretty mug. Tie the recipe onto the handle with a ribbon bow.

Variation: substitute brandy for the rum and ½ teaspoon vanilla for the nutmeg.

Give this with a can of plum pudding and a small bottle of rum or brandy for flaming the dessert.

Cinnamon-Spice Butter

Makes about 1½ cups
Preparation time: 10 minutes

  1 cup butter
  ¾ teaspoon cinnamon
  ½ teaspoon freshly grated nutmeg
  ⅛ teaspoon mace

This is wonderful on toast.

Cream butter; add all spices and mix well. Spoon into special small jars and sprinkle the top with cinnamon.

Make a memorable gift for newlyweds with an assortment of butters, a loaf of homemade bread, and an herbal tea. Pack all on a rattan breakfast tray so they can enjoy breakfasts in bed for years to come.

Fresh Fruit Butters

Makes 1½ cups
Preparation time: 10 minutes

1 cup butter, softened
¾ cup crushed strawberries, raspberries, or blueberries; or finely chopped apples, pears, or dates; or grated peel of 1 lemon
Juice of 1 lemon

Cream butter, stir in fruit or peel and lemon juice. Refrigerate or freeze.

These will keep up to 3 months in the freezer.

Save small pimiento jars, tiny mustard jars, or caviar jars for these elegant butters. Or buy the smallest soufflé dishes or the crocks designed for snails or butter. Browse in second-hand and antique shops, too, for odd, doll-size cups and other little pots for packing these butters. Spread the butters smoothly into the containers, then top with a piece of foil or cooking parchment cut to fit. A colorful holiday medallion can be stuck on top to decorate the gift, then wrap it in plastic film or a sandwich bag, caught with a bright ribbon.

CALICO JAR BONNETS

Calico prints
Compass
Rick-rack or lace trimming
Thread to match fabrics
Narrow elastic

Cut fabric into 5-inch squares. **Fig. A.** With a compass, inscribe 5-inch circles on the squares and cut them out. **Fig. B.** Sew rick-rack or lace trimming around edge of circle. **Fig. C.** Sew narrow elastic ½ inch from edge of circle on the wrong side of fabric. **Fig. D.** As a short-cut, you can attach calico circles to jars with rubber bands and tie on ribbon or yarn to conceal them.

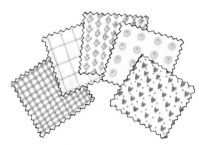

Fig. A

Fig. B

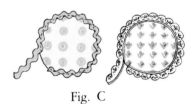

Fig. C

Fig. D

Here is a fresh idea for serving fruit and herb butters; pack them in hollowed-out fruits and vegetables. Shown here: Nut Butter in an orange, Parsley Butter in green and yellow peppers, and Strawberry Butter in a bright red apple. Also shown: Rum Butter, spooned into a mug and tied with a red ribbon; and Cranberry Butter packed in an old porringer and decorated with whole berries. A teddy bear mug of spicy Pfefferneusse seems to have snuck into the picture from Chapter 4.

½ cup finely ground nuts (walnuts, pecans, or hazelnuts)

Combine all ingredients and mix well. Shape into an attractive pat and top with a nut. Cover with plastic wrap and refrigerate.

Fill small jars with an assortment of butters. Pack into a basket with fresh fruits and unshelled nuts and include a fanciful animal-shaped nutcracker.

Variety Fresh Herb Butters

Makes 1½ cups
Preparation time: 10 minutes

1 cup butter, softened
2 tablespoons minced herbs
Juice of 1 lemon (optional)
Pepper (optional)

These herb butters are delicious on vegetables or on bread toasted briefly under a broiler.

Cream butter, add herb of choice and pepper and lemon juice if desired. Spoon into attractive containers and garnish with a sprig of the chosen herb.

For an outdoor luncheon, serve fresh herb butters that are mounded into sweet red, green, or yellow peppers and garnished with an herb leaf. Place on a flat straw serving basket with grape leaves around it. Make a holiday gift by placing an herb-butter-filled pepper on a bed of parsley; cover with plastic wrap and tie on a sprig of herbs.

Nut Butter

Makes 1 cup
Preparation time: 10 minutes

1 cup butter, softened
2 tablespoons confectioners sugar

CREATIVE CANNING

Organisms that cause food spoilage—molds, yeasts, and bacteria—are always present in the air, water, and soil. Enzymes that may cause undesirable changes in flavor, color, and texture are present in raw fruits and vegetables. When you can fruits and vegetables, you first heat them hot enough and long enough to destroy spoilage organisms and stop the action of enzymes.

The method of canning explained here is called "open-kettle" canning. In this method, food is cooked, uncovered, in a large pot, a "kettle." It is then packed into hot, sterilized jars while still boiling hot, and sealed without processing. Open-kettle canning is suitable for preserving jams, jellies, pickles, and relishes—all of which are high acid foods. It is not suitable for canning unprocessed fruits and vegetables, as the temperatures obtained are not high enough to destroy all the spoilage organisms present in raw food. If you are interested in canning unprocessed fruits and vegetables, the Department of Agriculture puts out an excellent booklet, "Home and Garden Bulletin Number 8, Home Canning of Fruits and Vegetables." It is available from the U.S. Government Printing Office, Washington, D.C. for a small fee.

Materials

You will need to purchase some special equipment for preserving. Your kettle should be a heavy-bottomed pot large enough to hold four times the volume of your ingredients. Screw-type canning jars are required for pickles and relishes, and recommended for jams and jellies as well. There are two types: those with metal screw bands and flat metal lids, and those with porcelain-lined zinc caps. The principal parts of each are illustrated.

Other materials required are a wooden spoon for stirring hot liquids, tongs for handling hot jars, a ladle or large spoon

Metal screw band

Metal lid with sealing compound

Seals here

for filling jars, and labels for identification. You can use any large pot for sterilizing jars, as long as you have a rack which will fit inside it on which to place them.

For jam- and jelly-making, you'll need glass jars and paraffin if you're not using canning jars, and a candy thermometer comes in handy. For most jellies, a jelly bag is a necessity, but you can use a cheesecloth-lined colander in a pinch.

The Jellying Point

Jams, jellies, and preserves that do not contain added pectin require you to "test for the jellying point." The most reliable way to do this is with a candy thermometer. The jellying point is 8° F above the boiling point of water, or 220° F at sea level and one degree less for each 500 feet in altitude. An alternate test is to put a few drops of the hot liquid on a chilled plate and place it in the freezer to see if the liquid will jell when cool. Remember to remove the kettle from heat each time you make the test.

Sterilizing Equipment

Before sterilizing jars, check all parts for cracks, chips, dents, or rust and discard any with problems. They could cause jars to seal improperly resulting in spoilage.

If jars are cloudy, fill with vinegar and allow to stand for two or three hours. Scrub with a brush or nylon scrubbing pad. Don't use steel wool which will scratch the glass.

Wash all jar parts, tongs, and a knife in hot soapy water or your dishwasher. To sterilize, place on a rack in a large pot and fill with water to one inch above jars. Bring to a boil and boil 15 minutes. Leave in water until you're ready to fill jars. Note: do not place rubber rings in dishwasher or sterilize them. Wash them with soapy water and keep wet until needed.

Filling and Sealing Jars

Remove hot jars with sterilized tongs and fill, leaving headspace indicated in recipe. Be sure that all pieces of fruit and vegetable are covered with syrup or they may darken. Run a sterilized knife around inside of jar between food and jar to remove air bubbles. Wipe off jar necks with a damp cloth and seal.

To seal screw-band canning jars, cover jar mouths with lids and screw on bands tightly.

To seal jars with porcelain-lined caps, fit rubber rings over jar necks and pull down carefully over screw threads. Be careful to stretch rings as little as possible. If rings do not lie flat, discard them. Screw on caps tightly.

Paraffin

Because it sometimes cracks or shrinks, paraffin does not form as dependable a seal as do canning jars. It should be used only to seal jams, jellies, and preserves, which cannot spoil because of their high sugar content. On the other hand, they can attract molds. It used to be thought that these molds were harmless and could simply be scraped off and the preserves below enjoyed. Now scientists believe that compounds called mycotoxins form in foods as a result of mold growth. Consequently, if you find mold on your preserves, the best advice is to throw them out, and, if you want a more dependable seal, don't use paraffin.

To seal with paraffin, melt it in a double boiler over low heat. Paraffin is highly flammable and should *never* be melted over direct heat. Fill and seal only one jar at a time. After filling, wipe inside of lip with a damp cloth and cover preserves completely with a ⅛-inch layer of paraffin and allow to cool.

After-canning Jobs

Test the seal on glass jars with porcelain-lined caps by turning each jar partly over in your hands. To test jars with metal lids, press center of lid; if lid is down and will not move, jar is sealed. Examine paraffin-sealed jars carefully for any signs of the paraffin's shrinking or cracking. If you find a leaky jar, use unspoiled food right away, or can it again. Before using the same jar or screw band again, check for defects. When jars are thoroughly cool, remove screw bands carefully. If a band sticks, covering it for a moment with a hot, damp cloth may help loosen it.

Before storing canned food, wipe jars clean. Label to show contents and date of canning. Wash screw bands and store in a dry place. Here's a neat trick for removing paraffin "lids" easily: lay a piece of string over cooled paraffin so that it extends over both sides of the jar. Cover with another layer of melted paraffin no more than 3/16-inch thick and allow to cool. Use the string to lift off the paraffin when you're ready to use the preserves.

Storing Canned Food

Properly canned food stored in a cool, dry place will retain its quality for at least a year. Canned food stored in a warm place near hot pipes, a stove, a furnace, or in direct sunlight may lose some of its eating quality in a few weeks or months, depending on the temperature. Heat is a particular concern when storing food canned by the open-kettle method as it is more vulnerable than food that has been processed. If you can't guarantee cool, dry storage, it's probably better to store your preserves in the refrigerator unless you think you will use them up within a few weeks.

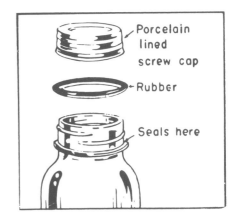

PICKLES AND RELISHES

This 18th-century pine cupboard holds summer's bounty in the form of jars of freshly put-up produce. The pickles shown include End of Season Relish, Refrigerator Cuke Pickles, Shaker Pumpkin Pickle, Pickled Watermelon Rind, and Chunky Vegetable Pickle.

⚔ 6 ⚔

Making pickles and relishes is an age-old art, but so rewarding! Perky, flavored condiments of this sort were devised to preserve fresh foods from the various ferments and spoiling organisms that made them so perishable centuries ago. Today your home-made pickles or relishes can be the very personal trademarks of your culinary creativity.

Any friend is lucky who receives a glowing cranberry chutney, spicy pickled watermelon rind, or golden pumpkin pickles. These elegant accessories to sandwiches, meats, and poultry can be packaged attractively, too. Fill salvaged olive jars, the thin tall ones, with chutney for a friend who dotes on curries or turkey sandwiches. Pack a fruit pickle in a small canning jar, seal it, and place it in a basket with a small roll of salami and a loaf of rye bread. Yummy!

Most of the pickles are prepared using the "open kettle" method of canning and so are impervious to spoilage. "Creative Canning," at the end of Chapter 5, will fill you in on canning techniques and specific equipment needs.

For perfect pickles, use pickling salt. Iodized salt will darken pickles and add an off flavor. Ordinary table salt contains additives that will cloud the syrup. Use whole spices for the best flavor, but tie them up inside cheesecloth. Remove the spices before filling the jars or the pickles will be bitter. Vinegars must have 5% acidity in order to prevent spoilage. Check labels carefully and don't use homemade vinegars whose strength it is impossible to gauge. White or cider vinegar may be used in all recipes.

Pickling can preserve flavor but it can't make an immature peach flavorful, or an over-the-hill cucumber crisp, so don't spend your valuable time on anything less than the best of the harvest.

End of Season Relish

Makes 8 pints
Preparation time: 1 hour
Cooking time: 10 minutes

    2 pounds onions, peeled
    1 medium head cabbage
   10 green tomatoes
   12 green peppers, seeded
    6 sweet red peppers, seeded
   ½ cup salt
    6 cups sugar
    1 tablespoon celery seed
    2 tablespoons mustard seed
   1½ teaspoons turmeric
    4 cups cider vinegar
    2 cups water

Grind vegetables in a hand shredder, using a medium blade. Or use a food processor, being careful not to puree vegetables.

Sprinkle with salt; let stand overnight. Place vegetables in colander and run fresh water through them, drain and squeeze gently with hands to remove water. Combine remaining ingredients in an 8 to 10 quart kettle, heat to boiling, stirring to dissolve sugar. Add vegetables and bring to a full boil; simmer 3 minutes. Ladle into hot, sterilized canning jars, leaving ¼-inch headspace. Seal and label.

The relish is a pretty red and green, just perfect for holiday giving. Give each jar a homey look by adding a tie around the top of printed ribbon or 1-inch strips cut from sprigged fabric. The fabric will crimp into a thin rope around the jar top, and stand up in a perky bow.

Cranberry Chutney

Makes about 2½ cups
Preparation time: 45 minutes
Cooking time: 30 minutes

2 cups cranberries
1 cup sugar
1 cup water
1 lime, including peel, chopped
1 medium onion, chopped
1 cup raisins
½ cup thinly sliced celery
½ cup chopped peaches (fresh or canned)
½ cup chopped pears
1 teaspoon ginger
½ teaspoon ground cloves

This is excellent served with holiday meats.

Wash berries, combine with sugar and water in large saucepan; bring to a boil. Simmer and stir for 5 minutes or until berries pop. Add remaining ingredients and cook until thick, about 20 minutes. Pour into hot, sterilized canning jars, leaving ¼-inch headspace. Seal and label.

An earthenware bowl that can go to the table is perfect for holding this relish. Wrap the bowl tightly in plastic film and tie a silver or white ribbon around it. A tiny Christmas ornament, the kind available in gift wrap centers, can be tucked into the bow.

Cranberry Nut Relish

Makes about 2 cups
Preparation time: 20 minutes

4 cups cranberries, chopped coarsely
1 medium orange

½ cup blanched almonds
1½ cups sugar
2 tablespoons brandy

Chop berries and place in 1-quart bowl. Cut orange into chunks and remove seeds. Chop with almonds, add sugar, and stir in brandy. Mix lightly with cranberries. Pack in small jars; keep refrigerated.

This relish will go from under the tree to the holiday lunch table if you pack it in a handsome glass. Cover with plastic film and finish with a gold or silvery white ribbon to set off the color of the relish.

Pickled Watermelon Rind

Makes 7 pints
Preparation time: 1 hour
Cooking time: 1 to 1¼ hours

4 quarts watermelon rind
½ cup salt
3 quarts water
8 cups sugar
2 teaspoons whole cloves
Three 4-inch sticks cinnamon
1 quart white vinegar

Prepare watermelon rind by cutting off dark green peel and pink flesh from rind. Cut white part of rind into 1-inch squares. Dissolve salt in 2 quarts water; pour over rind. Let stand overnight. Cook in water used for soaking until tender, about 20 to 30 minutes. Drain and rinse.

In kettle combine sugar, spices,

vinegar, and 1 quart water; simmer for 10 minutes. Add rind and cook until it is transparent. Ladle into hot, sterilized canning jars, including a piece of cinnamon and a clove in each jar. Cover with hot syrup, leaving ¼-inch headspace, and seal.

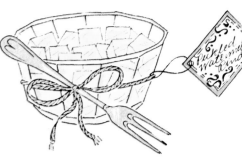

Tie some cinnamon sticks to a jar of this traditional pickle, or give in a table-presentable small bowl with a handsome pickle fork.

Chunky Vegetable Relish

Makes about 12 pints
Preparation time: 1 hour
Cooking time: 40 minutes

4 quarts sweet peppers—green, red, and yellow—seeded and cut into eighths
2 quarts carrots, cut into strips 1 to 1½ inches long
3 quarts small green tomatoes, cut into quarters
1 quart yellow onions, chopped
1½ quarts celery, cut into 1½-inch lengths
1 quart large lima beans (fresh or frozen)
1 pound beans, green or wax
1 cauliflower, medium head, cored and cut into flowerettes
1 quart white vinegar
1 quart water
6 cups sugar
3 tablespoons pickling spice (remove red peppers), tie in a cheesecloth bag for easy removal later
2 teaspoons turmeric

Cook vegetables separately in boiling salted water until just tender, drain. Place all in an 8 to 10 quart kettle. Combine remaining ingredients and bring syrup to a boil, pour over pre-cooked vegetables; bring to a boil. Ladle into hot, sterilized pint canning jars, leaving ¼-inch headspace. Seal and label.

Note: any remaining syrup may be used as a salad dressing.

This big deal pickle is so handsome that it deserves to be displayed flamboyantly—in a clear glass canister. To give to a family or enthusiastic host or hostess, paste a few colored foil medallions strategically on the jar. They will come off later when the relish is gone and the recipient wants to use the jar for other foods.

Refrigerator Cuke Pickles

Makes 3 pints
Preparation time: 40 minutes
  25 small pickling cucumbers, washed and sliced
   3 medium onions, sliced and separated into rings
  ½ cup salt
   4 cups vinegar
   5 cups sugar
   1 tablespoon turmeric
  1½ teaspoons celery seed
  1½ teaspoons mustard seed

Place sliced cucumbers and onions in pint jars. In saucepan mix together salt, vinegar, sugar, and spices. Heat to dissolve salt and sugar and pour into jars to cover vegetables. Refrigerate.

Since these pickles must be refrigerated, use waterproof, plastic ribbon or gummed tape for decoration. Try to find a brown-and-white check, or a star or heart design in red. Either will look nice against the green of these pickles.

Herb Mustard

Makes 1 to 2 cups
Preparation time: 15 minutes

  ½ cup dry mustard
   3 tablespoons brown sugar
  ¼ cup white wine
  ¼ cup tarragon vinegar
   2 egg yolks
  ½ cup vegetable oil
   3 tablespoons finely minced fresh herbs (savory, parsley, oregano, rosemary, sage, tarragon, or thyme)

Beat together mustard, sugar, wine and vinegars. Add egg yolks. Slowly pour in oil, beating well. Add herbs of choice. Spoon into small jars or crocks, cover and refrigerate.

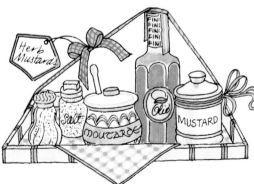

These small crocks of variety herb mustards go into a basket containing oils, vinegars, and savory salts for a gift to a special friend. Tie a green and white checkered napkin on the handle of the basket.

Pottsfield Pickles

Makes 7 pints
Preparation time: 1 hour
Cooking time: 30 to 45 minutes

  15 coarsely chopped green tomatoes
  15 chopped ripe tomatoes
  1½ medium heads chopped cabbage
   3 medium onions, chopped
   3 red peppers, seeded and chopped
  ½ cup grated horseradish
   2 bunches celery, coarsely chopped
   6 to 8 tiny cucumbers, coarsely chopped
  ½ cup salt
   3 pints vinegar
   6 cups sugar
  ½ teaspoon ground cinnamon
  ½ teaspoon ground cloves
  ½ cup mustard seed

Combine all vegetables. Add ½ cup salt and allow to stand overnight. Drain. Make a syrup of vinegar, sugar, and spices in large kettle. Add chopped vegetables and cook just until tender, stirring occasionally. Ladle into hot, sterilized pint canning jars, leaving ¼-inch headspace, and seal.

This pickle is rich and spicy looking. Cover jar tops with calico "bonnets" (Chapter 5), and give with a bar of fine old cheddar and a loaf of homemade bread.

Uncooked Pepper Relish

Makes about 2 pints
Preparation time: 40 minutes

 6 each red and green sweet peppers, chopped fine
 6 medium onions, chopped fine
 Hot water
 1½ cups vinegar
 1 cup sugar
 2 tablespoons salt

Place chopped red and green peppers and onion in large bowl. Pour hot water to cover peppers and onions; let stand 10 minutes; drain well. Combine vinegar, sugar, and salt; heat to dissolve sugar and salt; add ground vegetables. Ladle into jars and keep in refrigerator.

A crock with a small wooden spoon for dipping makes a homey gift. Tie a big green bow around the crock handle or neck.

Shaker Pumpkin Pickle

Makes 5 pints
Preparation time: 45 minutes
Cooking time: 30 minutes

 2 tablespoons whole cloves
 2 tablespoons broken-up stick cinnamon
 1 quart cider vinegar
 4 pounds sugar
 5 pounds pumpkin, rind removed and cut into 1-inch cubes

Tie cloves and cinnamon in double thickness of cheesecloth. Combine vinegar and sugar in an 8-quart kettle; add spices. Bring to a boil, add pumpkin, and cook until tender but not mushy. Ladle pumpkin cubes into hot, sterilized pint canning jars. Cover with hot syrup, leaving ¼-inch headspace, and seal.

These pickles are tawny-colored, so wrap a ribbon that is a slightly darker gold or rust-color around the neck of the jar and tuck in a twig of fresh evergreen and a tiny pine cone.

Good Hot Mustard

Makes 2½ cups
Preparation time: 30 minutes
Cooking time: 10 minutes

 1 tablespoon mustard seeds, coarsely crushed
 1 cup dry mustard
 1 cup cider vinegar
 1 cup sugar
 3 eggs, beaten
 2 tablespoons white wine

Mix together mustard seeds, dry mustard, and vinegar. Marinate in refrigerator overnight. In saucepan combine mustard mixture, sugar, and eggs. Cook, stirring until thick. Remove from heat; cool and add wine. Pour into small crocks, cover tightly, and refrigerate.

Spoon some mustard into a pretty mug and tie an herb sprig on the handle with ribbon. Cover with plastic wrap. Small jars salvaged from pimiento, caviar, or meat spreads are also ideal for this mustard. Cover the brand-name tops with colored foil medallions.

Dill Carrots

Makes 1 quart
Preparation time: 15 minutes
Cooking time: 5 minutes

 1 pound carrots, cut into strips
 ½ teaspoon salt
 1 teaspoon sugar
 2 large cloves garlic, sliced
 1 small onion, thinly sliced
 2 teaspoons dillweed or 2 heads fresh dill
 1 cup water
 1 cup vinegar

Fill jar with carrots; add salt, sugar, garlic, onion, and dill. Boil water and vinegar and pour into jar to fill. Cover tightly and turn upside down. Marinate overnight. Refrigerate.

For variation, try this recipe with other vegetables, such as zucchini, beets, cauliflower, or broccoli.

Give these bright pickles in a clear glass jar. Tie orange or bright yellow nylon net around the jar and catch it with a deep orange ribbon. A miniature pine cone tucked into the ribbon adds holiday atmosphere.

These jars of pickles are shown ready for giving. Wrap them in kitchen towels or cloth napkins—like this red linen one from Portugal—and tie with ribbon bows or fabric scraps.

THE FROZEN HARVEST

Think about wild blueberry muffins in December, or tender young asparagus in February. Both are possible if you have access to really fresh fruits and vegetables (preferably homegrown), and some spare freezer space.

Freezing is one of the best ways to put up fresh fruits and vegetables, and a life-saver when you're up to your neck in your garden's bounty. Freezing preserves taste, color, and food value better than any other method of preserving, and, compared to putting up jams or pickles, it's simple and *cool* work.

Each fruit and vegetable has different requirements, from blueberries, which require nothing more than a quick wash in cold water before being popped into freezer bags or containers, to artichokes, which must be blanched in an ascorbic acid solution and then cooled in ice water before packaging. Check any major cookbook for exact instructions for each fruit and vegetable.

Here are some neat tricks with frozen food:

Freeze fruit pie fillings in foil pie pans slightly smaller than the pan you will bake in. When fillings are frozen solid, remove from pans, seal, and label. Give with frozen homemade crusts for no-work pies. (Fillings should be allowed to thaw partially before pouring into crusts.)

Some elderly people have small appetites and are unable to use a whole package of frozen vegetables, especially if they live alone as so many do. A week's worth of seven different frozen vegetables packed in single-serve plastic containers or freezer bags (about one half cup per serving) is a thoughtful gift as fresh as summer sunshine. Pack vegetables in larger containers for a couple or family.

Herbs are particularly good freezers. Wash and dry fresh herbs carefully and chop fine. Place in ice cube trays and fill each compartment to the top with water. When frozen solid, pack in plastic bags and label. Use herb cubes as is in hot dishes or thaw and drain for salads.

Basil pesto is another great freezer. Blend together finely chopped basil, nuts, and oil, and package in baby food containers. To use, thaw, mix in softened butter and grated Parmesan, and stir into hot spaghetti.

Buy peppers when they're cheap or gather when they're plentiful in your garden. Chop and spread on cookie sheets or shallow trays. Freeze overnight, break up, and package in resealable plastic bags and they're ready to be measured out into spicy recipes all winter long. The same trick works well with onions and is a great time- and tear-saver.

For low-calorie sorbet, drop frozen fruits into a blender or food processor while the motor is running. Process just until mushy and add fruit liqueur to taste. Pop into the freezer for a couple of minutes if needed.

Never, never throw out mushy bananas. Mash them, add lemon juice or ascorbic acid to prevent discoloration, and freeze in one-cup containers to use in breads, muffins, pancakes, and shakes. Frozen whole bananas on a stick are wonderful, healthy treats for children. Roll in peanut butter and melted chocolate for an added treat.

Finally, if you're a city person with only a summer-time, country-house garden, the freezer is a great place to store composting materials. Finely chop all vegetable and fruit matter in a blender or food processor and store in plastic bags. Use as "green" compost or as a quick-start to your summer compost pile.

VEGETABLE YIELD CHART

	Quarts	Foot Row Length	Amount Seed	Pounds Yields	Bushels Raw Produce	Inches Between Plants	Inches Between Rows
Beans, snap	40	130	1¼ lbs.	80	1½	3–4	18–24
Beans, lima	16	265	2 lbs.	32	½	3–4	30–36
Beets	8	26	1 oz.	16	⅓	2–3	12–18
Broccoli	16	35	40 plants	32	1½	14–24	30–36
Carrots	14	40	1 oz.	26	½	2–3	12–18
Cauliflower	24	40	30 plants	48	1	14–24	30–36
Corn	24	130	½ lbs.	48	—	14–16	30–36
Peas	16	200	2 lbs.	32	1	1	18–24
Peppers	15	50	32 plants	30	1	18–24	18–24
Spinach	14	60	102 seeds	26	1	3–4	12–18
Squash, winter	14	16	8–10 seeds	26	—	Hills-4 ft.	6–8 feet
Tomatoes							
whole	40	65	35 plants	80	1½	30–36	30–36
juice	80	65	35 plants	160	3	30–36	30–36
Turnips	8	8	½ oz.	16	½	2–3	12–18

VINEGARS, INFUSIONS, AND OILS

American history can be traced through the designs on, and shapes of, glass bottles. Patriotic symbols were often used: eagles, flags, and sheafs of wheat, and national heros and heroines such as George Washington and Jennie Lind were sometimes portrayed. Collect old bottles to use as unique containers for your gifts of flavored oils and vinegars.

7

Any friend interested in new-wave cooking will adore you for giving a flavored vinegar or oil. A tiny jar of one of the salad dressings is a treat to an elderly person living alone. A salad enthusiast will appreciate a salad spinner filled with jars and bottles of assorted oils, vinegars, and dressings.

Both vinegars and oils easily absorb other flavors. By heating them, adding herbs or fruits, and allowing them to infuse, you can create unique flavor marriages.

Any kind of vinegar can be used as a base for flavored vinegars as long as it contains at least 5% acidity. For flavored oils you can use many of the inexpensive oils available at your supermarket—corn oil or such "vegetable" oils as safflower, soybean, olive, or blended oils. Because they are so highly refined that they are almost tasteless, they are the safest choice for an oil base to which you want to add a pure flavor.

If you want to try more flavorful oils, look for "unrefined, virgin, cold-pressed" oils at your gourmet shop or health food store. These are favorites of gourmets and are the healthiest as well as the most flavorful oils available. You can occasionally find a tasty olive oil in your supermarket. A dark green color is an indication of a stronger flavor.

The best quality oils are produced from the first pressing of the seed, nut, or fruit (the olive is classified botanically as a fruit) and are characterized by a dark color, distinctive flavor, and, usually, some sediment at the bottom of the bottle. Oils with strong flavors of their own, such as coconut, walnut, even peanut, may not combine well with other flavors.

When using one of the more flavorful vinegars (wine or malt), or one of the flavorful unrefined oils, arrange your flavor marriages carefully. For example, adding garlic to malt vinegar is an unappealing idea, and the intense flavor of walnut oil is a risky choice for most palates.

Decant oils and vinegars into bottles. Seal with corks and dip in paraffin that has been melted in a double boiler. Metal caps should not be used, particularly with vinegars, as they will corrode. By leaving a sprig of a flavoring herb in the bottle you will give your herb vinegars a fresh look, but don't try this with garlic as the flavor will become too pungent.

Flavored vinegars keep indefinitely and can be prepared weeks in advance. The oils may go rancid after six or eight weeks, so prepare flavored oils only a couple of weeks before giving. Salad dressings are pretty much last-minute gifts, but are so easy to prepare that they can be whipped together even a few minutes before you drive off on your gift-giving route.

Make this part of a dual gift—the handsome bottle of raspberry vinegar and another bottle of gift-quality olive or walnut oil. Tie gift ribbons or yarns around the necks of the bottles, and identify the vinegar and oil with tags.

Raspberry Vinegar

Makes 4 cups
Preparation time: 30 minutes

    2 cups red raspberries
    4 cups white vinegar

Add berries to vinegar. Heat gently for 15 minutes to infuse the flavor and red color, but do not boil. Strain and pour into pretty bottles. Use a sliver of bamboo or a long toothpick and thread some berries onto it, then add to vinegar. Cork bottle and seal top by immersing it in hot melted paraffin; label. Use with your favorite oil for a refreshing salad dressing.

Note: other fruit vinegars may be prepared by substituting strawberries, blackberries, blueberries, etc. Heat is necessary in order to extract the flavor and color.

VINEGARS, INFUSIONS, AND OILS

Some suggested herbal oils are basil, sage, lemon balm, and garlic.

Place oils in easy-pour bottles, so the recipient doesn't spoil the kitchen counter or best apron with splatters. Use wrappings that look fresh, or can be removed easily. Yarn in holiday colors is good. Or, for a change, tie a mesh dishcloth around the base of a bottle of oil, using kitchen twine for the tie. Tuck a basting brush and sprig of fresh herb in the tie, for a larger gift.

Herbal Vinegars

Makes 2 cups
Preparation time: 10 minutes
Infusing time: 4 to 5 days

  2 cups vinegar (white, cider, or wine)
    Minced fresh herbs

Bring vinegar to a simmer, remove from heat, and add 4 to 6 tablespoons herbs. Cover and allow to sit 4 to 5 days with occasional shaking. Strain into a bottle and add a fresh sprig of herb. Cork tightly and dip bottle neck in melted paraffin to seal. Label and store.

You can use almost any herb or combination of herbs. Try tarragon, chive (leaves or pink blossoms), basil, marjoram, dill, sage, rosemary, or winter savory. Onion adds a pungent note, and mustard, bay leaf, and chili add zest. Curry powder or garlic will add even more spice.

For a particularly pretty and flavorful vinegar, prepare tarragon vinegar and add a long, whole red pepper and a stalk of celery after straining into bottle.

Note: fresh herbs can be preserved by mincing the leaves and freezing in ice cube trays with water to cover. After freezing remove from trays and store in plastic freezer bags. To use, thaw and squeeze out excess moisture.

Use clear bottles for these pretty vinegars. Tie yarn or ribbon around necks of bottles and paste on a label with vinegar name and perhaps a favorite salad recipe. Small twig wreaths decorated with holiday greens and miniature flowers are also charming hung around the necks of antique bottles.

Garlic Vinegar

Makes 2 cups
Preparation time: 10 minutes
Infusing time: overnight

  2 cups wine vinegar
  1 clove garlic, quartered
  1 bay leaf

Heat vinegar to simmer, add garlic and bay leaf. Allow to stand overnight, strain, and bottle. Place in refrigerator.

According to the French, a salad must be dressed with oil, vinegar, and a good mustard. For an unusual gift put small jars of all three in a salad spinner or drainer and tie handles with pastel ribbons.

Herbal Oils

Makes 2 cups
Preparation time: 10 minutes
Infusing time: 4 to 5 days

  2 cups oil
    Minced fresh herbs

Use vegetable oils such as safflower, sunflower, corn, sesame, and walnut for making herbal oil infusions. (Coconut oil is high in saturated fat.)

Heat oil gently in a double boiler. (High heat discolors the oil and it becomes rancid quickly.) When oil is hot, add 10 to 12 tablespoons of selected herb, chopped. Allow to stand for 4 to 5 days; strain into the bottle and add a fresh sprig of herb.

Mustard Dill Sauce

Makes 1½ cups
Preparation time: 15 minutes

  ½ cup prepared mustard
  2 teaspoons dry mustard
  6½ tablespoons sugar
  ¼ cup herb vinegar
  ½ cup herb oil
  ½ cup minced fresh dill
    Salt
    Limes, sliced for garnish

Mix together prepared mustard, dry mustard, and sugar; stir in herb vinegar. Gradually add the herb oil, whisking briskly. Mix in dill; add salt to taste. A zesty sauce for fish!

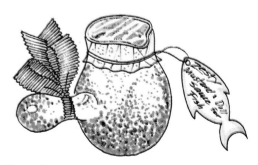

Spoon into an attractive mug, cover with plastic wrap, and tie with a ribbon. Garnish with lime slices before serving. Lime or lemon leaves tied in a white ribbon and attached to a jar of this mustard make a showy presentation. A fresh lime and a jar of the mustard in a salvaged strawberry or mushroom basket look good too.

Fresh Basil Dressing

Makes ¾ cup
Preparation time: 15 minutes

- ¼ cup wine vinegar
- ½ teaspoon sugar
- Salt
- Pepper
- ½ cup walnut oil
- 3 tablespoons minced fresh basil leaves

Heat vinegar to simmer, remove from heat. Stir in sugar, and salt and pepper to taste. Using a wire whisk beat in walnut oil slowly. Add minced basil. Bottle, label, and refrigerate.

Give this bottle a label—Christmasy or a design appropriate to the recipient, Victorian lady, art deco, etc. The label describes not only the dressing but also the essential instruction to beat before serving.

Sesame Dressing

Makes ⅔ cup
Preparation time: 5 minutes

- ⅓ cup sesame oil
- ⅓ cup lemon juice
- Garlic juice or garlic salt to taste
- 2 tablespoons minced fresh herb of choice: oregano, tarragon, or thyme
- Caraway, dill, or sesame seeds (optional)

Whisk oil into lemon juice and add garlic juice or salt. Add minced herb and ¼ teaspoon seeds (if desired). Refrigerate if not using immediately.

This fresh dressing in a clear glass beaker or cruet and a sprig of the appropriate herb in the bottle make a pretty picture. Tie a ribbon at the neck of the bottle and add a tag, with "Refrigerate" written on it. A pale yellow ribbon with a sprig of herb or evergreen is fresh looking.

Vinaigrette Dressing

Makes about ½ cup
Preparation time: 20 minutes

- 1 tablespoon prepared mustard
- 1 clove garlic, minced
- 2 tablespoons wine vinegar
- ¼ teaspoon minced oregano
- ½ teaspoon ground cumin
- ¼ cup olive or walnut oil
- Salt
- Pepper

Mix mustard, garlic, vinegar, cumin, and oregano, using a wire whisk to blend well. Gradually add oil, whisking briskly. Season with salt and pepper to taste.

Bottle in a small jar, wide enough to admit a miniature wire whisk. Tie the whisk to the neck of the jar with yarn. The recipient then can whisk the dressing together again when serving it, as this dressing tends to separate on standing. A superlative dressing for greens, asparagus, or artichokes.

Mason Jar Dressing

Makes about 2½ cups
Preparation time: 10 minutes

- ½-¾ cup herbal vinegar
- One 10½-ounce can condensed tomato soup
- 1½ teaspoons onion juice
- 1 teaspoon prepared mustard
- 1½ cups herbal oil
- ¼ cup sugar
- ½ teaspoon paprika
- Salt
- Pepper

Mix all ingredients together and shake well. Refrigerate and shake again just before serving.

Give half-cup sizes of this dressing in screw-top canning jars, with instructions "Shake before serving." Paste bright foil stickers on the jar tops and smaller foil stickers around the sides.

Chive Bacon Dressing

Makes 1 to 1½ cups
Preparation time: 30 minutes

¼ pound bacon, chopped
2 eggs, beaten
½ cup chive vinegar (or other herbal vinegar)
½ cup water
2 tablespoons minced, fresh chives
¼ cup sugar

This dressing is especially good on endive or lettuce and spinach salad with fresh mushrooms added.

Cook bacon and drain, reserving 1 teaspoon bacon fat. Combine fat, eggs, vinegar, and water. Cook, stirring with a whisk. Bring to a boil, cool. Stir in bacon, sugar, and cut chives. Bottle, label, and refrigerate.

A bouquet of fresh greens is the natural go-together with this gift. Try tying the spinach and other greens with bright pink or pale lavender ribbon for pizazz.

Vegetable Dressing

Makes ⅔ cup
Preparation time: 15 minutes

¼ cup herbal vinegar
2 tablespoons olive or walnut oil
1 teaspoon dry mustard
1 teaspoon sugar
½ teaspoon curry powder
½ teaspoon paprika
1 teaspoon minced onion
1 tablespoon butter
1 tablespoon minced parsley
1 egg, well beaten
Salt
Pepper

Heat together vinegar and oil, add mustard, sugar, curry, paprika, and onion. Mix well. Add butter and heat until melted. Add parsley and egg and stir over low heat until thick. Season with salt and pepper to taste. Pour over hot vegetables before serving.

This dressing can be reheated briefly in a double boiler or jar set in a pan of very hot, but not boiling water. So pour a batch into a 1-cup jar, close tightly and keep refrigerated until you're ready to take it to a good friend. Along with the jar of dressing, give a pound of the finest, freshest snap beans, baby carrots, or other premium vegetables available at your local green market.

Thousand Island Dressing

Makes 2 to 3 cups
Preparation time: 30 minutes

1 cup mayonnaise
½ green pepper, seeded and chopped fine
2 hard-cooked eggs, chopped fine
1 tablespoon minced fresh chives
1 tablespoon lemon juice
½ teaspoon salt
½ teaspoon paprika
2 tablespoons sugar
3 tablespoons chili sauce (optional)

Combine all ingredients and mix well. Pour into a jar, cover, and store in refrigerator.

This dressing goes with head lettuce salad or seafood, so wrap a bounteous head of lettuce in pale green nylon net or fresh-cooked shrimp, crab, or lobster in white or pink net. Give the dressing in a jar, salvaged or new, with a label on it and a ribbon tie matching the greens or seafood wrap.

Fruit Dressing

Makes about 2 cups
Preparation time: 35 minutes

  1 tablespoon flour
  2 tablespoons butter
  ¾ cup sugar
  2 eggs, beaten
  ½ cup orange or pineapple juice
  1 teaspoon kirsch liqueur (optional)
  ½ cup heavy cream, whipped

This is excellent over fruit salad or freshly prepared fruits for desserts.

In a saucepan melt butter, then stir in flour. Add sugar and eggs. Whisk over low heat until slightly thickened. Cool. Stir in fruit juice and Kirsch. Pour into a jar and refrigerate. For use stir into whipped cream.

A basket of the finest fresh apples, pears, or citrus fruit and a jar of this dressing make an impressive gift indeed. Tuck the jar, wrapped hobo-style in a square of gingham or checked kitchen towel fabric, into a corner of the basket.

French Dressing

Makes about 1½ cups
Preparation time: 15 minutes

  ¾ cup safflower oil
  ¼ cup herb vinegar
  3 tablespoons tomato juice
  3 teaspoons sugar
  ¼ teaspoon paprika
  ½ teaspoon salt
  ½ teaspoon dry mustard
    Pepper to taste

Shake all ingredients together in a bottle. Label and refrigerate. This is good on leafy green and vegetable salads.

Any family on your gift list will appreciate this dressing in a cruet tucked into a basket of salad garnishes—croutons (homemade, too, if you like), olives, capers, and a small bag of fresh shallots or high quality sweet onions.

Mint Dressing

Makes 1 to 1½ cups
Preparation time: 10 minutes

  1 cup honey
  ½ cup water
  1 tablespoon herbal or wine vinegar
  ½ cup fresh minced mint leaves

Good over fresh fruits or serve with roast lamb.

Combine honey, water, and vinegar; heat to a simmer, remove, and stir in mint. Bottle and label when cool.

Give this dressing in a small bottle with a sprig of fresh mint tied to the bottle neck with pale mint-green ribbon.

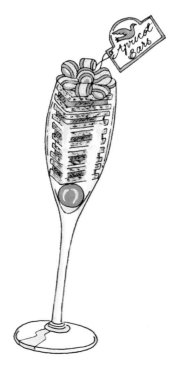

HERBS AND TEAS

Teas can be brewed with almost any combination of herbs and spices. Tea made from the flowers of the linden tree is popular in France, and the Greeks believe that sage tea has therapeutic effects. This antique white agate mortar holds wild rose hips, rich in vitamin C. Pack teas in baskets or tins for gift-giving. Seal them air-tight in plastic bags, or seal the tin, because eventually air will rob them of their flavor.

8

Does dried blueberry or orange cinnamon tea sound comforting? There are many flavors that you can blend into teas or other brewed infusions. These little gifts are simple to make, inexpensive, and appropriate for friends who enjoy drinking tea. A little packet of variety teas or dry drink mixes, packed for an elderly uncle or aunt living in a retirement home, can brighten his or her afternoons for several weeks to come.

The spice blends and seasonings in this chapter will be treasured by gourmet cooks and culinary dabblers alike. Those on limited diets will particularly appreciate the no-salt, no-caffeine blends. Tuck several packets of seasoning in a small basket with fruit and crackers.

In composing these flavorsome gifts, make sure your dried spices and herbs are not stale. If you have herbs in your own garden, it is not difficult to dry them yourself. Almost any herb can be grown outdoors, and mint, rosemary, marjoram, basil, dill, and tarragon do well in containers, too. When grown indoors, parsley seems to be attractive to a certain variety of very small black fly, but as it is available at most supermarkets year-round, there is no excuse for not using it fresh.

When making dry herb blends, use home-dried herbs or purchase new containers of herbs just before blending. To dry herbs, bundle them and hang upside-down in a warm breezy place until they are bone-dry; if not thoroughly dry they can mold or rot. Check dryness by placing a few leaves in an air-tight glass container for several days and watch for signs of mold, condensation, or discoloration. If any of these occur, allow the herbs to dry longer.

All herbs should be stored in tightly closed jars or tins in a dry but not too hot place. Although a shelf above the stove is a common storage place for herbs and spices, they will lose their flavor rapidly when exposed to the high heat in this location.

Whether you use home-dried or store-bought, dried herbs should be crumbled before use to release flavor and aroma. Mix herbs in china or glass bowls, as metal or plastic can impart an off taste. A tiny funnel folded of waxed paper will help you to fill jars and tins for giving. Seal all containers tightly with tape around the edge of the lid to prevent herbs from dusting out in packages.

Although in this country herbs are used solely to enhance other foods, in many parts of the world they are served on their own as an appetizer. For al fresco summer dining, try a platter of freshly washed basil, mint, dill, parsley, and coriander. Serve as is or with a bland cheese, and scallions, cucumbers, radishes, and tomatoes. Either way you have a light and refreshing first course that will stimulate the palate for the good things to come.

Dried Tea-berries

Preparation time: 5 minutes
Drying time: 2 to 3 days

Strawberries, blueberries, or black raspberries

Because they are small and don't contain much water, tiny wild berries are better for drying than cultivated berries.

Dry outdoors between pieces of fine wire or nylon mesh which will allow the air to circulate. Turn occasionally. Berries can also be dried in a microwave oven for 3 minutes. Use 1 teaspoon per cup of boiling water and infuse for 5 minutes.

Pack berries in a small jar or bag and tie with purple and gold ribbons. Be sure to include brewing instructions.

Fresh Herb Blend for Beef and Pork

Makes ½ cup
Preparation time: 15 minutes

- 1 tablespoon fresh summer savory, minced
- 1 tablespoon fresh thyme, minced
- 1 tablespoon fresh marjoram, minced
- 1 tablespoon fresh parsley, minced
- 1 tablespoon fresh sage, minced
- 1 tablespoon celery seed
- 4 crushed bay leaves, sharp stems removed
- 1½ tablespoons grated lemon peel

Combine all ingredients and refrigerate. Sprinkle over meat while roasting.

You can also make this blend with dried herbs in which case it is not necessary to refrigerate it.

A small crock of this herb blend and a favorite recipe for hamburgers or pork chops will be a special surprise on Christmas morning. Tie the package with a big red bow, and the jar of herbs with a miniature red bow.

Fines Herbes for Fish and Chicken

Makes 3 tablespoons
Preparation time: 15 minutes

- 1 teaspoon fresh chervil, minced
- 1 teaspoon fresh chives, minced
- 2 teaspoons fresh parsley, minced
- 1 teaspoon fresh tarragon, minced

Combine all ingredients and sprinkle over fish or chicken immediately after cooking.

A packet of this fresh herb blend and a fish-cooking gadget, such as a lemon zester, make a thoughtful gift. Tie the ensemble together with clear blue ribbon.

Herb Blend for Gravies and Stuffings

Makes ½ cup
Preparation time: 5 minutes

- ¼ cup salt
- 3 tablespoons celery salt
- 4½ teaspoons freshly ground white pepper
- 4½ teaspoons dried thyme
- 4½ teaspoons dried summer savory
- ¼ teaspoon cayenne
- ½ teaspoon ground cloves
- ¼ teaspoon ground allspice
- ¼ teaspoon ground mace

Combine all ingredients and mix thoroughly. Pour into a bottle, jar, or shaker and keep well corked!

A jar of this seasoning blend and a fresh capon make a lavish gift. Wrap the capon in foil over its market wrap and tie the jar onto the large package with a loop of red package-wrapping twine.

Bouquet Garni

Makes 4
Preparation time: 20 minutes

- Cheesecloth
- Dried herbs (see note)
- Thread

Cut cheesecloth into 4-inch squares. Mix herbs together and place 1 teaspoon of mixture in center of each square. Bring corners together and wrap and tie securely with thread.

Note: for meat, blend 1 teaspoon each of nutmeg, thyme, chervil, and tarragon; for fish, blend 1 teaspoon each of tarragon, mint, dill, and lemon peel; and for sauces, soups, stews, and vegetables, use 4 bay leaves, 1 teaspoon thyme, and 2 teaspoons parsley.

Label each bouquet and pack in a small basket. Tie a sprig of fresh herbs to the handle with pretty ribbon. If you want to make your gift really one to remember, a fine red wine is an excellent companion gift to these little bundles. Tie bottle neck and bundles with matching ribbons.

Rose Hip Tea

Preparation time: 10 minutes

Rose hips, dried

Naturally sweet, and rich in vitamin C, this is popular with children and an excellent substitute for caffeine- and sugar-laden soft drinks.

In a mortar finely crush seeds and pulp of dried rose hips to extract the maximum goodness from the herb. Use 1 teaspoon per cup of boiling water, and allow to infuse for 8 to 10 minutes. Sweeten with honey, if desired, or add a thin slice of lemon.

Pack a jar of tea and a twin jar of Strawberry Jam (Chapter 5) in a small basket with homemade cookies or bread—a gift of summer to dispel the mid-winter doldrums.

A teapot and a little plastic bag of crushed, dried rose hips make an attractive gift. A red Christmas rose makes it special.

Bergamot and Mint Tea

Preparation time: 15 minutes
Drying time: 2 to 3 days

This makes a refreshing afternoon tea.

Thoroughly dry herbs in cheesecloth bags. Crush, removing hard stems. Use 1 teaspoon per cup of boiling water and allow to steep 5 minutes. Serve with honey and lemon.

A tiny metal box of this tea makes a special treat for a live-aloner. Along with the tea, give a few of your choicest cookies: a pair of Pecan Bars (Chapter 4) or a plate of Teatime Tassies (also in Chapter 4).

Strawberry Leaf Tea

Preparation time: 5 minutes
Drying time: 2 to 3 days

Collect tiny wild strawberry leaves and allow to dry in a cheesecloth bag. (Hang it on your wash line and shake occasionally.) When thoroughly dried, crush the leaves and remove the stems. Use 1½ to 2 teaspoons per cup of boiling water. Allow to steep for 5 minutes and serve with a slice of lemon.

Almond Cranberry Tea

Serves 4
Preparation time: 15 minutes

6 bags almond-flavored tea
3 tablespoons diced fresh orange peel
2 cups boiling water
1½ cups cranberry juice
½ cup light brown sugar, firmly packed
Amaretto liqueur
Cinnamon sticks

In 2-quart saucepan combine tea bags, orange peel, and water. Brew covered for 5 minutes. Remove tea bags. Stir in juice and sugar; bring to a boil. Before serving add 1 tablespoon Amaretto to each cup. Serve with cinnamon stick stirrers.

Pack the ingredients for this holiday drink—the tea, orange peel, cranberry juice, brown sugar, and tiny bottle of the liqueur—in a small basket or bowl. Tie it all in colored cellophane. Attach the recipe, and let the family enjoy.

Orange/Cinnamon Tea

Preparation time: 10 minutes

¼ pound Ceylon tea
4 tablespoons diced orange rind
1 tablespoon ground cinnamon

Mix all ingredients together. Use 1 teaspoon per cup of boiling water and steep 4 to 5 minutes. Garnish with orange peel cut with miniature cookie cutters.

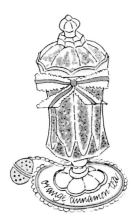

Pack this tea in a jar and wrap the neck with an orange velvet ribbon—sumptuous and befitting a richly flavored tea. For a special friend, give a good tea ball with this tea.

Coarsely grind spices and add to mixture. Pack into a tightly covered jar. Use 1 teaspoon per cup of boiling water and allow to steep for 5 minutes. Garnish with a clove-studded lemon slice.

Make an assortment of small plastic bags of herbal teas, label them and fill an attractive gift tin. Make a gift card with an amusing "fortune" verse and include it with your gift.

Christmas Brew

Preparation time: 10 minutes

3 cups water
1 cup pineapple juice
1 cup orange juice
2 cinnamon sticks
  Juice and chopped peel of 1 lemon
1 tablespoon whole cloves
  Apple parings

A brew to make your house smell nice at holiday time. Don't drink it—just enjoy the aroma!

Mix all ingredients together in a 3-quart saucepan or crock pot. Allow to simmer uncovered. Add water from time to time to prevent pot from boiling dry.

Herb Blend for Sauces and Soups

Makes 1 cup
Preparation time: 2 minutes

3 tablespoons dried parsley
3 tablespoons dried winter savory
3 tablespoons dried marjoram
3 tablespoons dried lemon thyme
3 tablespoons dried basil
1½ teaspoons dried powdered lemon peel

Combine all ingredients, mix well. Use ½ to 1 teaspoon flavoring to taste.

A jar or yarn-tied bag of this herb blend and a soup cookbook make an enchanting gift for a cook.

Kumquat Spice Tea

Preparation time: 30 minutes
Drying time: 2 to 3 days

1 pint fresh kumquats
¼ pound Ceylon tea
1 cinnamon stick
3 whole cloves

Slice kumquats in half and remove pulp. Arrange on nylon mesh and allow to dry thoroughly. Grind finely in a food chopper or processor and add to tea.

An envelope of these spices and the recipe for this old-time house-perfumer make a charming gift for a young couple starting their own family traditions.

THE IDENTIFICATION OF HERBS AND SPICES

The science of herbs is ancient and full of fascination for those who study it. As you use the various herbs called for in these recipes, you may wish to look at this chart and find out where the plants come from, what they look like, and what some of their reputed medicinal uses are.

The information on therapeutic uses of herbs is not necessarily verified by modern medicine, but derives mostly from ancient medical custom and folk wisdom. It is worth noting, however, that many of the old uses of herbs have been proven effective.

Since the terms describing therapeutic uses are medical, they may be unfamiliar to you. In alphabetical order: *anodynes* help relieve pain, *antiseptics* prevent breakdown of cellular tissues, *antispasmodics* allay spasms, *aphrodisiacs* stimulate the libido and sexual organs, *astringents* tighten the tissues. *Bitters* promote appetite, *carminatives* aid the heart, *demulcents* lubricate the digestive canals, *diaphoretics* induce perspiration, *diuretics* increase the flow of urine. *Emetics* compel vomiting, *emmenagogues* promote menstruation, *expectorants* clear the bronchial tubes, *hydragogues* drain water from the tissues. *Irritants* cause irritation to tissues, *laxatives* promote bowel movement, *nervines* allay nervous disorders, *parturients* aid childbirth, *pectorals* alleviate lung disorders, *rubefacients* bring blood to the surface when rubbed on skin, *soporifics* promote drowsiness, *stimulants* promote strength, *stomachics* relieve nausea, and *tonics* induce vivacity and a feeling of well-being.

Allspice (Pimenta dioica)
Also known as Jamaica Pepper or Myrtle Pepper
Found wild Jamaica, West Indies, Central and South America
Appearance Tree with purple berries. The berries are used.
Therapeutic or culinary uses An anodyne often used to relieve stomach disorders. It is added to some medicines for flatulence and diarrhea.

Aniseed (Pimpinella anisum)
Found wild European countries bordering the Mediterranean Sea and North Africa
Appearance An umbelliferous plant with much serrated leaves. Small, brownish-grey seeds have a strong pleasant odour, and a sweet spicy taste.
Therapeutic or culinary uses A pectoral. The distinctive flavour makes it a favourite ingredient for use in cough medicines and elixirs. It is most effective and quite safe for children.

Bay Tree (Laurus nobilis)
Also known as Laurel
Found wild Europe
Appearance An evergreen tree with lanceolate leaves which grows up to 25 ft. (8 metres) high. The leaves and fruit are used.
Therapeutic or culinary uses The laurel wreathes given to Victors at the Olympic Games were made of this tree. It is a stomachic and the oils are used in liniments for the relief of rheumatism.

Basil (Ocimum basilicum)
Also known as Sweet Basil
Found wild Northern Europe
Appearance A small plant, with a multitude of white and pink flowers, whose leaves have a strong clover-like scent. The leaves are used.
Therapeutic or culinary uses Formerly used as a carminative but now almost only used for culinary purposes.

Bergamot (Monarda fistulosa)
Found wild Southern Canada and Northern United States.
Appearance Hollow, grass-like stems with purple flowers. The stems are used.
Therapeutic or culinary uses A well-known soporific. Also popular in tea.

Caraway (Carum carvi)
Also known as Caraway Seed
Found wild Europe and North Africa
Appearance A hollow-stemmed herb usually grown in plantations. The seeds are used.
Therapeutic or culinary use A favourite flavouring. Especially recommended for children.

Cardamom (Elettaria cardamomum)
Also known as Malabar Cardamom
Found wild Ceylon
Appearance A boldly growing plant of exotic appearance. The seeds are used.
Therapeutic or culinary uses Its warming, aromatic, stomachic action is most beneficial for sufferers from flatulence and indigestion. It is also used to give 'note' to fine curries.

Cayenne (Capsicum minimum)
Also known as Chillies, Red Pepper, Bird Pepper
Found wild West Africa and tropical America
Appearance A small erect herb with brilliant dark green foliage. The fruit only is used.
Therapeutic or culinary uses One of the best and most positive stimulants known in herbal science. Also a carminative and rubefacient of great value, and a valued condiment.

Celery (Apium graveolens)
Found wild Europe
Appearance This is the familiar vegetable. The seeds are used.
Therapeutic or culinary uses Always regarded as one of the most effective aphrodisiacs. It is also a tonic, diuretic, and carminative and a most beneficial aid for the relief of rheumatoid troubles.

Chervil, Sweet (Myrrhis odorata)
Also known as Sweet Cicely
Found wild Throughout Great Britain
Appearance A very pretty, erect growing herb. The root and the leaves are used.
Therapeutic or culinary uses A herb with many uses. It is a carminative and an expectorant. It is also used as a remedy for coughs and is regarded as excellent for those who suffer from anaemia.

Chive (Allium schoenoprasum)
Found wild Europe, Canada, Northern United States
Appearance Hollow, grass-like stems with purple flowers. The stems are used.
Therapeutic or culinary uses Can be used to treat incontinence. Used more frequently for culinary purposes.

Cinnamon (Cinnamomum zeylanicum)
Found wild Ceylon
Appearance Another of the laurel family. An evergreen of noble appearance. The bark is used, rolled and dried in cylindrical quills.
Therapeutic or culinary uses As a carminative and stimulant it is indeed excellent, and it quickly ends vomiting. Also used as an aromatic and astringent and for culinary purposes as a flavouring and spice.

Coriander (Coriandrum sativum)
Found wild Southern Europe and the Near East
Appearance A diminutive herb. The fruit is used.
Therapeutic or culinary uses A valuable carminative taken to soothe and ease the bowels. Also acts as a stimulant to restore appetite and vigour. It is also a favourite flavouring.

Cumin (Cuminum cyminum)
Found wild North Africa and the Nile.
Appearance An erect and handsome herb with feathery foliage. The fruit is used.
Therapeutic or culinary uses A carminative. A favourite veterinary medicine for horses that are 'blown' through eating fresh spring grass.

Dill (Anethum graveolens)
Also known as Dill seed
Found wild Europe
Appearance An elegant erect herb with distinctive flower stems. The dried fruit is used.
Therapeutic or culinary uses One of the earliest medicinal herbs known in Europe. It is very effective for conditions of flatulence and dyspepsia and its carminative and stomachic qualities are well attested.

Garlic (Allium sativum)
Where found Universally cultivated
Appearance Similar to the shallot. The bulb is used.
Therapeutic or culinary use A most effective expectorant and diaphoretic. It is claimed that it also has an antiseptic effect upon the bowels. Garlic oil is much used in veterinary preparations.

Ginger (Zingiber officinale)
Found wild West Indies and China
Appearance Height about 3 ft. (1 metre) with glossy aromatic leaves. Its fleshy roots are dried and peeled. The rhizomes only are used.
Therapeutic or culinary uses Justly famed for its stimulative and carminative properties; can also be used as an expectorant. It aids digestion and promotes a feeling of warmth and well-being. Ginger also forms the basis of many sauces and flavourings and is much used in confectionery.

Horseradish (Cochlearia armoracia)
Found wild Europe
Appearance An herb growing up to 3 ft. (1 metre) tall with a pungent odour. The roots are used.
Therapeutic or culinary uses Warms the body and relieves flatulence and indigestion. It also promotes perspiration and is an excellent diuretic.

Licorice (Glycyrrhiza glabra)
Found wild Europe and the Middle East
Appearance A strong-growing perennial plant. The roots are used.
Therapeutic or culinary uses Licorice is of the greatest value in cough medicines. It is a demulcent and pectoral. It is, as well, a laxative with a gentle action.

Marjoram, Sweet (Origanum majorana)
Found wild Throughout Europe (also cultivated)
Appearance Commonly grown as a garden plant. The stalks and leaves are used.
Therapeutic or culinary uses Widely grown as a culinary seasoning.
Traditional and/or reputed uses Once regarded as a powerful stimulant

Mustard (Brassica nigra—Black Mustard)
(Brassica alba—White Mustard)
Found wild Throughout the Northern Hemisphere
Appearance A short-growing annual herb with bright yellow flowers. The seeds are used.
Therapeutic or culinary uses A powerful irritant and emetic. Mustard is much used in embrocations for the relief of rheumatic and arthritic pains, and is added to baths for the same purpose. It is also famous as a condiment for negativing the effects of fatty foods.

Nutmeg (Myristica fragrans)
Found wild East Indies
Appearance A tree of magnificent growth and habit. The seeds are used.
Therapeutic or culinary uses A valuable stomachic and carminative. However, it is chiefly used as a spice. If taken in abundance it can weaken the system.

Oregano (Origanum vulgare)
Also known as Wild Marjoram
Found wild Italy and Britain
Appearance Stalk with small leaves and purple flowers. The leaves are used.
Therapeutic or culinary uses An excellent anodyne with strong curative capabilities. Also a demulcent and diuretic. Used by women as both an expectorant and emmenagogue.

Parsley (Carum petroselinum)
Found wild Europe
Appearance Biennial umbelliferous plant with white flowers and aromatic leaves. The roots and leaves are used.
Therapeutic or culinary uses Parsley is one of the most beneficial of all diuretic herbs. It is excellent for the treatment of all kinds of kidney disorders and is used to eliminate stones and gravel. Also a strong emmenogogue and valuable for the treatment of amenorrhoea. One of the favourite culinary flavourings.

Pepper, Black (Piper nigrum)
Where grown India, Indonesia, Ceylon, Brazil
Appearance Vine with dark green leaves and red berries. The berries are used.
Therapeutic or culinary uses An effective bitter and hydrogogue. Also a demulcent.

Peppermint (Mintha piperita)
Also known as Curled Mint
Found wild Europe and North America
Appearance A stately herb with purple-hued stems. The leaves and oil are used.
Therapeutic or culinary uses Peppermint is one of the most highly regarded stomachic and carminatives. It relieves all forms of sickness, flatulence, and indigestion. It is also one of the finest flavouring agents known.

Poppy (Papaver somniferum)
Found wild Middle East, Turkey, India, China
Appearance An annual plant with greyish leaves and huge, single red flowers. The seed capsules are used.
Therapeutic or culinary uses The poppy seeds commonly used in confectionery and curries are from the same poppy plant used to produce opium. The seeds, however, do not have a narcotic effect.

Raspberry (Rubus idaeus)
Where found Under cultivation in most parts of the world
Appearance Produces cane-like growths that are 6 to 8 feet in height. Fruits are red and are profuse. The fruit and leaves are used.
Therapeutic or culinary uses A powerful astringent. Can be used with every expectation of success as a mouthwash, and to clean wounds and ulcers.

Rose Hips (Rosa canina)
Also known as Wild Briar
Found wild Europe and Middle East
Appearance The wild rose. The hips are used.
Therapeutic or culinary uses The hips yield ascorbic acid (vitamin C) and are of the greatest value when given to young children.
Traditional and/or reputed uses One of the best tonics for old dogs.

Rosemary (Rosmarinus officinalis)
Found wild Southern Europe and Near East
Appearance A hardy evergreen shrub with fragrant needle-like leaves. The leaves alone are used.

Therapeutic or culinary uses A most satisfying nervine, especially good for persistent headaches and migraine. It is known for promoting hair growth.

Sage (Salvia officinalis)

Also known as Red Sage
Found wild Europe and North America
Appearance A small herb. The leaves are used.
Therapeutic or culinary uses An astringent and most frequently used for sore throats, quinsy and laryngitis. Also a culinary herb.

Savory, Summer (Satureia hortensis)

Where found Commonly cultivated throughout the world as a flavouring herb.
Appearance A small shrubby plant. The leaves are used.
Therapeutic or culinary uses Good for the quick relief of flatulence and indigestion. Also used as a poultice to reduce inflammations.

Savory, Winter (Satureia montana)

Found wild Mediterranean region
Appearance Twelve inch perennial with purplish flowers. The leaves are used.
Therapeutic or culinary uses A good parturient or stimulant. Expels phlegm from the chest. Can be used to ease back and muscle ache.

Sesame (Sesamum indicum)

Also known as Semsem
Where grown Europe, Africa, South America, Southern United States
Appearance Tall, erect annual with white, trumpet-shaped flowers. The seeds are used.
Therapeutic or culinary uses A mild laxative. The leaves can be used to treat kidney and bladder disorders, and to soothe eye or skin irritations.

Spearmint (Mentha viridis)

Found wild Throughout the Northern Hemisphere
Appearance A strongly-growing perennial herb. The leaves and oil are used.
Therapeutic or culinary uses A very pleasant stimulant and one of the very best carminatives. Its action is certain and gentle, and is particularly suitable for the very young and the very old.

Star Anise (Illicium verum)

Also known as Badian Anise or Chinese Anise
Where grown Southern China, Southeast Asia
Appearance Small evergreen in magnolia family. The star-shaped fruit is used.
Therapeutic or culinary uses A good stimulant and diuretic. Also helpful for flatulence and nausea.

Tarragon (Artemesia dracunculus)

Where grown Throughout Europe
Appearance Bushy perennial, three feet high, with narrow sharp-pointed leaves and small grey-green flowers. The leaves are used.
Therapeutic or culinary uses Can be used as a hydrogogue and emmenagogue. Also good for relieving excessive evacuation.

Thyme (Thymus vulgaris)
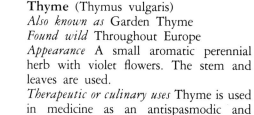
Also known as Garden Thyme
Found wild Throughout Europe
Appearance A small aromatic perennial herb with violet flowers. The stem and leaves are used.
Therapeutic or culinary uses Thyme is used in medicine as an antispasmodic and antiseptic, mostly for lung troubles.

Turmeric (Curcuma longa)

Found wild Asia
Appearance A sturdy herb. The rhizomes are used.
Therapeutic or culinary uses It is cultivated to make curry powder.
Traditional and/or reputed uses Very quickly relieves flatulence and indigestion and was regarded as an excellent liver tonic, but is not much used medicinally nowadays.

Vanilla (Vanilla planifolia)

Where grown Central and South America, Caribbean region
Appearance Climbing orchid with yellow pods. The pods are used.
Therapeutic or culinary uses Once considered to be a stimulant. Although no longer used medicinally, it was formerly common as an aid to digestion and as an aphrodisiac.

Herb Blend for Vegetables

Makes ⅓ cup
Preparation time: 2 minutes

    2 tablespoons rubbed sage
    2 tablespoons dried mint
    ½ teaspoon celery seed
    ½ teaspoon freshly ground white pepper

Place all ingredients in a mortar and crush fine. Store in a covered jar or a salt shaker with a piece of plastic wrap under the top. Use ½ teaspoon to season 4 servings of vegetables while steaming.

Give this in an antique crystal salt shaker and tie on a ribbon with the recipe attached.

Seasoned Salt

Makes 1 cup
Preparation time: 10 minutes

    ¾ cup salt
    1 teaspoon garlic powder
    1½ teaspoons paprika
    1½ teaspoons dry mustard
    1 tablespoon dried thyme
    ½ teaspoon dried dill
    1 tablespoon bay leaves, ground
    1 tablespoon dried basil
    1 tablespoon dried rosemary
    ½ teaspoon freshly ground pepper

Mix all ingredients and crush thoroughly in a mortar. Sift through a sieve and crush again. Store in a tightly closed container. This keeps for months, and is good on eggs, and in salads and breads.

A jar or small crock of this seasoning and a handwritten favorite recipe using it is a special gift. Pack in a discarded mushroom or strawberry basket, along with a pepper mill.

Star Anise Tea

Preparation time: 5 minutes

    1 teaspoon star anise
    ¼ pound Ceylon tea

Coarsely grind anise in a mortar. Mix thoroughly with tea. Use 1 teaspoon per cup of boiling water and allow to steep 4 to 5 minutes.

Tie a jar of this tea with green or gold ribbon and glue whole star anise pods to ribbon ends.

Flavored Sugars

Cinnamon Sugar

Makes 2 cups
Preparation time: 2 minutes

    2 cups sugar
    2 tablespoons cinnamon

Mix together, making sure lumps of cinnamon are broken up. Store in a large shaker; use for toast, cake, and cookie toppings.

Citrus Sugar

Makes 1 cup
Preparation time: 15 minutes

    Grated peel of 6 lemons or 4 oranges
    1 cup sugar

Peel is best grated in a food processor. If you don't have one, use a large grater, placed on waxed paper. Mix well with sugar. Refrigerate in a covered jar.

One tablespoon lemon sugar equals 1 teaspoon grated peel.

Vanilla Sugar

Makes 4½ cups
Preparation time: 5 minutes

    1 pound confectioners' sugar
    2 or 3 vanilla beans, slit lengthwise

Stir together vanilla and sugar, and store in a covered container. Use for dusting cakes and cookies.

Pack a shaker jar of flavored sugar and a package of pancake mix together in a colorful shiny shopping bag. Tie with contrasting yarn ties.

LITTLE HANDS HELPING

These cookie Bird Ornaments with their bright ribbon wings are easy and fun for children to make. Hang them on the Christmas tree or make a mobile that will spin and catch the light as it turns.

9

Children adore getting into the middle of holiday doings, so take advantage of their urge to help. Give them a job that they can manage—successfully and without too much mess. Even small children can wash and dry salad greens, or mix doughs and batters. Cutting-out and decorating Christmas cookies are made-to-order children's activities. Let your kids invite their friends, tie on dish towels for aprons, and arm the cookie-cutter brigade with dried fruits, nuts, and candies for decoration.

The read-alone projects in this chapter are ideal for children—with perhaps a little help from a parent or older brother or sister. Written in simple language with dozens of illustrations, they will help even beginning readers while away a rainy day. Children love to view their handiwork almost instantly and the greeting cards can go pretty fast after the cookies are cut and baked. Candy and Popcorn Strings, Window Greens, and Thumb Print Figures can be handled by tiny children almost alone, while Thread Balls and Feather Ornaments are challenging enough for older children. Cookie Brittle and Popcorn Cupcakes are easy and *inexpensive* gifts for your child to give to friends.

A Note to Children: People you give a gift to feel happy because you love them enough to think about them. When you make a gift with your hands, the person you give it to will feel even happier because you were thinking of them when you worked to make it, not just when you spent the money. So try to make something. Ask for help if you need it. Don't think it has to be perfect. If you put your love in it the person you give it to will know that.

Feather Ornaments

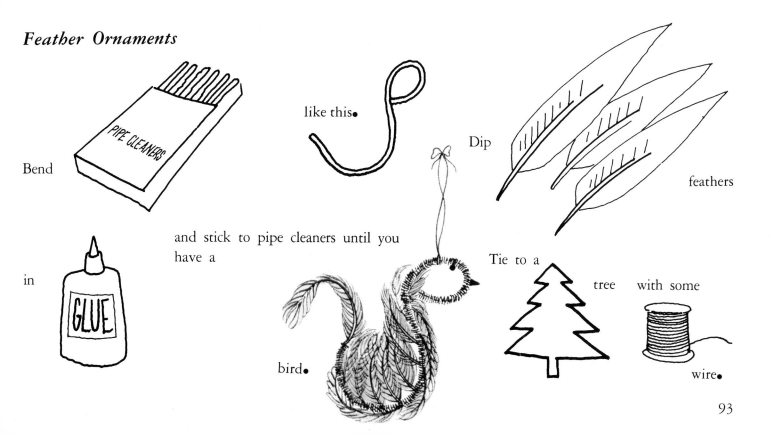

Bend

in

and stick to pipe cleaners until you have a

like this.

bird.

Dip

Tie to a

tree   with some

feathers

wire.

Kid's Cookie Dough

In big bowl mix with wooden spoon until everything is mixed together.

butter ½ cup SHORTENING

Add ½ cup SUGAR eggs and ¼ teaspoon VANILLA.

With grate the outside of a lemon and add this to a big bowl Mix well with

In small cup mix ½ teaspoon BAKING SODA and 3 tablespoons SOUR CREAM In medium bowl

mix 3 cups FLOUR and ½ teaspoon SALT.

LITTLE HANDS HELPING

Mix stuff in

small bowl

into

big bowl

Stir stuff in

medium bowl

into

big bowl

with

spoon

until you can't see any

FLOUR

Put in refrigerator

to chill for 15 minutes.

Use this dough to make Cookie Cards, Sign Language Cookies, and Bird Ornaments.

Bird Ornaments

If you want to see what these will look like when you're done, look at the big photograph at the beginning of this chapter. Make a cardboard pattern, roll out dough, and cut and bake cookies following directions in Sign Language Cookies project. Hint: use an apple corer to make a hole for the bird's eye and a smaller hole in the middle of its back for hanging. When cookies are completely cool, cut a piece of ribbon about 18 inches long. Thread the ribbon back and forth through the slot in the bird's back to make wings. Make a hanging loop by passing some nylon thread through the small hole in the bird's back. Hang on your tree or make a mobile.

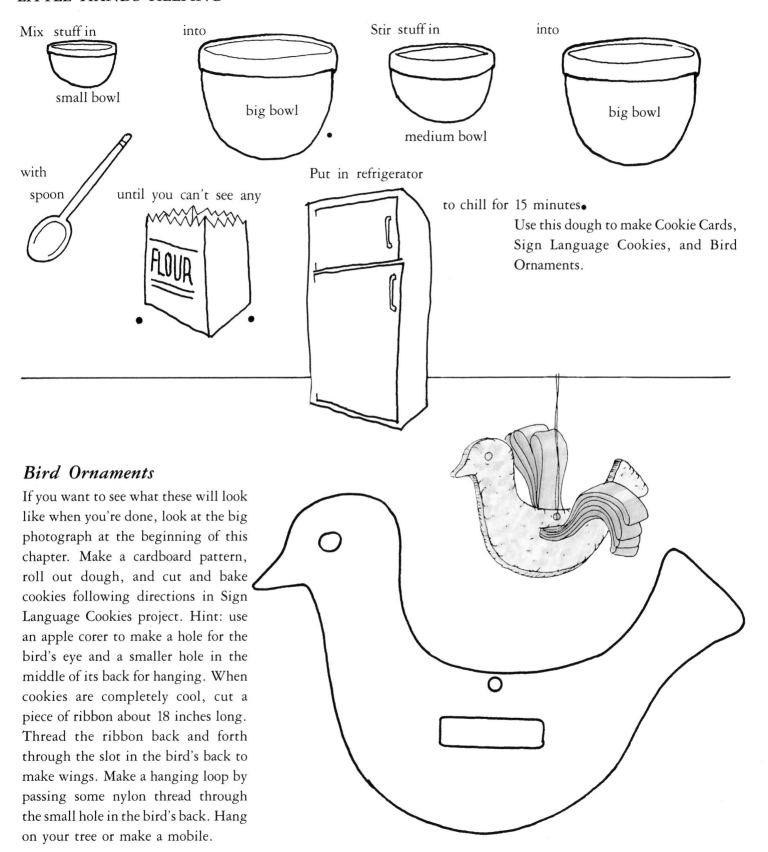

Cookie Brittle

If the grown-ups let you use the oven set it at 375; or ask an older friend to do it for you •

Find a big bowl •

Put in one stick of butter

and one of margarine

and 1 teaspoon VANILLA

and ½ teaspoon ALMOND

and ¾ teaspoon SALT •

Mix well with spoon •

Add ½ cup LIGHT BROWN SUGAR

2 cups FLOUR

and 1 cup CHIPS

chocolate, peanut butter, or butterscotch chips •

Stir together well with spoon •

and press down with a wooden spoon •

Empty into 10" 15" pan

Bake 25 minutes •

Take out of the oven and cool. Break into pieces and store •

0 25

Cookie Brittle

BARNUM'S ANIMALS

TIGER   LION

POLAR BEAR   BISON

For Mark and Nicky

Find a nice can to put it in •

Clay Stamp for Cookies

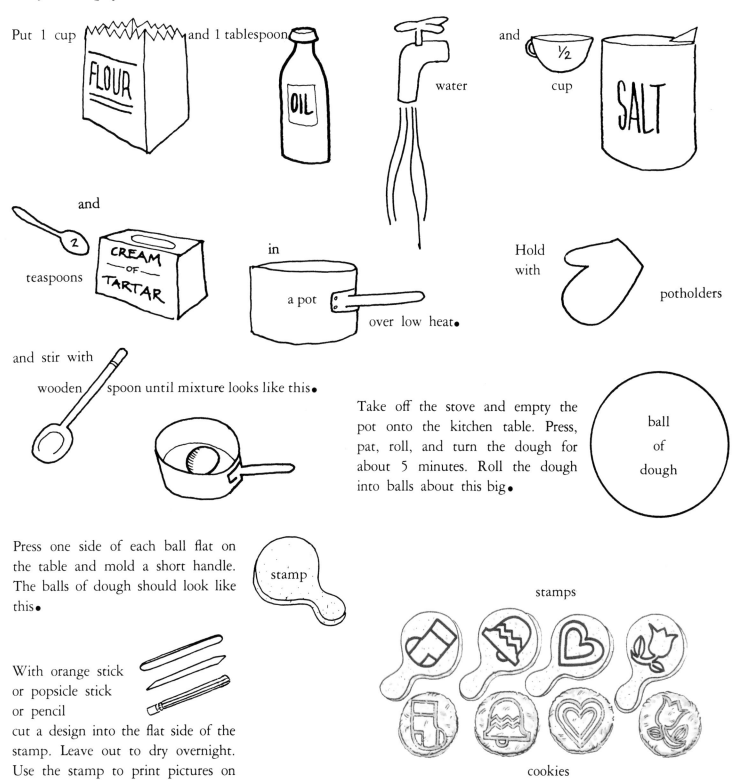

Put 1 cup FLOUR and 1 tablespoon OIL water and ½ cup SALT

and 2 teaspoons CREAM OF TARTAR in a pot over low heat. Hold with potholders

and stir with wooden spoon until mixture looks like this.

Take off the stove and empty the pot onto the kitchen table. Press, pat, roll, and turn the dough for about 5 minutes. Roll the dough into balls about this big.

ball of dough

Press one side of each ball flat on the table and mold a short handle. The balls of dough should look like this.

stamp

stamps

With orange stick or popsicle stick or pencil cut a design into the flat side of the stamp. Leave out to dry overnight. Use the stamp to print pictures on the spice cookies in Chapter 3.

cookies

Sign Language Cookies

Kids who are deaf talk with their hands. One of the languages they use is called American Sign Language. This cookie is the sign for "I love you." Wouldn't it be fun to learn to talk with your hands too? Then Mom and Dad wouldn't know what you were saying, and they couldn't complain that you were making too much noise!

To make a cardboard pattern, put tracing paper over the pattern printed in this book, and trace the outline with a

pencil. Make a sandwich with your finished tracing on top,

then  in the middle

then a piece of cardboard on the bottom.

The carbon paper should be in the middle with the shiny side down. Trace over your tracing, pushing down hard with your

pencil.

When you lift off the tracing

paper and carbon paper, the pattern will be printed right on the cardboard. Cut around the design with a

pair of scissors.

Make the recipe on page 94.

Sprinkle some

on the kitchen counter and roll out the dough with a rolling pin

until it's flat and not bumpy and about as thick as your pinkey.

Put some flour on your pattern and place it on the dough. Cut around it with a knife.

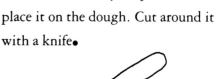

If the grown-ups let you use the oven

set it on 375, or ask an older friend to do it for you. Place cookies on cookie sheet and bake for 8 to 10 minutes until lightly browned. Take pan out of oven and put cookies on racks to cool. When they are completely cool, decorate with icing.

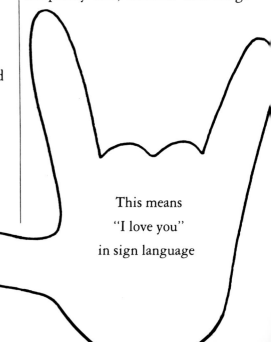

This means
"I love you"
in sign language

LITTLE HANDS HELPING

Thumb Print Figures

You will need:
Ink pad

and

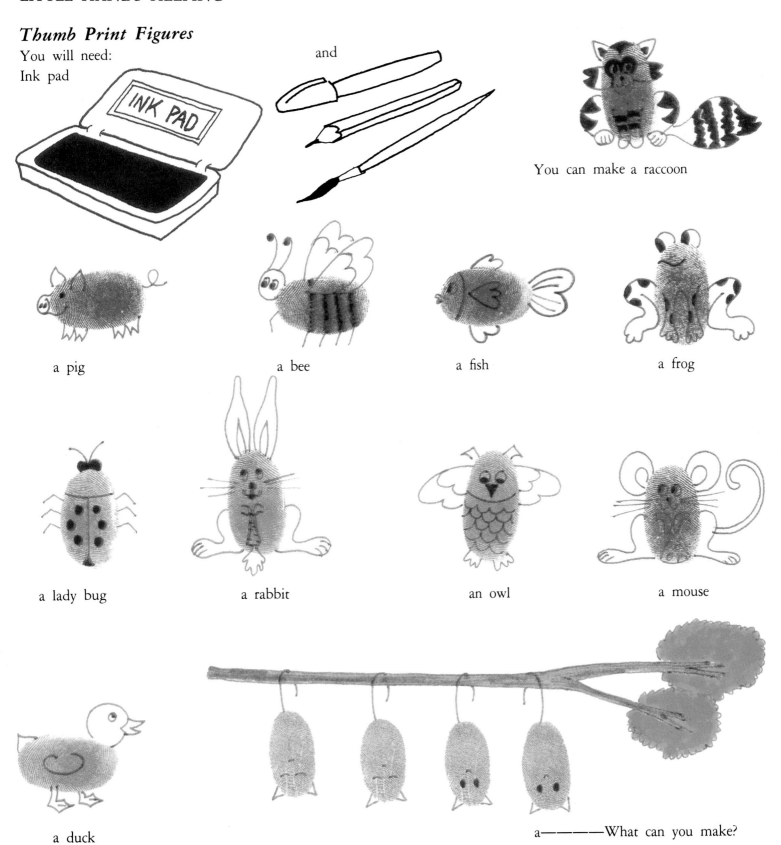

You can make a raccoon

a pig

a bee

a fish

a frog

a lady bug

a rabbit

an owl

a mouse

a duck

a————What can you make?

Raisin Stockings

Draw and cut out a  sock shape from cardboard. Use 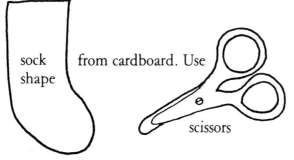 to cut around your picture and a point  to make a hole in the cardboard for hanging.

scissors

Put string through the hole and tie a  bow like your shoelaces so you can hang this decoration on the tree. Ask an older person to make some Royal Icing for you. Tell them the directions are in chapter 3. Or maybe there is some frosting in the refrigerator left over from making a  cake.

Spread frosting on stocking with 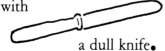 a dull knife. Press  into icing and allow to dry.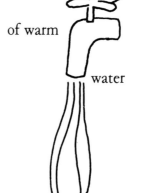

Hang it where the cat can't reach it.

Window Greens

Place ¼ lb. Beeswax 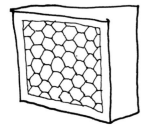 in  a pot of warm  water until the wax is soft enough to pinch. Break off pieces and roll into balls the size of marbles. Stick the balls on the wooden part of a window frame and

press in pretty twigs and leaves and flowers .

LITTLE HANDS HELPING

Popcorn, Cones, Cupcakes, and Balls

Put  1 cup light corn syrup and ½ cup SUGAR and 1 packet unflavored gelatin

in a pot.

Hold the pot handle with a pot holder.

Keep the heat low and stir all the time until it bubbles. Be patient. It is VERY HOT!! If it spits it will hurt.

Stir in ⅛ stick butter and take off stove.

Stir in ½ teaspoon of STRAW BERRY or MINT or LEMON flavors and 3 drops of food color. RED GREEN YELLOW

Pour popcorn into big bowl and pour the stuff in the pot on the popcorn. Stir with a wooden spoon.

Do not touch popcorn until it feels only a little bit warm when you hold your hand over it. Put some butter on your hands and squish popcorn into balls, or pack it into cones or cupcake liners.

Your friends will love them.

101

Thread Balls

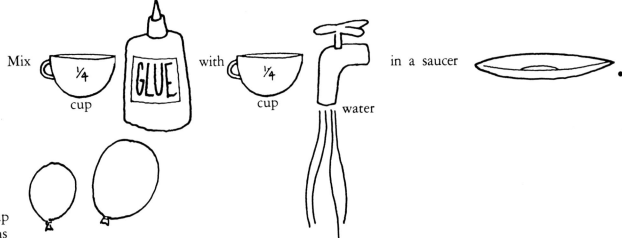

Mix ¼ cup GLUE with ¼ cup water in a saucer.

Blow up balloons and knot the ends. You might need to get some help with this. Soak the thread in the glue, and start wrapping it around the balloon like this

and keep wrapping the sticky thread around and around the balloon.

When you have covered up the whole balloon so you can hardly see the balloon through the thread, cut the thread with scissors

and stick the end of the thread to the balloon. Let it dry overnight. The next day pop the balloon with a needle.

The fun part!

Use tweezers to pull out the piece of popped balloon carefully so you don't tear the thread.

LITTLE HANDS HELPING

Cookie Cards

Make **KID'S COOKIE DOUGH** on page 94.

Sprinkle some **FLOUR** on the kitchen counter and roll out dough with a rolling pin until it's flat and not bumpy and about as thick as your little finger.

Cut dough into squares or rectangles or hearts or monsters with a dull knife.

If the grown-ups let you use the oven set it at 375, or ask an older friend to do it for you. Place the cookies on a cookie sheet and bake them for 8 to 10 minutes until they are a light brown color

Take the pan out of the oven with a potholder.

Slide the cookies onto racks to cool. When they are completely cool, use **ICING** to write out messages.

SUPER MOM WORKS HERE!

NO EL

Candy and Popcorn Strings

1. Cut a piece of thread long enough to stretch from hand to hand when you open your arms out wide.

2. Thread a needle.

3. Make the ends of the thread even and tie a knot. Poke the needle through the middle of a gumdrop or popcorn and push the candy carefully onto the thread and down to the knot.

4. Tie three good knots at the end of the thread so the candies can't fall off.

5. Hang it on your tree.

PARTIES GREAT AND SMALL

This traditional turkey dinner is served with all the trimmings—six vegetable side dishes, Gooseberry and Pumpkin Chiffon pies (Chapter 3), and an unusual, uncooked cranberry relish (Chapter 6). If your guests aren't too full, pass dishes of Spiced Nuts and Rainbow Crystals (Chapter 1) after dinner.

10

Inviting friends in for a carol sing around the piano, to exchange Hanukkah gifts, or just because you want to see them for a special time is one of the nicest gifts you can give.

The menus in this chapter are the essence of good entertaining: varied enough to delight the eye as well as the palate and so well-organized that you'll actually be able to spend time with your guests!

Turkey dinner here is made special with a richly flavored stuffing and an assortment of vegetables that make this the proverbial groaning board. Yet any competent cook can produce this feast with only minor help from friends or family. The sweet potatoes, carrots, and turnip soufflé can all be assembled the night before and baked in the oven after the turkey has been taken out to cool. The no-bake pumpkin pie is unusual and a god-send to the harried host or hostess. The gooseberry pie can be assembled and frozen long before the big day and baked during dinner to serve hot.

The ham dinner is distinguished by its trimmings—savory corn pudding, buttery beans, and homemade relishes. Make the ham glaze the night before. Reheat and spoon it over the ham at the last minute. Both desserts are good keepers and the pea soup is even better if allowed to mellow for a day or so. Wash and dry the salad greens and cover with a damp paper towel until you're ready to toss with the vinaigrette just before serving.

The spring luncheon is a snap. Both the mousse and the jellied salad can be prepared ahead and refrigerated for up to 24 hours. Use a frozen, pre-baked pie shell to cut your preparation time in half for the quiche. Bake the cake in the morning so it will have a chance to cool thoroughly, and assemble while the quiche is baking.

The Party for Neighbors is ideal for impromptu entertaining. The cake will keep for months in your refrigerator if wrapped air-tight in foil. Make the decorative iced wine containers the night before (or have one on hand in your freezer). The tea punch can be served hot and whipped up at the last minute or prepare it earlier in the day and chill for hot-weather entertaining. Cookie trays can be arranged, covered tightly with plastic wrap, and kept in a spare bedroom to whisk out at party time.

The Hanukkah meal is a simple one but a favorite with young and old. Who could refuse crispy potato pancakes served with applesauce and a dollop of fresh sour cream? Keep the finished pancakes warm in a low oven while you're making more and you'll be able to sit down and enjoy them too.

Once you've decided on your menu, organize the dinnerware and serving pieces. In case you need a platter, gravy boat, or cake knife, borrow it or give it to yourself as a holiday gift. Press table linens and try some fancy napkin folds just for fun (see the end of this chapter). Some table settings and buffet layout suggestions on the following pages explain the mystery of what to do with Great-aunt Sophie's finger bowls.

Not all of the recipes mentioned above appear in this chapter. Consult the index for page numbers for the others. Serving suggestions are given in italics at the end of each recipe. Note that the suggested garnishes are not included in the lists of ingredients.

Roast Turkey with Cornbread Sausage Dressing and Giblet Gravy

Serves 15 to 20
Preparation time: 2 hours
Roasting time: 14 to 17 pounds—3 to 3¼ hours
18 to 21 pounds—4½ to 5¼ hours

A 14- to 21-pound turkey
1 medium onion, sliced
3 stalks celery, sliced
Cornbread Sausage Dressing (recipe follows)
End crust of bread
2 tablespoons vegetable shortening
Giblet Gravy (recipe follows)

Preheat oven to 325°F. Remove giblets from turkey and reserve for gravy. Place onion and celery in shallow roasting pan. Stuff turkey with dressing, cover cavity with end crust of bread, and tie turkey legs together with string. Rub skin with shortening. Place bird in pan and roast until browned (1½ to 2 hours). Cover with foil and baste occasionally until done. Remove turkey to hot platter and allow to stand 20 minutes before carving. Serve with giblet gravy.

Cornbread Sausage Dressing

4 cups dried cornbread cubes
½ pound sweet pork sausage
2 medium onions, chopped
2 stalks celery, chopped
½ teaspoon poultry seasoning
½ teaspoon rubbed sage
⅓ cup fresh chopped parsley
1 egg, slightly beaten

Christmas Dinner

Cranberry Champagne Sparkler

Roast Turkey
with
Cornbread Sausage Stuffing

Giblet Gravy

Pecan Brussel Sprouts

Creamed Dill Onions

Creamed White Potatoes

Candied Sweet Potatoes

Turnip Soufflé

Ginger Baked Carrots

Cranberry Nut Relish

Gooseberry Pie

Pumpkin Chiffon Pie

Spiced Nuts   Rainbow Crystals

½ cup water
Salt
Pepper

Remove sausage from casing and cook until brown and crumbly. Drain off fat. Place bread cubes in large bowl, add sausage, onions, and celery and mix well. Add poultry seasoning, sage, and parsley. Combine egg and water and pour over dressing. Add salt and pepper to taste. Mix well.

Giblet Gravy

1 turkey gizzard
1 turkey heart
1 medium onion, chopped
2¼ cups plus 2 tablespoons water
½ teaspoon salt
1 turkey liver
Drippings from turkey
3 tablespoons flour

Place turkey gizzard and heart in saucepan. Add onion, 1½ cups water, and salt. Simmer 35 minutes. Add liver, simmer an additional 15 minutes. Remove giblets, chop finely and return to liquid. Discard fat and vegetables from turkey roasting pan and add ¾ cup of water to pan. Stir to loosen brown bits and add to gravy. Make a paste with flour and 2 tablespoons water. Over low heat stir flour paste gradually into gravy with a whisk. Heat to a simmer, continuing to stir as gravy thickens; adjust seasoning.

Serve on a traditional white turkey platter on a bed of kale. Scatter fresh cranberries or red and purple grapes.

Pecan Brussels Sprouts

Serves 8
Preparation time: 20 minutes

2 cups fresh brussels sprouts or 3 packages (10 ounces) frozen
Water
¼ teaspoon salt
¼ cup butter
½ cup coarsely chopped pecans

Wash and trim brussels sprouts. Cook in ½ inch boiling salted water in covered saucepan until barely tender, 8 to 10 minutes. Drain and return to pan. Heat butter in skillet, add pecans, and stir over low heat until nuts are a warm brown, about 10 minutes. Pour over sprouts, toss well, and turn into a hot bowl.

A sunny yellow or warm pumpkin-colored bowl complements the rich green and brown of this dish.

Creamed Dill Onions

Serves 8 to 10
Preparation time: 30 minutes

   3 pounds small white onions, peeled
     Water
  ½ teaspoon salt
   3 tablespoons butter
   2 tablespoons flour
   1 cup milk
     White pepper
     Fresh dill

Place onions in saucepan with water to cover. Add salt and simmer just until tender. Drain.

In small saucepan melt butter and add flour, stirring with a whisk. Add milk, pepper to taste, and 1 tablespoon minced dill. Cook and stir until thick. Pour over onions and garnish with a fresh dill sprig. Serve at once.

These creamy onions need a brightly colored dish to set them off. Try a grape-leaf green vegetable dish.

Creamed White Potatoes

Serves 10
Preparation time: 30 minutes

   3 pounds potatoes, peeled and quartered
     Water
  ½ teaspoon salt
  ¾ cup milk, warmed
  ¼ cup butter
     Salt
     Pepper
     Parsley for garnish

Place potatoes in saucepan with water to cover and salt. Cook until tender, drain. Mash potatoes with a potato masher, fork, or electric mixer while adding milk and butter. Season with salt and pepper to taste. Garnish with parsley.

Show this family favorite in a brightly colored bowl. For a lovely brown crust, dot with butter and sprinkle with Parmesan or bread crumbs and place under broiler for a few minutes before serving.

Candied Sweet Potatoes

Serves 10
Preparation time: 30 minutes

   3 pounds sweet potatoes
     Water
  ¾ cup dark molasses
  ½ cup dark brown sugar, firmly packed
  ¼ cup butter
     Salt
     Pepper

Cover potatoes with water and simmer until barely tender. Drain and peel. Cut in halves. Preheat oven to 325°F. Place sweet potatoes in greased, shallow baking dish. Drizzle molasses over them and sprinkle with brown sugar. Dot with butter and add salt and pepper to taste. Bake 30 minutes, basting now and then with juices. Serve hot.

Bake and serve in an earthenware casserole or an oven-proof glass dish that comes with its own serving basket.

Turnip Soufflé

Serves 8
Preparation time: 30 minutes
Baking time: 35 to 40 minutes

   1 medium turnip (1½ pounds), peeled and quartered
     Water
  ¾ teaspoon salt
  ¼ cup plus 1 tablespoon butter, softened
  ½ cup uncooked farina
   1 egg, slightly beaten
   1 tablespoon sugar
     Salt
     Pepper
     Parsley for garnish

Place turnip in 2-quart saucepan with water to cover and salt. Cook until tender. Drain and mash with fork or potato masher. Preheat oven to 325°F. Grease a 2-quart soufflé dish with 1 tablespoon butter; add mashed turnip, butter, farina, egg, and sugar. Mix well and season with

salt and pepper to taste. Bake 35 to 40 minutes.

Serve this in a classic white soufflé dish. Garnish with parsley.

Ginger Baked Carrots

Serves 8 to 10
Preparation time: 30 minutes
Baking time: 30 minutes

   2 pounds carrots, scraped and sliced
  ½ cup minced onion
  ⅓ cup water
  ¼ teaspoon ginger
   1 teaspoon salt
  ½ teaspoon sugar
  ¼ cup butter

Preheat oven to 375°F. Place carrots in greased casserole and add onion and water. Sprinkle with ginger, salt, and sugar, and dot with butter. Bake 30 minutes.

A hollowed-out pumpkin or large squash makes an attractive natural container for these golden carrots.

Country Ham Dinner

Rose Wine   Cranberry Shrub

Currant Glazed Ham

Home-style Pea Soup

Southern Cornbread

Corn Pudding

Buttered Green Beans

Tossed Green Salad
with
Vinaigrette Dressing

Pickled Watermelon Rind

Mustards

Apple Cider Cake   Pecan Pie

Assorted Cookies

Candied Nuts

Currant Glazed Ham

Serves 12
Preparation time: 45 minutes
Baking time: 3¼ hours

A 10- to 12-pound, fully-cooked, smoked ham
¼ cup water
Thinly sliced peels of 6 oranges
2 cups water
⅓ cup currant jelly
¾ cup orange marmalade
4 tablespoons red wine

Preheat oven to 325°F. Remove skin and trim fat from ham. Place in shallow roasting pan and add water. Bake about 16 minutes per pound (3¼ hours for a 12-pound ham) or until meat thermometer registers 140°F. If ham browns too quickly, place a tent of foil over it. Do not seal. When done remove from oven and allow to rest while making glaze.

To make glaze, combine orange peels and water in saucepan and boil for 10 minutes. Drain and repeat. Combine jelly, marmalade, and orange peels in saucepan and simmer for 10 minutes. Remove from heat and stir in wine. Spread on ham.

Arrange on a bed of dark kale strewn with raw cranberries and orange slice twists.

Home-style Pea Soup

Serves 10 to 12
Preparation time: 10 minutes
Cooking time: 2 hours

1 pound split peas
2 quarts water
Bone from ½ a smoked ham
1 medium onion, chopped coarsely
1 carrot, scraped and thinly sliced
Freshly ground pepper to taste
2 tablespoons pickling spice, wrapped in a square of cheesecloth and tied securely

Place all ingredients in 3-quart pot. Bring just to boiling and simmer gently for 2 hours, stirring occasionally. Add more water if necessary. Remove ham bone and pickling spices before serving.

Serve this in an old-fashioned soup tureen. Sprinkle with croutons, chopped parsley, and crumbled bacon.

Corn Pudding

Serves 6
Preparation time: 30 minutes
Baking time: 45 to 50 minutes

2¾ cups milk
2 cups whole kernel corn (fresh or frozen)
2 tablespoons butter
4 eggs, slightly beaten
2 tablespoons finely chopped onion
1 teaspoon sugar
1 teaspoon salt
¼ teaspoon freshly ground pepper

Preheat oven to 300°F. Scald milk in a large saucepan, add corn and cook 10 minutes. Remove from heat and allow to cool. Blend eggs with cooled corn mixture, add remaining ingredients, and pour into buttered casserole. Set casserole in pan of boiling water on oven rack and bake 45 to 50 minutes or until knife inserted in center comes out clean. Serve hot.

Bake and serve in a cast iron skillet or souffle dish.

This hearty ham dinner is just the thing for cold-weather appetites. The ham, glazed with currant jelly and shredded orange peels, is shown here with a pressed glass pickle dish of Pickled Watermelon Rind (Chapter 6). The menu also includes Southern Cornbread (Chapter 2), Cranberry Shrub (Chapter 11) and steamed green beans. The recipes for two quite different mustards, and Vinaigrette Dressing, are in Chapter 7. You'll find the dessert recipes in Chapter 3 and the recipe for Candied Nuts in Chapter 1.

This amusing Majolica water jug was given away as a premium by a grocery company in the late 1800s. Its fishy shape is appropriate to a meal which includes Tuna Mousse and zesty salad made in a fish mold. You'll find the bread recipe in Chapter 2 and the lavish dessert in Chapter 4. Sparkling Yogurt Drink is in Chapter 11.

Tuna Mousse

Serves 8 to 10
Preparation time: 45 minutes
Chilling time: 3½ hours

1½ packages unflavored gelatin

½ cup cold water
Juice of 1 lemon
1 cup mayonnaise
1 can (7 ounces) flaked tuna
2 cups peeled and chopped cucumber
½ cup thinly sliced celery
¼ cup sliced stuffed olives
2 teaspoons onion juice (scrape a cut onion with a spoon)
1½ teaspoons prepared horseradish
1 teaspoon salt
¼ teaspoon paprika
1 cup heavy cream, whipped
Sliced stuffed olives for garnish
4 or 5 limes for garnish

Combine gelatin, water, and lemon juice in small saucepan. Heat and stir until gelatin is completely dissolved. In large bowl combine mayonnaise, tuna, vegetables, and seasonings. Mix carefully and stir in gelatin mixture. Gently fold in whipped cream. Oil a 4 x 8-inch metal loaf pan. Decorate bottom with slices of

stuffed olives and spoon mixture into pan. Chill until firm, about 3½ hours. To remove, dip pan in warm water and invert onto serving dish.

Line serving dish with lettuce and watercress. Garnish with limes cut in sawtooth-edged halves. Dip half the limes in chopped parsley and half in paprika. Serve one lime half to each person.

Crab Quiche

Serves 10
Preparation time: 30 to 45 minutes
Baking time: 35 to 50 minutes

2 baked 10-inch pie shells or Cheese Crust (recipe follows)
1 pound (3 cups) cooked crabmeat
¼ cup dry vermouth
3 or 4 scallions (green onions), chopped
2 tablespoons butter

2 cups heavy cream, lightly whipped
4 eggs, slightly beaten

Prepare, bake, and cool Cheese Crusts (if not using baked pie shells). Preheat oven to 450°F. Soak crabmeat in vermouth while preparing rest of ingredients. Sauté scallions in butter and add to crabmeat mixture. Stir in cream and eggs and pour into pie shells or Cheese Crusts. Bake 15 minutes, reduce heat to 350°F, and bake an additional 20 minutes.

Note: you may use lobster or chopped ham instead of crabmeat.

Cheese Crust

2 cups flour
1 cup butter
2 cups shredded extra-sharp cheddar

Preheat oven to 400°F. Combine flour, butter, and cheese. Mix thoroughly with a pastry blender. Press into quiche pans and bake 15 minutes.

This lovely pale pink quiche needs no garnish. Serve in a porcelain quiche pan or on individual Limoges plates.

Zesty Salad

Preparation time: 20 minutes
Chilling time: 3½ hours

1 package (6 ounces) raspberry-flavored gelatin
⅔ cup boiling water
3½ cups stewed tomatoes, chopped coarsely
1 medium onion, chopped
½ cup chopped celery
1 medium green pepper, chopped
4 to 6 drops hot pepper sauce

Dissolve gelatin in hot water and stir in tomatoes and juice. Add remaining ingredients and stir well. Pour into oiled 6-cup mold and chill until set, about 3½ hours. To serve, dip mold in warm water and invert onto serving dish.

Arrange Belgian endives on serving dish and garnish with watercress bunches twisted into bouquets. Serve creamed horseradish in individual relish dishes.

Spring Luncheon

White Wine

Sparkling Yogurt Drink

Tuna Mousse

Crab Quiche

Zesty Salad

Creamed Horseradish

Favorite Buttermilk Bread

Great-Grandmother's
Strawberry Cake

Hanukkah Feast

❧ ❧

Wine   *Juice*

Potato Latkes

Applesauce

Sour Cream

Fresh Fruits

Wine Cookies

Potato Latkes

Serves 6 to 8 (24 to 30 large pancakes)
Preparation time: 45 minutes

- 4 large Idaho potatoes (about 2¼ pounds), washed and chopped
- ⅔ cup coarsely chopped onions
- 1 teaspoon lemon juice
- 2 eggs, lightly beaten
- ¼ cup matzoh meal
- ½ teaspoon salt
- ¼ cup minced chives (optional)
  Vegetable oil for frying

Use a food processor or grate potatoes by hand. Add lemon juice and stir. Press potatoes in sieve to remove excess liquid. Transfer potatoes to large bowl and add eggs, matzoh meal, and salt. Stir. Heat about ½ inch of oil in an iron skillet. Form patties or pancakes using a heaping tablespoon of mixture for each. Fry, turning once, until golden crisp. Drain on absorbent paper. Keep warm in 250°F oven until ready to serve.

Spoon a pool of applesauce in the center of each plate and arrange pancakes around it. Top each pancake with a dollop of sour cream and garnish with bunches of watercress twisted into flower shapes.

This Hanukkah feast is a simple one of potato pancakes with sour cream and applesauce. Wine Cookies (Chapter 4) and fruit are a simple desert.

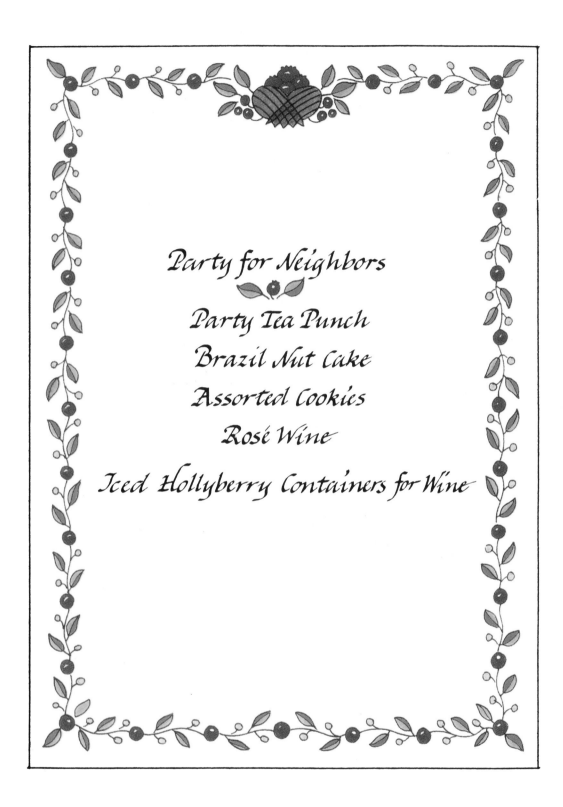

Party for Neighbors

Party Tea Punch

Brazil Nut Cake

Assorted Cookies

Rosé Wine

Iced Hollyberry Containers for Wine

The rosé wine complements the candied cherries in the Brazil Nut Cake, and the Iced Hollyberry Containers are an attractive way to keep it chilled (see Chapter 11 for directions). The Party Tea Punch (Chapter 11) can be served hot or cold and is a pleasant alternative to wine. Pass plates of assorted cookies and candies, such as Rainbow Crystals (Chapter 1) shown here in a pressed glass dish.

NAPKIN FOLDS

Simple Luncheon Fold

This fold is quite close to the flower folds of origami. A plain or bordered napkin shows off it's delicate lines, and a flower-painted napkin ring picks up the floral theme. The perfect fold for an elegant spring luncheon with friends.

1. Fold napkin in half diagonally to make a triangle pointing up. Bring right point to the center and repeat with left point.

2. Fold right edge in.

3. Repeat with left edge.

4. Fold napkin in half with folds facing out. Slip into napkin ring and fluff top points.

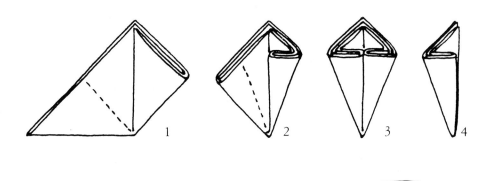

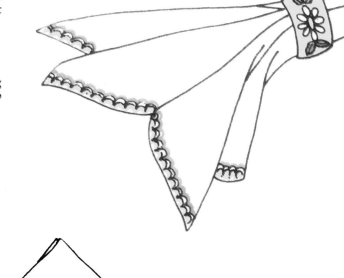

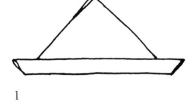

Sommelier Fold

A wine steward knows that condensation from a cold wine bottle can leave rings on a wood table. This fold will protect your table and add a touch of elegance as well. Use a large square napkin of absorbent cotton or linen.

1. Fold napkin in half to make a triangle pointing up and fold up bottom 1 to 1½ inches.

2. Fold up another 1½ inches.

3. Fold down top layer of napkin over bottom fold and place bottle as shown.

4. Lift front and back of napkin and tie in back of bottle, being careful to catch back triangle in tie.

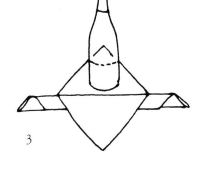

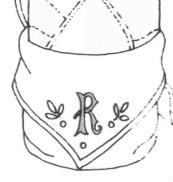

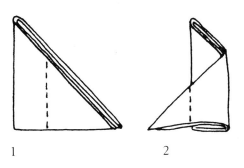

1   2

Buffet Fold

This is a quick and easy fold to use when entertaining casually but on a large scale. It would be perfect for the Party for Neighbors, or a family reunion barbecue. Use striped napkins for a dramatic look.

1. Fold napkin in half to make a triangle pointing up. Fold in half again to make a right triangle.

2. Fold right side to the left and back again to the right to make a zig-zag.

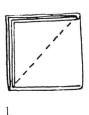
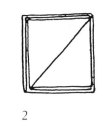

1   2   3

Buffet Pouch

This comes in handy when serving a buffet to lots of people. Napkins can be folded a day or two before and tableware inserted. The bundles can then be stacked until needed. Use any large square napkins, either cloth or paper.

1. Fold napkin in quarters and place so open edges are at upper left corner.

2. Fold upper left corner down as shown.

3. Fold under corners as shown.

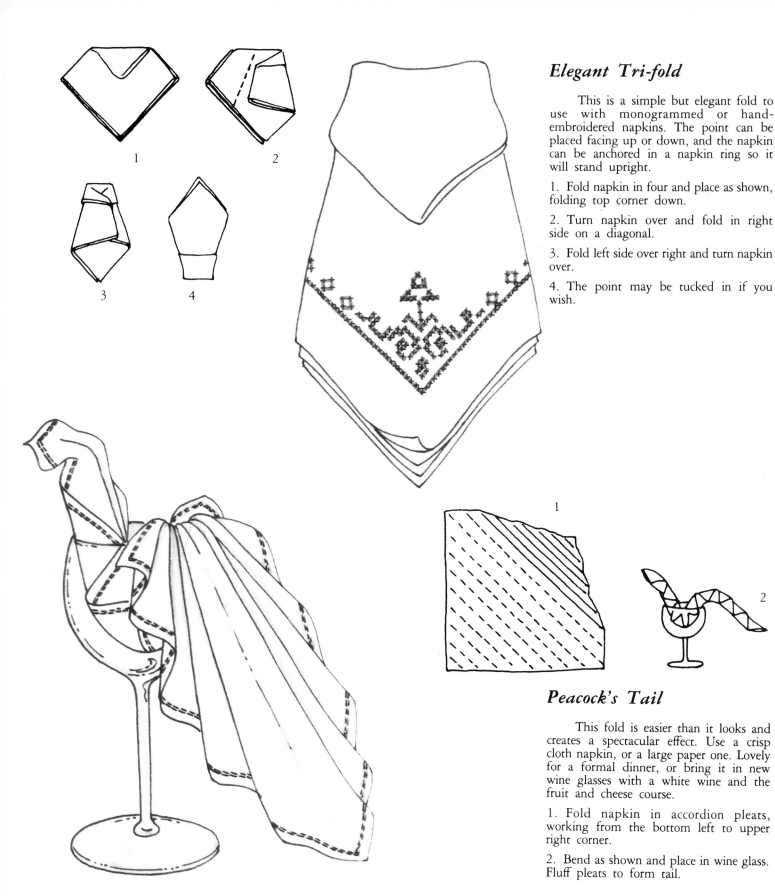

Elegant Tri-fold

This is a simple but elegant fold to use with monogrammed or hand-embroidered napkins. The point can be placed facing up or down, and the napkin can be anchored in a napkin ring so it will stand upright.

1. Fold napkin in four and place as shown, folding top corner down.

2. Turn napkin over and fold in right side on a diagonal.

3. Fold left side over right and turn napkin over.

4. The point may be tucked in if you wish.

Peacock's Tail

This fold is easier than it looks and creates a spectacular effect. Use a crisp cloth napkin, or a large paper one. Lovely for a formal dinner, or bring it in new wine glasses with a white wine and the fruit and cheese course.

1. Fold napkin in accordion pleats, working from the bottom left to upper right corner.

2. Bend as shown and place in wine glass. Fluff pleats to form tail.

Bishop's Mitre

This is a very common restaurant fold that can be accomplished easily at home. It is equally lovely in plain linen or a colorful print. Use a fairly stiff napkin for best results.

1. Fold napkin in half to make a rectangle. Fold should be at bottom. Fold right corner down and left corner up.

2. Turn napkin over and fold bottom edge to top edge.

3. Napkin should look like this.

4. Holding napkin firmly at top center, turn napkin over. Two triangles should now show at top edge. Fold right side under, tucking in point.

6. Turn napkin over and fold in right side, tucking in point. Stand up napkin and place in center of plate. Tuck in a placecard if you wish.

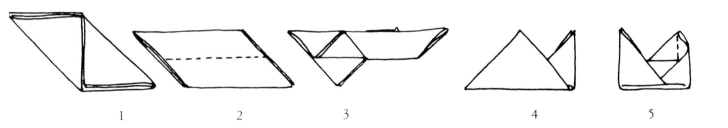

| 1 | 2 | 3 | 4 | 5 |

TABLE LAYOUTS

Fig. A

A perfectly appointed table is a joy to behold, eliciting oohs! and aahs! from adults much as the first sight of the Christmas tree does from children. Sparkling with crystal, and laden with a gay assortment of platters, serving dishes, and glowing glass bowls of colorful relishes, the buffet sets the mood for your dinner—sumptuous but relaxed.

It is one of the best ways to serve a large group of people, and may be your only choice, unless you have a really large dining room and table. Guests enjoy a buffet because they can serve themselves only what and as much as they want. The host and hostess enjoy it because they are free to spend more time with their guests.

There are no rules concerning buffets and only a few suggestions. If possible, allow guests access to both sides of the table to cut down on traffic problems. Arrange foods logically in the order in which they would be served at a sit-down meal (see **Figs. A** and **B** for possible arrangements). Meat should be carved in advance so guests need only help themselves with a fork. Side dishes should be served in small bowls that can be replaced or refilled as needed with hot food kept warm in a low oven. Napkins folded so that they will hold the flatware (see **Fig. A**) are a help to guests burdened with filled plates. Centerpieces may consist of candles, flowers (fresh or dried), fruits, vegetables, or nuts. A centerpiece adds a lot to the look of a buffet, so be inventive. Remember that it can be as high as you wish, as,

unlike a sit-down meal, guests will be looking down on it. Finally, remember that your guests came, most of all, to see you, and strive for a "lillies of the field" look, with no sign of your toiling and spinning.

A formal dinner should be reserved for special occasions, not least because it requires one or more family members to play "server" unless you can afford to hire someone for the evening. On the other hand, you needn't wait for visiting royalty. Graduation from high school or college, a big promotion, or a wedding anniversary (ask the kids to serve) is sufficient reason to celebrate.

"Serve from the left, and clear from the right" are all most of us know about formal entertaining, and, in contrast to buffet dining, the rules are complex and many. An etiquette book will give you all the details, but some general guidelines follow.

The host and hostess should sit one on either end of the table. The honored guest, if female, should be seated to the immediate right of the host, if male, to the immediate right of the hostess. The remaining guests should be seated alternately, male and female.

A formal menu consists of a first course of soup, melon, or seafood cocktail. This is followed by fish, meat with accompanying vegetables, salad, dessert, and coffee. For a slightly less formal dinner, one or more of these courses may be dropped, as the fish course often is.

Centerpieces should be low so that guests

can talk to each other comfortably across the table. And linens, china, glasses, and flatware should obviously be of the best. Borrow from friends or rent if you don't have sufficient tableware of your own.

Flatware required will depend on the menu. No more than three pieces should be placed on each side of the plate. If more are needed, they can be brought in later with the appropriate course. Flatware should be placed in the order in which it will be used, working from the outside in. Knives and spoons should be on the right, and knife edges should face the plate. Forks should be on the left, with the exception of the cocktail fork, which should be placed at the extreme right. A soup spoon should be used for soup, and a teaspoon or dessert spoon if melon is served. The fish course requires a special fish knife and fork. The fish knife has a dull, rounded blade and is somewhat smaller than the dinner knife. The fish fork looks much like a salad fork (which can be substituted for it if need be) but the central tines are slightly longer. Both the knife and fork are often notched.

Very fancy napkin folds are considered out of place at a formal dinner party, but a simple fold may be used. The napkin should be placed on the plate if the first course is to be soup, and on the extreme left if melon or seafood cocktails will be served, as these will be on the plate when diners are seated.

China and glassware used will depend again on the menu. At least two glasses should be provided—one each for water

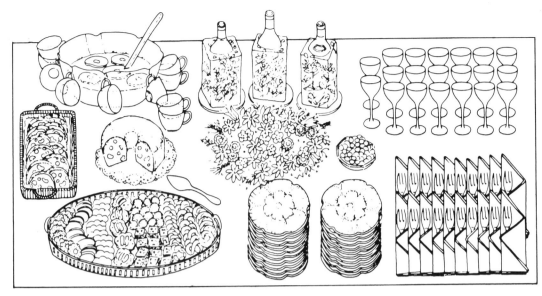

Fig. B

and wine. Add a third glass if two wines are served (see **Fig. C**). An empty or filled plate should be present in front of each guest throughout the meal, except immediately before the dessert course, when the table should be completely cleared and crumbed. A service plate is on the table at the start of the meal. When the melon or seafood cocktail is served before the guests come to the table, place it in its own dish or glass, on its own plate, and place both on top of the service plate. Soup is served in individual bowls on small plates, usually after the guests are seated. (**Fig. C** shows the table setting for a formal meal—the Country Ham Dinner—which includes soup but not a fish course.)

After guests have finished the first course, the service plate and soup plates are removed and replaced with succeeding courses each requiring its own plate and flatware. Bread-and-butter plates are not used, and sets of salt, pepper, and condiment dishes are placed between every two to three diners. If finger bowls are required, they are only partially filled with water. Float a slice of lemon or lime, a sprig of a scented herb, or a flower in each one. Unless they are needed earlier for a finger food, bring them to the table just prior to the coffee. Coffee is served black in demitasse cups, with sugar, and sometimes milk, offered to each guest as his or her coffee is poured.

Each course should be served either on filled plates, or presented by the server on platters from which guests can help themselves. Relishes, crackers, and breads should be passed by the server throughout the meal, and he or she should keep wine and water glasses filled as well. As you can see, the server has a lot to do. If guests are not to be kept waiting an unacceptable amount of time, one server shold not be responsible for more than six to eight guests.

If it seems like a lot of work, it is! But a formal dinner party can turn an already special occasion into a glittering memory.

Fig. C

NOGS AND TODDIES

This pewter punch bowl set dates from the 1820s and makes a lovely container for Party Tea Punch. If you don't own an heirloom punch bowl, the introduction to this chapter offers some ideas for improvising one.

122

11

You'll find the traditional drinks of the holidays here and with them a batch of new ideas for holiday drinking, including non-alcoholic drinks for children and the increasing number of adults who prefer to abstain. Rosy punches made with cranberry juice look festive, and children will love hot chocolate served with peppermint stick stirrers. A slow cooker will keep mulled cider or wine hot and flavorful for unexpected guests, and the drink will perfume the house with its spicy holiday fragrance. Ice containers with greens and berries frozen right in are an elegant way to keep wines cold.

Punches demand a punchbowl, and small glass cups with handles are preferred, especially for hot punches. A large glass salad bowl or ceramic mixing bowl with ceramic cups or juice glasses are adequate substitutes if you're short on heirloom glassware and don't care to rent some. Camouflage the bowls with tissue or foil and surround them with evergreens or flowers. If you must use a kitchen ladle, tie a bow to the handle and tuck in a tiny Christmas rose.

When hot beverages must be served in straight glasses, here's how to keep your fingers from being burned.

Fold a napkin into a strip an inch or two wide.

Wrap it around the hot glass.

Pinch ends together with your fingers so napkin wraps tightly around glass.

Ice floats or rings will give punch a festive look and are easy to make. Fill a ring mold half full with water (stir water several times to remove air bubbles) and freeze until the water is very cold. Add leaves, non-toxic evergreen (boxwood, holly berries, and mistletoe are poisonous), pour on more cold water, and freeze until firm. Fresh citrus slices or quarters, and candied or maraschino cherries, make festive-looking ice decorations too, but don't add too many garnishes, or you'll have to pass out forks with the punch cups.

Christmas Bowle

Serves 12 to 16
Preparation time: 15 minutes
Chilling time: overnight

  4 cups strawberries, hulled
  1 cup sugar
  1 cup cognac
  3 bottles of May or Rhine wine, chilled

Combine strawberries, sugar, and cognac. Cover tightly and allow to stand overnight in refrigerator. Before serving stir in chilled wine. Add a fresh strawberry to each glass.

Serve in a cut-glass or old pitcher on a tray decorated with lemon leaves. Or decant into a clear glass bottle and wreathe the neck with a miniature circlet of evergreens.

Mulled Wine

Serves 18
Preparation time: 10 minutes

  6 cups red table wine
  1 tablespoon sugar
    Spiral-cut peel of 1 orange
    Spiral-cut peel of 1 lemon
    Nineteen 3-inch cinnamon sticks
  1 whole nutmeg, grated
  5 whole cloves

Combine wine, sugar, citrus peels, 1 cinnamon stick, nutmeg, and cloves in saucepan. Simmer gently for 5 minutes. Strain. Serve hot in mugs with a stick of cinnamon.

The spice packet for this holiday drink and the orange, lemon, and jug of red wine in a basket make an impressive gift brought to a holiday party.

Party Tea Punch

Serves 50
Preparation time: ½ hour

2 quarts boiling water
1 cup loose tea
1 tablespoon whole cloves
  Five 4-inch cinnamon sticks
1 cup lemon juice
1 cup orange juice
1½ cups rum
1½ cups brandy
  Sugar to taste

Bring 2 quarts water to a boil; add tea and spices. Brew for 5 minutes. Strain into large punch bowl; add fruit juices, rum, and brandy. Stir, taste, and stir in sugar. Serve hot or cold.

This is a big-bowl punch, so show it in your best punch bowl. Garnish with slices of clove-studded apples, lemons, or oranges, and surround the base with evergreens and silver balls or magnolia leaves sprayed gold.

Cranberry Champagne Sparkle

Serves 25
Preparation time: 15 minutes
Freezing time: 6 hours or longer

  Rosebuds
  Mint leaves
1 cup sugar
1 quart cranberry juice
1 bottle sauterne, chilled
1 bottle champagne, chilled
1 bottle (1 pint, 12 ounces) ginger ale, chilled

Freeze small rosebuds and mint leaves in water in ice cube trays. Dissolve sugar in cranberry juice and add sauterne. Pour into punch bowl and garnish with rose/mint ice cubes. Set punch bowl in a wreath of green ivy. Add champagne and ginger ale just before serving.

Tuck a few rosebuds among the ivy—red for Christmas, white or pink for springtime parties.

Rum Tea Toddy

Serves 4
Preparation time: 15 minutes

4 cups water
1 teaspoon grated lemon peel
6 whole cloves
5 tea bags or 5 teaspoons tea
  Honey
4 jiggers rum
  Four 3-inch cinnamon sticks
4 slices lemon

Combine water, lemon peel, and cloves in a saucepan. Bring to a boil. Allow to stand 3 minutes. Pour over tea. Brew for 5 minutes, strain, and add honey to taste. Pour into mugs and add rum to each. Garnish with cinnamon sticks and lemon slices.

A plastic bag of the spices, tea, and peel for this drink with a small bottle of rum make a warm-hearted holiday gift. Attach the instructions for brewing this bracing drink.

Spicy Hot Chocolate

Serves 4 to 5
Preparation time: 5 minutes

4 cups milk
  Five 1-ounce squares semisweet chocolate
1 teaspoon vanilla
  Four 4-inch cinnamon sticks
  Rum (optional)

Combine milk, chocolate, and cinnamon in a saucepan. Heat until chocolate melts. Remove from heat and stir in vanilla. Serve in warm mugs. Add rum for a spirited drink

A Mexican chocolate beater (available at specialty food stores) or a set of good-looking mugs and the spices and chocolate for this drink, along with the recipe, look special under a Christmas tree.

New Year's Punch

Serves 30
Preparation time: 40 minutes

    2 cups cranberry juice
    2 cups apple juice
    2 cups orange juice
    1 cup lemon juice
    2 cups light corn syrup
    1 large bottle club soda or champagne
       Sliced orange and lemon
       Sprig of mint

Combine juices and corn syrup, stir and chill thoroughly. When ready to serve, add club soda or champagne. Garnish with fruit slices, or an ice ring containing tiny crab apples and mint leaves.

A silver punch bowl is perfect for this, but if you don't have one use a large white or stainless steel mixing bowl. Wrap it nattily in a folded napkin in a color to accent your table decorations and sprinkle confetti around the base of the bowl.

Cranberry Shrub

Serves 16 to 18
Preparation time: 5 minutes
Chilling time: 20 minutes

    1 pint cranberry juice cocktail
    1 pint grapefruit juice
    1 pint apricot nectar
    1 pint pineapple juice
    1 pint orange sherbert

Mix juices together and chill thoroughly. Serve with spoonfuls of orange sherbert in punch glasses.

This is a favorite punch for teen-age parties or for children. As a time-saver, serve it in plastic glasses, each marked with the child's name in red or green china-marking pencil.

Holiday Egg Nog

Serves 20
Preparation time: 40 minutes

    1 dozen eggs, separated
    1 cup sugar
    1¼ quarts rum
    1 quart milk
    1 pint heavy cream, whipped
       Nutmeg, freshly grated

Beat egg yolks and sugar until light; add rum a little at a time while beating. Add milk. Stir in whipped cream until incorporated. Beat egg whites until stiff and fold in. Pour egg nog into a pretty punch bowl. Sprinkle fresly grated nutmeg on top and place within a wreath of holly.

Your most handsome punch bowl is the only container for this traditional holiday drink, and if you don't have a punch bowl you can rent one from a party goods shop or party rental company.

Mulled Cider

Serves 8
Preparation time: 30 minutes

    2 quarts apple cider
    ½ cup light brown sugar, firmly packed
    4 whole cloves
    4 whole allspice
       One 2- to 3-inch cinnamon stick
    1 tablespoon dried orange peel
       Fresh orange and lemon peel
       Rum (optional)

Heat apple cider; add sugar and stir until dissolved. Tie spices and dried peel in cheesecloth and add to cider. Simmer for 15 minutes. Pour into mugs. Garnish with orange slices or use a tiny cookie cutter and cut animal shapes from orange and lemon rinds. Serve warm.

Note: add jigger of rum to each serving if desired.

A plastic bag of homemade cookies and a small jar of this spiced cider with instructions attached for reheating (in the jar in a pan of hot water) make a charming gift for a singleton. Tie red ribbons around the cider bottle and cookies.

Sparkling Yogurt Drink

Serves 2
Preparation time: 5 minutes

⅔ cup yogurt, plain or flavored
1¼ cups club soda
½ teaspoon salt
    Sprig of mint

Combine yogurt, club soda, and salt. Mix well. Pour over ice and garnish with a sprig of mint.

Give the ingredients for this light drink to the fitness and diet enthusiasts on your gift list, along with the recipe for mixing it. Two handsome glasses make a good accompanying gift.

The cast iron rooster just might unbend a little after he samples some of the Mulled Wine—shown here in a hand-blown glass flask dating from 1840.

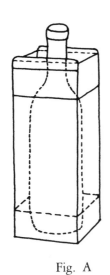

Fig. A

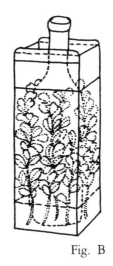

Fig. B

Making Ice Wine Containers

½ gallon paper milk container, washed and dried
Water
Assorted leaves, evergreen sprigs, flowers, ferns, etc.
Empty wine bottle

Open up top of milk carton and pour about 2 inches of water in container. Place an empty wine bottle of the same size as the bottle that you will be serving in center of carton. **Fig. A.** Insert flowers, leaves, etc. (stem ends down) into water around bottle; freeze. **Fig. B.** Fill carton to shoulder of bottle with water and freeze again. **Fig. C.** To remove bottle pour hot water into bottle. **Fig. D.** Tear away carton. **Fig. E.** Insert bottle of wine and place in a dish lined with a pretty white napkin. **Fig. F.**

Note: if serving vodka or gin you may freeze these bottles directly in ice.

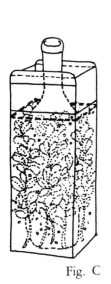

Fig. C

Fig. D

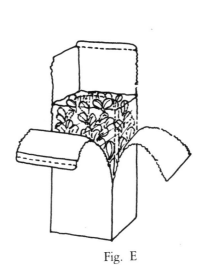

Fig. E

Fig. F

DECORATIONS AND TRIMMINGS

This fragile Dried Flower Wreath will keep for several years if, between seasons, you wrap it in tissue paper and store it away from light and heat.

12

Making your own decorations is a glorious tradition to start. The decorations will be unique—handmade always is! The projects in this chapter are simple and interesting enough for the whole family to share.

Encourage even the youngest children to make one of their own to hang on the tree or to trim a mantel. If you save them, they become part of the family tradition; they act as "memory steps" as the children grow up—"Yes you were, Becky, you were four when you made that wreath. I remember because we were living in Clinton then."

One evening spread the dining table with newspapers or an old, faded tablecloth, put out the materials, and let everybody design his or her own ornament.

When you are working with greens, have good flower clippers or kitchen shears, florists' wire or tape, and other floral design equipment handy. Ask your florist to cut evergreens to different lengths if you don't gather them yourself. For paper, threads, and other novelties, you need a good pair of shears and, for some projects, gummed tape is a help. Each decoration has a list of the materials you need.

When working with glue or other sticky substances, it is a good idea to have a damp sponge on the table to wipe up any spills immediately, or to keep fingers wiped clean.

There are ideas for decorations of all kinds, for the Christmas tree or holiday table and almost every nook indoors, and exciting outdoor decorations for every season. Many of the smaller projects are ideal for decorating packages of homemade goodies, and a gloriously fragrant herbal or pomander wreath is an heirloom gift that will last for years. So get your clippers ready, and don't forget the mistletoe!

Dried Flower Wreath

Preparation time: 1½ hours

Foundation wreath
Dried flowers
No. 28 or 32 gauge wire
Green floral picks
Florist's holding spray or hair spray

Foundation wreath may be of straw wound with nylon thread or green styrofoam. Or make your own of willow branches, honeysuckle vines, or grapevines, wound with wire or florist's tape.

Flowers to use include: lavender, tansy, rose and golden yarrow, feverfew, baby's breath, santolina, mint, hydrangea,

blue and white statice, pink and yellow rose buds.

Tie wire around foundation wreath, forming a loop for hanging. Make small bouquets of flowers and wrap with wire. Insert in foundation wreath or anchor to wreath with floral picks. Distribute colors evenly to achieve a balanced effect. Fill in with single dried flowers to cover flower stems.

When wreath is complete, take outside and spray generously with florist's holding spray or hair spray.

Or make a delicate wreath for a baby's christening with baby's breath; lemon thyme to symbolize courage; chamomile flowers to symbolize patience; and lavender, mint, and statice.

Kissing Ball

Preparation time: 1 hour

> Large, round potato
> 12-inch length of heavy wire (coat
>   hanger wire)
> Pliers
> Ribbon
> Mistletoe
> Awl or knitting needle
> Evergreen sprigs: boxwood, privet,
>   ilex, or pine

Pierce potato through with wire. Bend end of wire with pliers so potato will not slide off. Securely tie six 12-inch lengths of ribbon onto bend of wire, and tie on mistletoe to hang below kissing ball when completed. Bend other end of wire to form loop for hanging. Make holes in potato with awl or knitting needle and insert 4-inch pieces of evergreen until potato is filled and fluffed with greens. Snip ends to form even ball of evergreen. Tie a pretty red bow on top and hang in your entrance-way.

Tin Lanterns

Preparation time: 20 minutes

> Styrofoam cups
> Tin foil or colored foil
> Nail or awl

Wrap foil around cup, draw a simple pattern and punch holes along outline with nail or awl. Insert a small candle. Lovely, delicate lighting for an evening meal.

Rose Hip Wreath

Preparation time: 1 hour

> No. 28 or 32 gauge wire
> Foundation wreath of straw wound
>   with nylon thread
> Rose hips clipped to 3- to 6-inch
>   lengths
> Clippers

Tie wire around foundation wreath, forming a loop for hanging. Snip off thorns from rose hips and insert in straw wreath, working counterclockwise. This makes a dense and compact wreath that will last for several years.

Spice Wreath

Preparation time: ½ hour

> No. 28 or 32 gauge wire
> Foundation wreath of grapevines
> Spices: cardamom pods, peppercorns,
>   bay leaves, cloves, star anise,
>   cinnamon sticks
> White liquid glue

Tie wire around foundation wreath, forming a loop for hanging. Glue small piles of spices to foundation wreath with white glue.

Herbal Wreath

DECORATIONS AND TRIMMINGS

Preparation time: 1½ hours

No. 28 or 32 gauge wire
Foundation wreath of grapevines, honeysuckle, or privet
Dried herbs: rosemary, thyme, oregano, marjoram, savory, bay berries, and chive blossoms

Tie wire around foundation wreath, forming a loop for hanging. Make bundles of herbs and tie around wreath with wire.

Note: a microwave oven can be used for drying herbs. Place herbs on paper towels and put in oven at lowest heat setting for 2 to 3 minutes. Stir herbs and repeat.

Dried Apple Swags

Preparation time: 20 minutes
Soaking time: overnight
Drying time: 4 hours in conventional oven
6 minutes in microwave oven

10 apples: Winesap, Cortland, or other winter apples
6 tablespoons powdered ascorbic acid, or fruit color preservative
2 quarts water
Heavy thread or string

Core and peel 10 apples, slice into ¼- to ½-inch rings. Prepare a solution of 6 tablespoons ascorbic acid in 2 quarts water (or prepare solution of fruit color preservative according to package directions). Soak apple slices in solution overnight, drain. Place on wire mesh in a 250°F oven for 4 hours, turning occasionally. Alternatively, place on paper towels and cook 3 minutes in microwave oven at lowest temperature, rotate, and cook for another 3 minutes. Air-dry overnight. Thread and hang as swags.

Reconstitute apples by soaking in water for 20 minutes or until soft. Good in Fruit Compote (Chapter 5).

Bird Feeders

Preparation time: 45 minutes

Heavy, white cardboard
Waterproof felt-tip markers
One 6-inch wooden dowel (¼-inch width)
No. 28 or 32 gauge wire
¼ cup suet, softened
½ cup bird seed

Cut bird shape out of cardboard and decorate with markers. Cut a hole in center of bird and insert dowel. Insert a wire for hanging. Brush suet on both sides of bird tail or wings and press in bird seed. Neighborhood birds will really appreciate this colorful decoration.

Apple Bobeches

Preparation time: 15 minutes

1 red apple
1 green apple
Juice of 1 lemon
Cloves

Core apples and enlarge holes until apples will fit over a candle. Slice apples ¾ inch thick. Brush both sides with lemon juice or soak in juice for 10 minutes. Decorate with cloves and slide over candles to catch drips—a delightful, fresh centerpiece.

Tiny Cookie Wreath

Preparation time: 10 minutes

Kid's Cookie Dough (Chapter 9) or dried peels of lemons, limes, and oranges
White liquid glue
Small foundation wreath of grapevines

Cut out and bake cookies, using the smallest cookie cutters available. Or cut cookie shapes from dried citrus peels. Glue to foundation wreath.

A Bread Wreath may be used, as shown here, as a decoration, but it makes good eating too! Try using it as part of an edible centerpiece.

132

DECORATIONS AND TRIMMINGS

Pomander Wreath

Preparation time: 2 hours

 6 small, firm oranges
 Cloves
 Knitting needle or nail
 Foundation wreath of green
  styrofoam, 10–12 inches in
  diameter
 3-inch finishing nails

Stud oranges with cloves, puncturing oranges with knitting needle or nail if needed. Draw 6 circles evenly around foundation wreath, and drive 3 nails through each circle. Place oranges on nails and hang in kitchen or dining room.

Path Lights

In Scandinavia candle-lit snow houses light a visitor's way to the door. They're easy and fun to make and children will be more than happy to help.

Build a mound of snow balls 4 feet high, hollow out niches for candles, and pack snow firmly. Use thick candles that will burn for several hours

Candle Tree

Browse through antique shops for the glass jars with wire loops that were used to light Christmas trees before electricity. They can still be found in old milk glass and pretty colors. Old-fashioned canning jars can also be used. Place scented small candles in jars and hang from the branches of a tree. A quaint, Christmasy decoration for winter, and the perfect lighting for a spring party or summer barbecue.

Beeswax Ornaments

Preparation time: 40 minutes

 Beeswax
 Candy molds
 Non-stick compound
 String

Melt beeswax in a double boiler. (Wax is quite flammable and must not be melted over direct heat.) Spray molds with non-stick compound and place a loop of string in each mold. Pour in beeswax and allow to cool and harden, about 20 minutes. Unmold, trim off excess wax, and hang on tree or in windows.

You can also make braided ropes of wax and decorate with tiny ribbons, cloves, and berries.

Bread Wreath

Preparation time: 40 minutes
Rising time: 1½ hours
Baking time: 20 minutes

 French Loaves (Chapter 2)
 Yolk of 1 egg, lightly beaten

After first rising, punch down dough and knead slightly. Cut dough into 3 equal portions and form into ropes about 16 inches long. Braid and shape into a circle, tucking ends under. Place on greased cookie sheet sprinkled with cornmeal and allow to rise for 1 hour. Brush with beaten egg yolk and bake in preheated 350°F oven for 20 minutes until nicely brown. Cool on wire racks.

This gives a country touch to a kitchen window.

Tie on a checked ribbon and make a pretty bow on top.

Candle Centerpieces

Preparation time: 15 minutes

Hollow out green, red, and yellow apples, and pears and quinces. Place a fat candle in each and arrange as a centerpiece. For spring place on lemon leaves. In late summer use huge grape leaves. Evergreens add a seasonal touch for a winter table.

For an amusing summer centerpiece use purple and white turnips, kohlrabi, squashes, or gourds, or carve a squash basket and place several small candles in it.

133

PLAY-CLAY ORNAMENTS

These charming ornaments look like gingerbread, but they're actually made from a durable, inedible dough that can be painted and sprayed with a clear sealer so they'll last for years. The dough clay recipe given here, which can be cut in half, makes about 2 pounds of clay—that's enough for 10 to 15 ornaments, the largest of which is about 3½ x 6 inches. You can make your own patterns by tracing these full-sized pictures, or you can use cookie cutters.

In addition to dough ingredients, you will need: ribbon; paper clips; waxed paper; sculpting tool or orange stick; artist's paintbrush; acrylic paints, poster paints, or watercolors; quick-drying clear plastic spray, clear nail polish, or clear shellac.

To make hangers, straighten a paper clip, leaving a hook on each end. Cut the paper clip in half and you have two ready-made hangers.

Play-Clay

1 cup cornstarch
2 cups (1 pound) baking soda
1½ cups cold water

In medium-sized saucepan, stir together cornstarch and baking soda. Add water all at once and stir until smooth. Stirring constantly, cook over medium heat until mixture reaches consistency of *slightly* dry mashed potatoes. (Mixture will come to a boil, then start to thicken, first in lumps and then in a thick mass; it should hold its shape.) Turn out onto plate, cover with damp cloth, and let cool.

When cool enough to handle, knead thoroughly on cornstarch-dusted surface until smooth and pliable.

If not to be used immediately, store completely cooled clay in tightly closed plastic bag or container with tight-fitting cover. Clay may be kept in cool place up to two weeks. Knead stored clay thoroughly before using.

Forming the Ornaments

1. Working with a small amount of clay at a time, roll it out to ½-inch thickness on waxed paper or on a work surface lightly dusted with cornstarch.
Hint: to keep waxed paper from wrinkling, slightly moisten work surface before laying paper down. Keep remaining clay in tightly closed container.

2. Cut out ornament shapes.

3. Smooth and shape outer edges of each cookie using a sculpting tool or an orange stick from a manicure kit.

4. Press this same tool gently into clay to define certain lines, such as the snowman's legs; the gingerbread house windows, door, and lattice work; the stocking heel and toe.

If you wish, you can add three-dimensional hand-shaped details such as buttons, scarf, and bow-tie for the snowman; a toy bag for Santa Claus; trimming on the star and bell; buttons, scarf, and tassel on the gingerbread man's hat; the angel's book and hands; the reindeer's ear and harness; a base and garland on the Christmas tree.

Hint: to join pieces of clay or add one layer to another, moisten the area of contact on the ornament with a wet paintbrush, then gently press on the detail pieces.

5. Insert a hanger into top center of each ornament.

6. To dry ornaments, place finished pieces, decorated side up, on wire rack or protected surface. Clay will dry and harden at room temperature. When ornament fronts are dry to the touch (several hours or overnight), turn them over and continue drying, turning occasionally.

Hint: if small pieces should come off in drying, let dry completely then glue them back in place with white glue.

To speed-dry ornaments, preheat oven to 350°F. When this temperature is reached, turn oven off. Place clay ornaments on cooling rack or on waxed-paper-covered cookie sheet and put in oven. Let dry in oven until oven is cold, turning occasionally. If necessary, continue drying at room temperature, turning occasionally.

Decorating

1. When ornaments are thoroughly dry, give them an overall coat of paint in a light brown (gingerbread) color using acrylic paints, poster paints, or watercolors. Let this coat dry thoroughly.

2. Paint over gingerbread color with whichever other colors you choose, following the defining lines and details you outlined earlier.

3. For a shiny finish and extra strength, spray completely dry, painted ornaments with 3 to 4 coats of quick-drying clear plastic spray. Allow ornaments to dry thoroughly between coats. Or, you can paint them with clear nail polish or dip them in clear shellac.

THOUGHTFUL GIFTS

Candy the flowers from your garden for a charming gift. Use superfine sugar, or try vanilla sugar for an interesting flavor variation.

13

Here's a potpourri of gifts from your kitchen and garden that, for the most part, require no cooking. Some, like the play-dough bear that hangs from a jar of jelly, or drip-catching collars for a teapot spout, make perfect companion gifts to homemade edibles from other chapters. Others will appeal to the fragrance lover on your list: two old-fashioned potpourris, and citrus pomanders to hang on a chair back or doorknob.

The gourmet cook will appreciate fresh herb plants, or a garlic or bay leaf wreath. Try making the strings of chilis, traditional Christmas decorations in New Mexico kitchens. And anyone will appreciate ''April in December''—spring flowers to brighten up the dreariest winter days. Our chart gives complete forcing instructions for 11 varieties of spring bulbs.

You'll find thoughtful gift ideas in every chapter in this book, but what about combining projects in special gift baskets that you tailor to suit each friend? Here are some ideas to get you started:

For a friend on a diet, give a loaf of bread baked without salt and with a low-cholesterol margarine instead of butter. Add one of the no-sugar fruit spreads in Chapter 5, and a no-caffeine herb tea. A selection of the no-salt herb blends in Chapter 8 will convince your friend that giving up salt does not necessarily mean giving up gourmet cooking. Pack everything in a non-stick fry pan since your friend is probably trying to cut down on fried foods, too.

For a lucky Mom on Mother's day, give a fully-appointed breakfast tray (complete with bud vase and single rose), laden with an assortment of homemade breads, butters, jams, and teas.

And how about a gourmet basket for the man who has everything. Money can't buy delicacies like Kumquat-Spice Tea, Rose Hip Syrup, and Shaker Pumpkin Pickles.

For physical-fitness folks, give an athletic bag jammed with Health Bread, a jar of Sparkling Yogurt Drink, and maybe some Green Apple Squares for quick energy.

If you choose your container with care, you'll have a gift to be enjoyed immediately, and one that will remind the recipient of your thoughtfulness for years to come.

Candied Flowers

Flowers
Small artist's paintbrush
Egg white, slightly beaten
Superfine sugar
Paper towels

The choice of flowers is almost limitless. Just be sure that blossoms are not poisonous. Some possibilities are: early violets—yellow, white, and blue; strawberry blossoms; borage blossoms; periwinkles; small single roses; buttercups; small pansies; and mint leaves.

Pick single blossoms early in the day. Paint with egg white and sprinkle thoroughly with sugar. Allow to dry on paper towels for 3 to 4 days. Package and store each flower separately in its own glass jar. Use to decorate cakes and candies, or float in a punch bowl.

Grapefruit Bird Baskets

1 grapefruit
¾ cup suet, softened
1 cup bird seed
String

This gift is for the birds! It will also be appreciated by bird-loving friends who will lure new species to their backyard feeding stations with this tasty treat.

Slice grapefruit in half and scoop out juice and pulp completely. Make a hole on each side to accommodate a string for hanging. Place in a 275°F oven for 3 to 4 hours until firm and dry, or dry in a microwave oven for 6 minutes at lowest setting. Mix suet with bird seed and generously fill each half. Thread a string through holes and hang outside near a window.

Baskets made from hollowed-out grapefruit and filled with food birds like are a thoughtful gift to neighborhood birds, especially when snow covers the ground and food is hard to find.

Honey Bears

1 cup flour
½ cup salt
2 tablespoons cream of tartar
1 tablespoon oil
1 cup water
Food colors
Raisins

Combine flour, salt, cream of tartar, oil, and water in saucepan. Cook over low heat 2 to 3 minutes, stirring. When cool enough to handle, knead dough until soft and smooth. Divide into portions and knead in food coloring. Mold tiny teddy bears with raisins for eyes, and hang over a honey pot or jelly jar to harden. Store remaining clay in tightly closed tin or plastic bag. A whimsical gift for a bear-loving gourmet. Hang on a jar of homemade jam or jelly.

Tussie Mussies

Fresh or dried herbs
Fresh or dried flowers
Grosgrain ribbon
Perfume

These nosegays were popular in colonial times and were often given as gifts to people making a journey. Different flowers and herbs symbolized different things: rosemary and forget-me-nots for remembrance, violets for loyalty, and marigolds for happiness, for example. Soak ribbon in perfume before tying around bouquets. They will dry and last for years.

Chili Ristras

Brown thread
A button
Fresh ornamental red and green peppers

Cut a piece of thread about a yard long. Tie a button on one end to prevent the peppers from falling off. String peppers on thread and allow enough thread left over to make a loop for hanging. Hang to dry.

Note: peppers contain capsaicin, an irritant to skin and eyes. Work with rubber gloves outside or in a well ventilated place.

Heart Picture Cookie

Kid's Cookie Dough (Chapter 9)
Photograph
Royal Icing (Chapter 3)

Preheat oven to 350°F. Roll out dough ¼-inch thick and cut out a large heart shape. Use small heart cookie cutter or paring knife to cut out inside of heart to fit picture. Bake on ungreased cookie sheet for 8 minutes. Cool on wire racks. Pipe or spread icing on back of cookie and press photograph on top so portrait shows through. Decorate front of cookie with icing. (See "Tip Tips," Chapter 3).

Teapot Cuffs

Heavy paper towels
Felt-tip markers
Hole puncher
White liquid glue

These ruffled collars are popular in Austria and Germany. They come in handy

Garlic Wreath

Dream Bags

catching spout drips.

Fold 1 sheet of paper towel into fourths. Draw scalloped-edge 2-inch circles on towel with marker and punch a hole in the center of each. Cut out circles and cut rays from each center hole so circles will slip over teapot spout. Glue 4 circles together for each collar and decorate with markers. A charming companion gift to a box of herbal tea.

Calico
Needle
Thread
Sweet Dreams Potpourri (recipe in this chapter)
Ribbon

Sew little bags of calico. Stuff with potpourri and tie tightly with ribbon. Place under pillows for sweet dreams.

Gardener's Basket

This is a gift that any good cook will treasure, and use!

Late in October pull garlic bulbs from the soil. Braid stems and leaves and tie ends together to make a wreath. Hang to dry. Wreath should last a year.

Herb Sampler

Bouquet Garni (Chapter 8)
Thread
Gift tags
Wide ribbon
Scissors

Tie gift tags around Bouquets Garni with thread, and label each one for vegetables, for meat, etc.

Sew bundles to a wide ribbon and tie on a small pair of scissors with a long ribbon so the cook can snip off the little bundles when needed.

Fill a rattan harvesting basket with an assortment of fruit, vegetable, and flower seeds. Add a shiny new trowel and a pair of gardening gloves or knee pads.

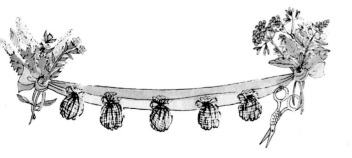

Garden Markers

Styrofoam from meat and produce trays
Waterproof felt-tip markers
Waterproof glue
Garden stakes or small dowels

Cut out flower and vegetable shapes from styrofoam and color with markers. Glue to stakes and use to mark garden rows.

Sachet Hearts

Red Satin
Dry Rose Potpourri (recipe in this chapter)
Needle
Thread
Lace

Cut out hearts from satin. Place right sides together, add lace edging, and sew around heart. Leave a 2-inch opening. Stuff with potpourri, insert a length of ribbon for hanging, and sew opening shut.

Hang on a chair or bedpost, use as a pin cushion, or store in your dresser drawer for an everlasting fragrance.

Potpourri

The basic ingredients of a potpourri are herbs, flowers, spices, essential oils, and a fixative.

Lemon verbena, lavender, and scented geraniums are among the most commonly used herbs and flowers. More easily obtained are rosemary, marjoram, marigolds, pansies, and roses. Spices include cinnamon, cloves, nutmeg, cardamom, and allspice. They should be used ground, and the formula is 1 tablespoon of spice to 4 cups of herbs and flowers. You may also add chopped dried citrus peels.

Essential oils or perfumes can be used to emphasize certain notes in a potpourri. A few drops of your favorite perfume will make the potpourri uniquely yours.

Most mixtures will lose their aromatic potency after drying. By adding a fixative the life of the potpourri is extended immeasurably. Tincture of benzoin, styrax, orris root, or a synthetic called muskene are possible fixatives.

To make a potpourri, combine spices, fixative, and essential oils (if desired). Mix thoroughly with dried herbs and flowers. Allow to cure for 4 to 6 weeks, stirring or shaking occasionally to guarantee a uniformly blended fragrance.

Here are 2 potpourri recipes to try:

Dry Rose Potpourri

3 cups dried rose petals
2 cups dried lavender
1 cup dried lemon verbena
1 tablespoon dried lemon peel
1 tablespoon allspice
1 tablespoon cinnamon
1 tablespoon cloves
1½ tablespoons orris root

Combine lemon peel, allspice, cinnamon, cloves, and orris root. Combine with remaining ingredients. Store in a covered jar and allow to cure for 4 to 6 weeks. Shake frequently.

Sweet Dreams Potpourri

1 cup dried rosemary
1 cup dried lemon verbena
2 cups dried pine needles
Rose or lavender oil or perfume

Crush and mix together rosemary, lemon verbena, and pine needles. Add a drop of lavender or rose oil, or, if oils are unavailable, a drop of perfume.

Recipe Collection

Write your favorite recipes clearly on index cards (you might want to try your hand at calligraphy for the recipe titles) and tie around a plant with a ribbon.

Bay Leaf Wreath

No. 28 or 32 gauge wire
Foundation wreath of straw wound
   with nylon thread
Heavy-duty green thread
Needle
Bay leaves
Ribbon

Wrap wire around foundation wreath and make a loop for hanging. String bay leaves on thread and wrap around wreath, placing leaves carefully. Repeat until wreath is covered. Tie on a glossy red ribbon bow.

Pomanders

Fruits: apples, oranges, lemons, and
   quinces
Whole cloves
Spices
Nail or knitting needle
Ribbon

Stud fruits with cloves (use nail or knitting needle to pierce the tough skins of citrus fruits) and roll in ground spices. Different spices complement different fruits. Try these combinations: apples and cinnamon; oranges and orris root; lemons and cloves; and quinces and allspice. Wrap studded fruits with ribbon and give to scent a closet or kitchen.

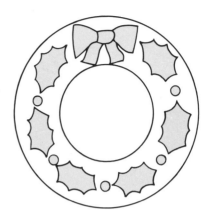

APRIL IN DECEMBER

Forcing spring bulbs for winter blossoms

Spring flowers make perfect winter gifts, and forcing bulbs is not at all difficult if you follow directions carefully. When choosing varieties for forcing, check with your florist or nursery to pick ones that are adaptable. Bulbs may be potted in containers of several different sizes: standard, three-quarter, or half. The pointed tips of the bulbs should show. Bulbs require a medium potting soil to which compost has been added.

A few varieties, hyacinth and paperwhite narcissus for example, can be forced in water as well as soil. Special bowls are available for this purpose. Paper-whites can also be forced in a pebble-filled bowl. Press bulbs into pebbles so that they almost touch each other, and add water to cover pebbles. Add a piece of charcoal to each dish to keep the water clear and delay bacterial formation and growth.

All bulbs need a period of darkness and relatively cool temperatures in order to form root systems. See the chart below for time and temperature requirements. After roots have formed, bulbs should be moved gradually into sunight to develop top growth and flowers. Start bulbs at different times and you'll have fresh flowers all winter long.

Flower	Best planting time	Pot	Weeks to root	Weeks to force	Temperature nights and cloudy days (°F)	Fragrant
Amaryllis	Nov. to Dec.	Standard pot	4 to 6	8 to 12	65 and over	No
Calla-lily, yellow	Nov. to Dec.	Standard pot	4	12 to 14	65 and over	No
Cape lily	September	Standard pot	4	6 to 8	60 to 65	No
Daffodil	October	Half pot or ¾ pot	6 to 8	8	55 to 60	Yes
Freesia	Aug. to Oct.	Half pot or flat	6	12 to 14	50 to 55	Yes
Hyacinth, Dutch	October	Half, ¾, or standard pot	6 to 8	4 to 6	50 to 55	Yes
Hyacinth, French and Roman	Sept. to Oct.	Bowl or half pot	4 to 6	6 to 8	55 to 60	Yes
Iris	September	Half pot	4	6 to 10	55 to 60	No
Lily, Easter	November	Standard pot	6 to 8	8 to 12	60 and over	Yes
Narcissus, paper-white	Oct. to Nov.	Bowl	1 to 4	5 to 10	55 to 60	Yes
Shamrock	Sept. to Oct.	Bowl or half pot	4	8	65 and over	No

COLLECTING NATURAL MATERIALS FOR DRIED BOUQUETS

Nature offers a wealth of materials that can be used to create attractive, dried arrangements and bouquets in winter. However, the collection of such materials is a year-round project. People who wait until late in the season may lose out on many choice items; such materials should be gathered as they become available throughout the year.

Driftwood, for example, can be obtained in all seasons, but the best selection can be found in late spring and early summer after spring thaws and rains have washed the material onto lakeshores and seashores.

Other natural materials that can be collected at various times of the year, include a host of different, intriguing seed pods, foliages, branches of trees and shrubs, cones, nuts, multicolored gourds, colorful flowers, seeds, grasses, small grains, and even lichens, mosses, and fungi.

Many of the grasses are available in mid-summer and should be harvested before they go to seed. Small grains—such as wheat, oats, millet, and barley—should be gathered before their seeds begin to drop in the late summer.

Seed pods of tulip, daylily, peony, and baptisia, among other flowering plants, should be gathered from the flower border while they are still small and green in the summer, or in the early fall when they are fully mature. In the fields and meadows, milkweed, teasel, dockweed, staghorn, sumac, and mullein, among other wildings, produce attractive seed pods. Harvest seed pods at different stages of development to get a nice gradation of color ranging from green to dark brown.

Flowers that will be dried in their natural shape, or pressed flat, must be picked before they are fully mature; otherwise they may shed petals as they dry. Strawflowers should be picked when the center petals are just unfurling. Other flowers that dry well include blue salvia, globe amaranth, tansy, catananche, cockscomb, statice, globe thistle, artemesia, and pearly everlasting. Some common flowers that retain their color and shape well are larkspur, red salvia, marigold, zinnia, ageratum, and the old-fashioned cabbage rose.

Almost any flower can be dried in dry sand, or a mixture of sand and borax, or fine silica gel. In all cases, a 1-inch layer of the granular material is spread out in a box, the flowers are laid on the bed of granular material, and more material is carefully sifted around the flowers until they are covered. The box is then put in a warm place for one to three weeks until all moisture is removed. The granular substance will prevent the flower petals from withering while they are drying. Be sure to use very fine-grained sand, or the petals will look pebbly. Fine white children's play sand, or washed sea sand, works well.

Placing pans of dried flowers in one of the granular materials in a warm 200°F oven for several hours will speed up the drying process. When flowers are dry, they can be very carefully removed, and will be quite natural in shape. In some cases, colors will change. White and yellow flowers hold their color very well. Red and pink flowers tend to fade, as do blue.

Flowers may also be dried quickly in sand in a microwave oven. You will need to experiment, but results can be excellent.

Whether dried flower petals are processed in a granular material, or dried by hanging in a warm, dry room, after the flowers are arranged in a bouquet, it is advisable to spray the arrangement with a clear plastic. A dull, clear spray—available in hardware and paint stores—is the least expensive, although you can even use hair spray, if you wish. The spray not only gives strength to the papery dry petals, but it also prevents them for absorbing water and becoming droopy on humid days.

Seed pods and flowers can be dried naturally by stripping off their leaves, tying them in bundles with rubber bands, and hanging them upside down in a warm, dry, dark, place to prevent fading and loss of color.

Cones of pines, hemlocks, larch, and other evergreens—as well as beech and oak leaves and mosses, lichens, and acorns—can be obtained from the woodlands.

Some of the pine cones will be ready for collection in mid-summer when they usually drop off the trees; these cones should be gathered while their beautiful tan and brown colorings are strong and fresh and not yet spoiled by lying on the ground.

Nuts, such as acorns, horse chestnuts, hazelnuts, beechnuts, walnuts, hickory nuts, and pecans, may also be gathered at various stages of development to have variations in size. Husks of horse chestnuts, Chinese chestnuts, pecans, and hickory nuts can be used effectively in making decorated plaques.

Shapely branches of shrubs and trees, such as the winged euonymus, sweet gum, larch, or thorn apple, can be cut in the late fall when curved or angled branches become more visible after leaves have fallen.

Leaves of many kinds of trees and shrubs should be collected while they are still green or at later stages of development, but don't wait until they drop off the branches. Leaves of palmetto, seagrape, eucalyptus, and mullein can be dried in their natural form. Fern fronds are collected in the late summer before they curl and shrivel. They should be pressed flat between sheets of newspapers weighted with stones and boards.

Decorative gourds should be harvested before the first frost in the fall hits the garden. They should be washed and dipped in household disinfectant before drying them on layers of newspaper in a warm dry place, rotate the gourds often to ensure even drying.

Weekly trips to the garden, fields, and woodlands, as well as vacation trips to more distant areas, will result in a large collection, and an expanded appreciation of nature.

WRAPPING AND PACKING

With this gaily painted sleigh from the 1890s, you're ready to set off on your gift-giving rounds. Directions for making a Scandinavian Delivery Sled are given in this chapter.

⚔ 14 ⚔

When you give a homemade gift it should look as good as it tastes, and it should taste as fresh as if it just came from your kitchen that morning. Of course some edibles are better keepers than others. This chapter will give you a complete rundown on what can be sent by slow boat to China, and what should go no farther than across the street.

When sending gifts to far-flung friends and family, most of us depend, willingly or not, on the U.S. mail. They guarantee to get it there come rain, or snow, or glut of holiday mail, but they don't say in what condition. This chapter will take you through the maze of postal regulations and includes hints for packaging for freshness and protection, like a "vacuum seal" for baked goods and popcorn cushioning for breakables.

For picture-perfect wrapping, step-by-step drawings and instructions are included for making gift bags from salvaged wrapping paper, and tying ribbon bows that will make even the simplest gift look special.

Don't forget the aids to wrapping that make it easy: a good supply of tape, transparent or in pretty colors; a utility knife for cutting cardboard; and a sumptuous supply of yarns, ribbons, tags, and papers.

Preparing Gifts for Mailing

Generally speaking, a gift in transit has three mortal enemies: time, handling, and the elements—heat and moisture. Time is the implacable foe. If the edible you are sending cannot keep fresh for five days, then try sending something else, because it is not worth risking spoilage.

Careful attention to packing will protect your package against damage during handling. Use a firm metal or cardboard container and wadded waxed paper, wadded newspaper, or styrofoam pellets. Some extra precautions for particular gifts are spelled out below. A general rule is the more delicate the gift, the more packing it will require.

Lastly, one must occasionally contend with the elements. Sealing your gift in plastic film, or a self-closing plastic bag, will fend off wetness. Heat, the more

difficult foe, can be countered by placing your gift in a bed of styrofoam beads. Thick layers of flat, un-wadded newspaper are also good insulation. (An easily available substitute for styrofoam beads is popcorn. Just be sure to tell the person who receives the gift that the stale, unsalted popcorn is not for eating.)

Vacuum sealing keeps food fresh because it removes air from around the food and keeps it out. "Homemade" vacuum sealing can be accomplished with thin, but airtight, plastic bags and good lungs. Here's how to do it:

Put food in plastic bag and gather neck of bag in fist. **Fig. A.**

Hold open neck of bag tightly against mouth and suck out air. **Fig. B.**

When bag presses in against food, twist neck opening closed quickly before air can get back in. **Fig. C.**

Double twisted neck back on itself, and tie shut with a twist-tie. **Fig. D.**

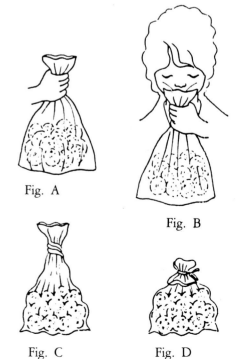

Fig. A

Fig. B

Fig. C

Fig. D

Candies and Comfits

The easiest candies to send are hard candies such as Rainbow Crystals or Salted Oven Pecans, that are not spoilable by time or handling. Moisture may make them sticky, so wrap them in plastic or seal in a waterproof tin with a strip of tape run around the seam between the bottom of the lid and the top of the can.

Most of the other candies fall into two groups—either sticky or soft. Sticky candies, such as Spiced Nuts or Walnut Crunchies, must be carefully sealed in plastic, or individually wrapped in the paper or foil cups sold commercially for candies. Overwrap in waxed paper or plastic film. Soft candies, such as Southern Penuche, Cream Caramels, or Fruit and Nut Divinity, are especially susceptible to handling problems. Wrap individually in plastic as above and pack with styrofoam beads or popcorn.

The only candies that cannot be sent at all are chocolate-dipped candies, which require refrigeration (Chocolate Creams, Chocolate Peanut Butter Buckeyes, and Chocolate-dipped Fruit).

Breads and Muffins

Breads and muffins can go stale in as few as three days. Muffins and yeast breads (Country White Bread, English Muffin Loaves, Favorite Buttermilk Bread, Challah, and French Loaves) simply do not outlast the shipping time and should not be sent. At the other extreme are Coriander Gingerbread, Health Bread, and the aptly named Traveller's Date Nut Bread. These are heavy breads that will not only last well, but will resist crumbling.

Sweet breads such as Berry Cornbread or Spiced Zucchini Bread will not last as well as the harder breads, but can still withstand shipping. All breads can benefit from "homemade" vacuum sealing. To ship, pack carefully with a firm insulation of styrofoam beads or popcorn. There are no special ways of keeping breads from going stale or crumbling. Simply recognize that some types are more vulnerable than others.

Cakes and Pies

Pies cannot be shipped no matter how well packed they are. The same holds true for frosted cakes. Among the unfrosted cakes, however, there are some excellent shippers—especially Brazil Nut Cake, Black Fruitcake, and Pork Cake. Other unfrosted cakes should be shipped much as you would ship breads, and, like breads, the softer the cake the riskier it is to send it. Lastly, if you simply must send the Apple Cider Cake or Breakfast Stollen, leave off their simple toppings and send directions for the toppings with the cake.

Cookies

None of the cookies in Chapter 4 are highly perishable, but some are extremely delicate. The fragile Lace Cookies should probably not be shipped at all. Four of the others require special protection. Cookie Greeting Cards and Crystal Cookies must be stacked with waxed paper between them to prevent them from sticking together. Walnut Speculaas and Teatime Tassies are even more delicate. When stacking them, use paper cupcake liners to prevent crumbling or cracking. All cookies should be sealed in a rigid container and insulated with crumpled waxed paper, or styrofoam beads, or both.

No cookie was ever hurt through cautious packing, but some seem to require less of it. The harder cookies, such as Heart Molasses Cookies, Wine Cookies, or Pfefferneusse, are the strongest. The Cookie Cards, Sign Language Cookies, and Heart Picture Cookie in the other chapters are also excellent for mailing. Other kinds of cookies may crumble more easily, and can be packed with whatever materials best suit each type: cupcake liners, styrofoam, or sheets of paper towels sandwiched between sheets of waxed paper.

Gifts in Jars and Bottles

Jams and jellies, pickles and relishes, vinegars and oils, will not deteriorate as long as the jars or bottles are properly sterilized and tightly sealed with screw tops or corks and paraffin as described in any basic cookbook or "Creative Canning" at the end of Chapter 5. Use strong corrugated cardboard boxes to protect the glass, and use cardboard dividers if sending more than one jar per package.

The U.S. Post Office requires that breakable containers with a capacity of more than four fluid ounces be cushioned with an absorbent material sufficient to take up all the leakage (popcorn or wadded paper towels will absorb moisture) and sealed within a waterproof container (a sealed plastic bag should do). If capacity exceeds thirty-two fluid ounces, two layers of waterproofing must be provided. If you know you will be shipping liquids through the mail, save plastic containers and use these instead of glass ones.

The butters included in Chapter 5 are perishable if not refrigerated and cannot be mailed. Any dressing that contains eggs (such as Thousand Island Dressing) spoils easily and must be refrigerated.

Most of the nogs and toddies in Chapter 11 cannot be shipped since it is illegal to send alcohol through the mail. Non-alcoholic beverages can be sent. Follow the general instructions for sealing and packaging above.

Herbs, Spices, and Teas

These are among the safest gifts to mail. They hold their flavor for up to one year, are obviously unbreakable, and can withstand a reasonable degree of heat and moisture. Vacuum-seal them so that they will keep their fragrance, and enclose in a container that will not leak or become punctured during shipping. Even a thick envelope with a self-closing plastic bag inside will work.

Decorations and Trimmings

The decorations in Chapters 9, 12, and 13 range in mailability from the dangerously fragile Dried Flower Wreath to the sturdy Spice Wreath. Since freshness is not really a concern, the main question is whether the wreath will hold together. The Pomander Wreath is a poor shipper that should probably not be sent. Dried Apple Swags, Chili Ristras, and the Old-fashioned Kissing Ball, are among those that will do fine if packed in cardboard and cushioned with crumpled newspaper.

Other decorations you might consider sending: Beeswax Ornaments (wrap individually in waxed paper and insulate from heat with styrofoam beads or popcorn); Raisin Stockings (pack flat in a box with wadded paper for protection); and Popcorn Cones, Balls, and Cupcakes (wrap securely or vacuum seal in plastic to prevent moisture from entering, and surround with firm insulation to prevent crumbling).

U.S. Postal Regulations

Containers

Cardboard boxes are the most commonly used containers for sending gifts. Even the lightest corrugated cardboard box can securely hold up to 20 pounds. Paperboard containers, such as shoe boxes, can hold up to 10 pounds.

Tubes, used most often for sending posters, are also attractive containers for candies or hard cookies. Use purchased mailing tubes or cardboard tubes from paper towels. Tubes up to 18 inches long may have sides as thin as 1/16-inch. The length of the tube must not exceed ten times the tube's girth.

Manila envelopes will work for gifts weighing under one pound that are less than one-inch thick. Special reinforced envelopes can hold up to five pounds. Envelopes will not protect their contents, so use them only for sending herbs or hard candies.

Wrapping

Wrapping is not allowed on the outside of a package unless it contributes to the proper sealing of the container. Unnecessary markings are also not allowed.

Sealing

For boxes and tubes, use tape to seal the flaps or ends. Pressure-sensitive and reinforced tapes provide the strongest seal. Paper tape, of at least sixty pounds basis weight, is also widely used for sealing, but not for reinforcing the package. See "Sealing Tapes" in this chapter for instructions on how to seal packages using the three most common types of tape. On envelopes, staples or adhesive should be adequate. Note that staples must be covered with tape or the post office will refuse to mail your package.

Addressing and Marking

If you wish to say "fragile" on the container, write it below the postage and above the name of the addressee. All markings, especially the address, should be written in ink that will not dissolve, rub off, or smear. A copy of the address should be placed inside the container in case the outside is defaced.

Private and Express Mail Services

The regulations above apply only to the U.S. Post Office. If you use a private delivery service, ask them about their rules and regulations. Private services are listed under "Delivery Service" in the Yellow Pages. Be sure to weigh your package before you call, as this information will be requested.

If you're determined to send something perishable, or you want to send something overseas, you might consider an express mail service. One such service is available at any local post office. You are guaranteed 24-hour delivery to most parts of the U.S., and 48 hours to many foreign countries. Many private delivery services offer express mail service too, so call around and compare prices. Note that when using private delivery services, the charge will always be lower if you drop your package off at their offices yourself.

SEALING TAPES

How to seal packages using the three most common types of wrapping tape to meet U.S. Government postal regulations

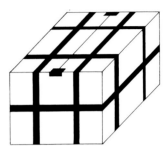

Pressure Sensitive Filament Tape
This tape is composed of filaments imbedded in pressure sensitive adhesive. It is extremely strong and only short "L" or "C" shaped strips are needed to accomplish effective closure. However, closure and reinforcement may be accomplished by complete banding as illustrated. It is important to tape down the ends of the flaps.

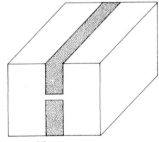

Reinforced Paper Tape
This tape is about three inches wide and is composed of several laminated layers with filaments running both lengthwise and across. It is extremely break resistant and has excellent adhesive qualities. Reinforced tape is preferred over plain paper tape. Equivalent plastic tapes may be used in the same manner.

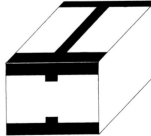

Paper Tape
This is a one-thickness tape available in many widths and strengths. It must be correctly applied, both as to positioning and adhesion, and must be graded in use according to the size, shape, and weight of the package. It is not adequate for heavy packages. Of particular importance is the absolute necessity for fully taping down the ends of the package flaps.

RIBBON BOWS

Copy-Cat Bow

This is a simple, but effective, bow that saves on ribbon, since it uses only 1½ yards.

Cut ribbon in half and form the first loop by folding and creasing the ribbon (right sides together) at the bottom of the first loop. Make sure that the crease is angled to the left or right, so each loop is offset from the previous loop. **Fig. A.** Continue until you have four loops and 1 streamer. Staple ends together. **Fig. B.** Repeat step 1 again with the second half of your ribbon. Glue one of the two sections of ribbon under the edge of the item (flowers, basket, etc.) that you are decorating. Place the second section of ribbon under the opposite edge, splaying off in another direction. Glue in place.

Glue-On Bow

Use 1½ yards of ribbon.

Cut 3 pieces of ribbon 8″ long. Fold ends of one piece to center, gluing wrong sides together. **Fig. C.** Cut the second 8″ piece in half. Fold each length in half to form loops, gluing wrong sides together at ends. With the third 8″ ribbon, fold as illustrated in **Fig. D**, tacking with glue to hold, forming a larger circular loop with a smaller teardrop loop below it. Cut two 12″ pieces from the remaining ribbon for streamers.

To assemble bow, glue the two single loops under the center bow section made in step 1. Glue the piece made in step 3 directly on top, with larger circular loop at top. **Fig. E.** Attach streamers and glue in place on back of bow.

Fig. A

Fig. B

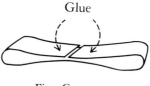

Glue

Fig. C

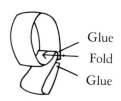

Glue
Fold
Glue

Fig. D

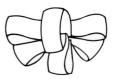

Fig. E

Single Ribbon Loops

Fold the ribbon lengths into loops or puffs. Tie a 6″ length of fine tie wire around base. Twist wire to secure. **Fig. F.** Loops may be wired to picks or stems for added length or may be used flat with no wire to glue under or around an object. **Fig. G.**

Fig. H

Fig. F

Fig. G

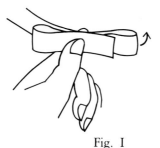

Fig. I

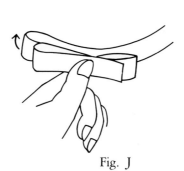

Fig. J

Twisted Bow

Form a small loop with the ribbon and hold with your thumb on top and index finger on the bottom. **Fig. H.** Twist the ribbon so the right side is up and make another loop the same size, opposite the first loop. **Fig. I.** Twist the ribbon again and make a larger loop opposite the second loop. **Fig. J.** Continue twisting the ribbon and making loops. Make sure that each loop is on the opposite side from the previous one and that each layer of loops is progressively larger. Hold all loops firmly between your thumb and index finger. When the bow is of the desired size, wrap a piece of tie wire around the middle and twist tightly to hold loops securely. Separate the loop to the right and left to form a full bow. **Fig. K.** If desired, add streamers. Cut a piece of ribbon twice the length of the finished streamer. Twist the ribbon one *full* turn in the middle and secure at the base of the bow with the same wire. As many streamers as desired may be added.

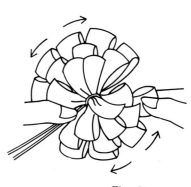

Fig. K

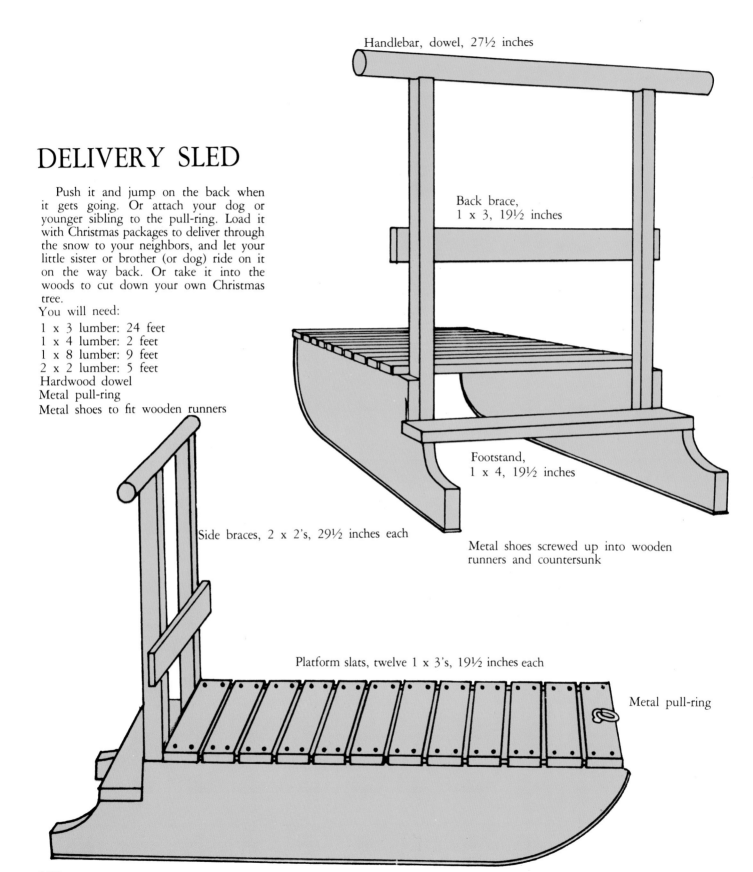

Handlebar, dowel, 27½ inches

Back brace,
1 x 3, 19½ inches

DELIVERY SLED

Push it and jump on the back when it gets going. Or attach your dog or younger sibling to the pull-ring. Load it with Christmas packages to deliver through the snow to your neighbors, and let your little sister or brother (or dog) ride on it on the way back. Or take it into the woods to cut down your own Christmas tree.

You will need:

1 x 3 lumber: 24 feet
1 x 4 lumber: 2 feet
1 x 8 lumber: 9 feet
2 x 2 lumber: 5 feet
Hardwood dowel
Metal pull-ring
Metal shoes to fit wooden runners

Footstand,
1 x 4, 19½ inches

Metal shoes screwed up into wooden runners and countersunk

Side braces, 2 x 2's, 29½ inches each

Platform slats, twelve 1 x 3's, 19½ inches each

Metal pull-ring

Wooden runners, two 1 x 8's, 47¼ inches each

Gift Bags

Center box on wrong side of wrapping paper. Allow 2 inches on each side. **Fig. A.** Wrap paper over box allowing a 2-inch overlap. Glue. **Fig. B.** Turn box so end is facing you. Fold sides in, top and bottom down. Glue. **Fig. C.** Remove box and turn bag right-side up. Fold in 2-inch allowance and glue. Make a hole on each side and string yarn or ribbon through holes for a handle. Knot ends. **Fig. D.**

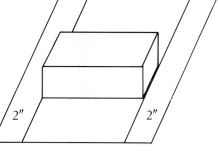

Fig. A

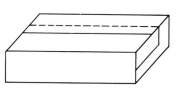

Fig. B

Fig. C

Fig. D

Tags, Labels, and Cards

With these illustrations and a photocopying machine, you can make each gift unique. Enlarge them, reduce them, copy them on plain or colored paper, or gummed labels. Use parchment paper for an antique look, and color them with delicate pastel pencils. Or, for a bolder look, use white paper and felt-tip markers. Back them with cardboard for placecards, and try your hand at calligraphy for the names. Some designs can even be used as placemats if you enlarge them sufficiently. Enlarge and copy others on cardstock for instant postcard party invitations. The sky's the limit. You may never have to visit a card shop to buy gift cards again.

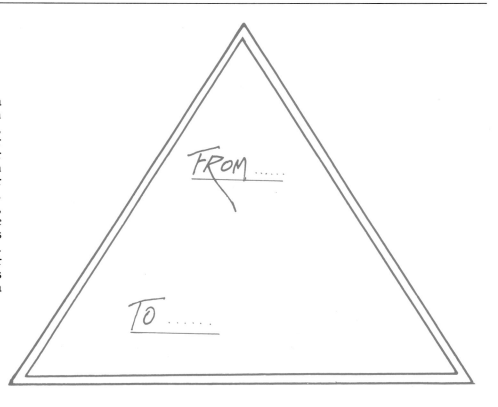

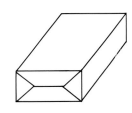

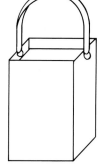

To:

From:

O Fresh from the oven
for
from

To:

From:

From the kitchen of:

From my garden

Thank you

To:

From:

WRAPPING AND PACKING

Merry Christmas

happy holidays!

CONSUMER'S GUIDE TO SELECTING FRESH PRODUCE

Anise . . . an unusual substitute for celery with an anise-like taste • greenish white bulbs and inner stalks may be eaten raw in salads or lightly cooked • highest quality is firm, light, greenish white and not wilted • available periodically with peak season Nov.–Dec.

Apples . . . popular varieties are Red Delicious, Golden Delicious, and Macoun for eating; Cortland, Gravenstein, McIntosh, Granny Smith, Spartan, Red Rome, Puritan, and Northern Spy for both eating and cooking • some varieties available year round and others featured only in the fall • highest quality are fresh, firm, unbruised, and have good color • always wash before eating; apples may be lightly waxed to prevent drying • peeling reduces nutrient and fiber content • are best stored refrigerated • most important nutritionally for fiber.

Apricots . . . available only in June and July • highest quality are plump, juicy looking with golden-orange color; avoid dull, soft, very firm, or greenish fruit • nutritionally important for vitamin A.

Artichokes . . . a thistle-like, prickly plant with strong, deeply cut leaves • available most of the year; peak supply Mar.–May and Oct.–Nov. • highest quality are compact, plump, heavy for size with tightly clinging leaves and good green color • over-mature artichokes are tough and woody and have opening leaves • watch for worm injury near base which may extend deep into the heart • size has no bearing on quality or flavor • nutritionally important for fiber.

Asparagus . . . available Jan.–June • highest quality is firm, unwilted, and has closed tips; stalks should be brittle • rapidly loses flavor and quality with storage, is best eaten right away • nutritionally important for vitamin C and fiber.

Avocados . . . varieties differ in color, size, and pebbling of the skin • available most of the year, peak Apr.–June • highest quality are free from bruises, freezing injury, and discoloration • ripe fruit are slightly elastic when squeezed very gently • underripe fruit mature easily at home at room temperature • use when ripe as flavor, texture, color and nutritional value decline markedly with storage • browning of the cut fruit is retarded by acid (lemon juice, vinegar) and by storing the unused portion with the seed • relatively high in fat, most of which is saturated • very high in potassium and fiber; and moderate in niacin, riboflavin, and vitamin C.

Bananas . . . picked green as mature fruit develop split skin and decay • in ripening the starch is converted to sugar, increasing the sweet taste but not the calorie content • available all year • highest quality are plump, firm, bright in appearance, and free from bruises • high in potassium and very easy to digest.

Beans . . . include green and yellow wax beans • green available all year; yellow wax periodically • highest quality are crisp, unwilted, well colored, free from scars and discoloration, and should break with a snap • nutritionally most important for fiber.

Beets . . . edible portion includes the fresh leaves and the root; both are available periodically • *Roots:* highest quality are smooth, firm, and unshriveled • *Greens:* come from early or new crop beets or from very young plants grown especially for leaf development • best quality are tender, clean, and not ragged, torn, or yellow • moderate source of vitamin A.

Blueberries . . . cultivated blueberries vary in size from ⅛″–1″ and in color from whitish blue to blue-black • the powdery grey "bloom" is due to minute grains of wax produced by the plant • available May–July • highest quality are plump, dry, clean • freedom from moisture is essential for preserving quality • high in fiber, moderate in vitamin C.

Bok Choy . . . elongated cabbage-like vegetable with shiny dark green leaves and snowy white stalks; popular in Oriental cuisine • resembles both Swiss chard and celery • all parts edible; mostly eaten cooked but may be consumed raw • available all year; peak Feb. • moderate source of calcium, vitamin A, and fiber.

Broccoli . . . all portions of the plant are edible, with the leaves and flowers containing the highest amount of nutrients • may be eaten raw or cooked • available fresh nearly all year • peak Mar.–Apr. and Oct.–Nov. • best quality is firm, dark green, or green with purplish cast with compact closed flower clusters • over mature or aged broccoli has spreading bud clusters, open or yellowish flowers • rich source of vitamins A and C, fiber, moderate in riboflavin and calcium.

Brussels Sprouts . . . a form of tall, stemmed cabbage with tiny heads along the stem • peak Sept.–Apr. • highest qualities are hard, compact, and bright green • aged sprouts may be wilted or yellowed • rich in vitamin C and fiber.

Cabbage . . . includes the common green cabbage, the red or purple variety, and Savoy • highest quality are compact, free from wilting or yellowish leaves • Savoy has crinkled leaves, a loose head, and is usually darker green than the common cabbage • available most of the year • keeps well in refrigerator if protected from excess moisture • moderate source of vitamin C and fiber, especially if consumed raw • dark green outer leaves are richest in vitamins and minerals.

Carrots . . . available all year; marketed either fresh or after storage • freshly grown carrots are smaller, more tender, and sweeter than those produced for storage • highest quality are firm, well-formed, and well colored • avoid carrots which are flabby or shriveled • rich in carotene, which is converted to vitamin A in the body; moderate source of fiber.

Cauliflower . . . may be eaten raw, cooked, or pickled • available most of the year; peak Sept.–Nov. • highest quality is white or cream-colored, compact, free from spots or speckles • moderate source of vitamin C and fiber.

Celery . . . although yellow and green types exist, the green type, "Pascal," is most widely sold • highest quality is bright green, firm, and brittle • available all year • may be eaten raw or cooked • both leaves and stalks are edible with the leaves being richer in nutrients • moderate source of fiber.

Cherries . . . Bing is the best known sweet cherry; red tart cherries are mostly sold for processing • available mid-May–July • highest quality are firm, plump, bright, sweet, and juicy, free from bruises or decay.

Chestnuts . . . sweet chestnuts or marrons • brown, smooth, thin-skinned nuts sold after the spiny husk has been removed • may be eaten raw but ususally consumed roasted or boiled • available Oct.–June • provide fiber.

Chives . . . related to onions • long slender green tops are used for seasoning both raw and cooked • mild onion-like flavor • best are from tender young plants, are very slim, deep green, and unbruised • flowers may be used to flavor and color vinegar • available Feb.–Mar. and potted through summer.

Coconut . . . the nut produced by cultivated palm trees, sold with the husk removed • usually has a brown shell covered with coarse fibers; the center is filled with a thin, watery liquid • dense moist white "meat" of the nut is removed from the shell and eaten fresh; liquid may also be consumed • fresh ripe coconuts have firm "eyes" and liquid sloshes inside • fresh coconut is rich in fiber and also very high in saturated fat.

Collards . . . similar to kale in flavor • bright green flat leaves formed on spreading heads • available all year • usually eaten cooked • highest quality are bright, tender, unwilted, free from yellow, damaged, or discolored leaves • rich source of vitamins A and C.

Corn . . . maize or sweet corn • varies in color according to variety from creamy white to deep yellow • usually cooked • available most of year, peak Apr.–Sept. • quality and sweetness are directly related to the length of time between harvesting and eating as the sugar is rapidly converted to starch • provides considerable fiber but may be hard to digest.

Cranberries . . . available Sept.–Dec. • highest quality are firm, plump, rich red in color, dry, and free from soft spots • may be consumed raw as in relish, or cooked • cranberries alone are low in calories but as consumed in juices, relishes, or desserts have considerable amounts of sugar added.

Cucumbers . . . three types are: *Table,* green with white spines; *pickling,* smaller, less tapered than table variety; *greenhouse,* adapted for greenhouse culture under heat • English or European cucumbers are a long seedless variety grown in greenhouses • usually eaten raw with or without the rind, but may be cooked • available all year, peak May–Sept. • highest quality are green, firm and free from puffiness or soft spots; yellowness is a sign of age • fairly perishable and may be lightly waxed to preserve quality.

Dandelions . . . better known as a weed, the tender young central leaves may be eaten raw or cooked, much as spinach • have a pungent, bitter but pleasant flavor • available occasionally • highest quality are from young plants, are tender, have good green color, and still have roots attached to retard wilting; yellow color indicates age • nutritional value best when eaten raw; rich source of vitamin A; moderate in fiber, iron, vitamin C, calcium, thiamine, and riboflavin.

Eggplant . . . or aubergine • small varieties are known as Italian eggplant • "fruit" varies in color from white to deep purple and in shape from round to oblong • should not be eaten raw • available all year; peak season June–July • highest quality are young, slight immature fruits which are firm, glossy, heavy for size, rich in color, and free from scars, bruises, or dark brown spots • moderate source of fiber.

Escarole/Chicory . . . belong to the chicory family • *curly endive* or *chicory* is the variety with deep cut curly leaves held in large, spreading heads • *escarole* has straighter, broader leaves with ruffled edges • *Belgian endive* has an elongate, fairly tightly packed head whose leaves are mostly white, with yellow edges and very little green • all forms may be eaten raw or cooked • highly prized for their distinctive, somewhat bitter flavor • highest quality are young, tender, crisp, and bright green (except Belgian endive) • moderate in fiber.

Grapefruit . . . includes both white and pink fleshed varieties • available all year; peak Jan.–May • highest quality are firm but not hard, well-rounded and heavy for their size • high in vitamin C.

Grapes . . . available all year; peak supplies July–Nov. • color is a good guide to ripeness; darker varieties have no green tinge; light varieties become yellowish • grapes do not ripen after picking. Most popular varieties are: *Thompson,* green, seedless, and the leading table grape, firm, tender and sweet • *Italia Muscat,* green

with a thick skin and heavy sweet flavor; used for wine • *Calmeria,* green-white and elongated with firm pulp and a thick skin • *Perlette,* white and small, firm, juicy, and with a thin skin, seedless • *Emperor,* red-purple, seeded, moderately firm with a thick skin • *Tokay,* brilliant red, seeded, very firm with a thick skin and neutral flavor • *Concord,* purple-blue, round, seeded, tart and highly perishable • *Ribier,* purple-black, seeded, firm with a thick skin and neutral flavor.

Jerusalem Artichoke . . . knobby tuber somewhat resembling a small potato • cooked, it has a bland, mildly artichoke flavor • available occasionally • highest quality are clean, firm, free from shrivelling and decay • moderate source of iron, thiamine, and fiber.

Kale . . . has dark green to blueish, somewhat heavy, very curly leaves • edible portion is the leaf, with coarse stems and ribs removed; leaves are eaten cooked • highest quality is young, and deep blueish-green; avoid yellow, brown, wilted or bruised leaves • rich source of vitamins A and C; moderate in calcium and fiber.

Kiwi Fruit . . . has a light to medium brown "furry" skin with an attractive, pale, greenish pulp and small black seeds; about the size and shape of an egg • allow to ripen at room temperature until fully softened but not mushy • may be eaten peeled and sliced or scooped directly from the skin; seeds are edible • has a tangy flavor which mellows on ripening • contains the enzyme actinidin which prevents gelatin from setting • available periodically.

Leeks . . . resemble an enlarged, coarser version of green onions with a white stalk and heavy green top • are prized in French cooking for their delicate onion flavor • available year round, peak season Sept.–Nov. • edible portions are the white and light yellowish parts of the stalk • highest quality have at least 2"-3" of white stalk and are firm, crisp, unwilted, and without yellow leaves at the top • moderate in fiber.

Lemons . . . available all year, peak Mar.–Sept. • excellent keeping qualities, may be stored 1–5 months • highest quality have fine textured skin and are heavy for their size • slightly greenish lemons are preferable in taste and keeping quality to those which may be deep yellow but old and dry • both lemon juice and lemon peel are moderate in vitamin C.

Lettuce . . . three types are: *head lettuce,* which includes the familiar Iceberg, Butter, Boston, and Bibb varieties • Boston and Butter varieties tend to have very tender leaves and a delicate buttery flavor • with Iceberg, avoid heads which are very hard, lack green color, and have irregular bumps • *Romaine lettuce,* the major variety of this type; recognized by its elongated shape and narrow leaves • *leaf lettuce,* with spreading leaves which are moderately to very curly • most common varities are Salad Bowl with all green leaves, and Red or Ruby, with red-edged leaves • highest quality for all varieties should be moist, tender, unwilted, crisp in the stalk, and have undamaged leaves and bright color • modest source of fiber.

Limes . . . seedless citrus fruit with deep green outer rind and green flesh • Key limes are a smaller, more acidic variety • available all year with peak season June–Aug. • highest quality have glossy green skins and are heavy for their size; avoid those with yellow, brown, dull, or dry skins indicating age.

Mangos . . . oval and may be 4"-10" in length and weigh up to a pound • often deep green in color when mature, but may also be rich yellow to red • edible portion is the deep orange flesh surrounding the large central white seed coat • its flavor is somewhat like a tangy peach • highest quality mangos have smooth outer skin, and are free from bruises or discoloration • allow to ripen fully before eating • peak season is May–Aug. • rich source of vitamin A, moderate in vitamin C and fiber.

Melons . . . *Cantaloupe,* also know as muskmelon due to its aroma when ripe • has rough or netted skin • available Feb.–Oct. • highest quality are sweet, juicy, finely textured, at least 5" in diameter, and free from bruises or cracks • melons picked at maturity are well netted and have rounded depressed scar at the stem end where the fruit has come off the stem smoothly • may require ripening at room temperature • avoid eating cantaloupe too soon; allow it to take on a yellow background appearance, acquire an aroma, and soften • rich source of vitamins A and C • *Honeydew,* has a smooth creamy outer

color, waxy feel, and pale green flesh • available Feb.–Nov. • highest quality are sweet, juicy, and finely textured • look for ripe fruit, indicated by cream to yellow rind and pleasant fruity aroma • moderate source of vitamin C • *Watermelon,* has a green outer rind which varies from dark green to light green, with green or white stripes or a light green mottled appearance • the flesh is pink to red in color and very watery • available Feb.–Nov. • highest quality has firm texture and bright color; mature melon has velvety bloom, dull surface, and yellow underside.

Mushrooms . . . different varieties are white, golden, and brown in color • abundant all year owing to domestic cultivation • washed mushrooms may be eaten raw • cap and stalk are edible, with caps considered to be a delicacy • highest quality are free from blemishes, firm, with short stems and unopened veil at the base of the cap • mushrooms with spots or slight darkening or exposed gills may still be fresh and safe, but will not keep well • moderate source of riboflavin and fiber.

Mustard Greens . . . usually eaten cooked • highest quality are fresh, tender, rich green in color, and may have a bronze tint; avoid wilted or yellow greens • rich source of vitamin A; moderate in calcium and vitamin C.

Napa . . . variety of cabbage with elongated compact head and broad, large, light green crinkled leaves • eaten raw or cooked; more tender than common cabbage • available all year; peak Feb.

Nectarines . . . smooth skinned genetic variant of the peach • vary in color from amber-yellow to deep purplish red with yellow • peak June–Aug. • highest quality are plump, rich in color, and have a slight softening along the seam • hard fruits may require 2-3 days ripening at room temperature in order to develop peak quality • rich in potassium, moderate source of Vitamins A and C.

Okra . . . or gumbo • long, slender, yellowish green pods with lengthwise ribs • commonly used in soups, "gumbos," or "creoles" • remains firm if batter-fried; becomes slippery and soft if steamed or boiled • available all year, peak June–Aug. • highest quality pods are tender, fairly uniform in shape, and free from discoloration • moderate in fiber.

Onions . . . dry onions are harvested as mature bulbs; green onions or scallions are pulled before a large bulb has formed • available all year • dry onions are usually "cured" or dried prior to marketing to prevent plant disease • adequate ventilation is critical for optimum storage of dry onions • highest quality onions are hard, dry, and have small necks; avoid those with blemishes, sprouts, or woody centers; quality is unrelated to size. Common varieties are: *Yellow,* pungent, generally globe-shaped, hard, store well • *Spanish,* mild, large, round, medium firm flesh, dark yellow skin • *Red,* mild to pungent, red skin with red and white flesh • *White boilers,* mild, small, round, white • *Green onions/Scallions,* mildly pungent, no bulb, white stalk with long green tops, both parts edible.

Oranges . . . early Florida varieties may ripen before the rind turns orange so ethylene is used to "de-green" the orange • some oranges may be lightly waxed • highest quality are firm, heavy for size, have fairly finely textured skin, and are free from decay or soft spots; some varieties may be "russeted," i.e., have a brownish net on the rind; this does not affect quality or flavor • rich in vitamin C, modest in thiamine. Major varieties are: *Navel,* seedless, with rather coarse flesh, easy to peel and readily divided into segments; easily recognized by presence of umbilicus or "navel" at flower end; most widely available Nov.–June • *Valencia,* or juice oranges, generally medium to large, round, have a smooth skin, are seeded and heavy for their size, and have a medium grained flesh; available Apr.–Nov. • *Temple,* believed to be a hybrid of the tangerine and sweet orange; deep orange-red color, easy to peel and segment, has some seeds and a thin leathery rind; juicy and sweet.

Papayas . . . pear-shaped with greenish yellow skin, rich orange flesh, and many small black seeds • papayas are the source of the enzyme papain, which is used to tenderize meat • most often eaten with seeds removed • milk sweet flavor • available all year, peak Apr.–July • highest quality are smooth, at least half yellow, and free from bruises • may be ripened at room temperature • high in vitamin C, moderate in vitamin A and fiber.

Parsnips . . . edible portion is the pale

yellow tap root resembling a carrot but thicker at the crown • flavor is mild, sweet, and nutty • available all year, peak Sept.–May • highest quality are smooth, firm, well-shaped, and small to medium in size • high in fiber.

Peaches . . . vary in color from pale yellow to deep yellow with extensive red blush; flesh may vary from pale cream to deep yellow • varieties may be freestone or cling depending on how readily the flesh parts from the stone • available May–Oct. • highest quality are bright, firm, neither hard nor soft, and free from bruises • if too green or hard, peaches will not ripen well • moderate source of vitamin A and fiber.

Pears . . . pears do not successfully ripen on the tree and are picked when green; carefully controlled storage conditions permit gradual ripening and the availability of fresh fruit long past harvest season • ripen at room temperature away from direct heat • different varieties available most of the year • highest quality have well developed color, are firm but not hard, should yield to gentle pressure at the stem end, and have finely textured flesh • skins are edible in most varieties, but are peeled in cactus and prickly. Major varieties are: *Anjou,* main winter pear; oval to globular shape with yellowish green skin occasionally having russet or red shading; flesh is yellowish-white, fairly fine, buttery, juicy, and sweet • *Bartlett,* most widely produced variety; bell-shaped with thin skin, yellow when ripe, may be blushed; other varieties are red; texture fine and free of grit; sweet and juicy • *Bosc,* second most common winter pear; unique shape and color having long neck and cinnamon color; yellowish flesh, juicy and flavorful • *Comice,* large, plump, bell-shaped fruit; greenish yellow, often blushed, other varieties may be red; very fine flesh, sweet and very juicy; regarded by many as the standard of dessert quality • *Seckel,* small fruit with brownish yellow skin frequently blushed with red; flesh somewhat granular; prized for its sweet, spicy flavor and juiciness.

Peas . . . *Green,* sold fresh in pods • edible part is the seed, which is noted for its sweetness and delicacy • best eaten as soon after harvest as possible as the sugar content is rapidly converted to starch • must be refrigerated to retain sugar • available occasionally • highest quality are young, fresh, with bright green velvety pods; immature pods are flat; yellowish appearance indicates age or damage • rich in fiber; moderate in thiamine, niacin, and vitamin C • *Snow or sugar snap,* specially developed variety with small seeds and edible pods; usually sold with stems attached • prized for their sweetness and delicate flavor • available occasionally • highest quality are young, tender, with bright green flat pods, free from wilting and yellowing.

Peppers . . . two main types are: *sweet,* which may be large and square shape or long and tapered; vary in color from bright green to deep red or red and green, others are yellow • *hot or chili,* which are generally elongated and small and may be green or red • both available all year, peak May–Sept. • highest quality are plump, firm crisp, unwrinkled, and free from spots or blemishes • green peppers are rich in vitamin C; mature red peppers are a modest source of vitamin A • hot chili peppers are rich in vitamins A and C.

Persimmons . . . vary from plum to tomato or heart-shaped, and in color from yellow to orange-red • for best flavor, allow to fully ripen until soft as jelly to touch; if underripe, will be tart • ripening may be hastened by storing in an unventilated plastic bag with a ripe apple • rich source of vitamin A and fiber; moderate in vitamin C.

Pineapples . . . available all year • do not sweeten after harvest, but lose their acidity and become softer and more yellow • highest quality are plump with fresh deep green crown leaves and pleasing fragrance • ease of leaf pulling and "thump testing" are of no value in determining quality • avoid fruit with bruises or soft spots, and those with dried, withered leaves.

Plantain . . . closely related to and resembles a banana, but longer and thicker, with coarse rough blemished skin • may be green, pink, red, or blackish brown in color with cream to yellowish flesh • fruit is starchy and used cooked as a vegetable • available occasionally.

Plums . . . different varities are yellow, red to purple-black, and green in color and round to oval in shape • available May–Aug. • highest quality are firm, not hard or soft, and free from breaks or discoloration. Major types by color are: *Red,* including La Roda, Queen Rosa, Queen Ann, Fire Queen, Late Santa Rosa, Frontier, Simca Rose; red to purple skin, yellow to red flesh; very juicy • *Black/purple,* including Italian prune, Nubiana, Fresno Black, Zona Black, Friar, El Dorado; deep red/purple to black skin, whitish yellow to amber flesh; less juicy • *Green,* including Kelsey, Wickson; greenish to yellow skin with yellow to whitish yellow flesh; juicy.

Pomegranates . . . a curious fruit consisting of many bright red, seeded kernels embedded in a pithy inedible center and covered by a brownish-red rind • kernels have a tangy, pleasantly acid taste • usually eaten raw • available Oct.–Dec. • highest quality are heavy for size with fresh, not dried-out appearance.

Potatoes . . . *White,* varieties differ in size, shape, skin, texture, and suitability for various cooking methods • available year round • "new potatoes" are newly harvested potatoes of any variety sold without prior storage; available May–Sept. • store in cool, dark, well ventilated place; do not refrigerate • some varieties darken after cooking; dark areas are harmless and may be prevented by serving immediately after cooking • highest quality are firm, well shaped, relatively smooth, and free from black spots, cracks, decay, and sprout; size does not affect quality • avoid greenish potatoes which have been overexposed to sun and may taste bitter; peel any green areas • rich in potassium, moderate in vitamin C, thiamine, and niacin; skins are an excellent source of fiber. General categories are: *Round White,* creamy buff color, smooth skin, very firm texture • *Long White,* elongated with light brown smooth shiny skins; very firm texture • *Round Red,* reddish skins with some netting; firm and white inside • *Russet,* long and cylindrical with heavily netted brown skins; white mealy texture • *Sweet,* not botanically related to white potatoes • may be white or yellow to deep orange in color and are typically sweet in taste • two types are dry and moist; dry are firm with light tan skin and usually light yellow to orange when cooked; moist have tan-brownish red skins and are deep orange and soft when cooked • the term "yam" frequently refers to the moist variety of sweet potato which is soft when cooked and orange in color; the true "yam" belongs to a different botanical genus • available Sept.–Feb. • highest quality are clean, firm, thick, medium-sized, and free from shrivelling, soft or wet spots • fairly perishable and should be stored at room temperature only for short periods • orange sweet potatoes are a very rich source of vitamin A, modest in vitamin C and fiber.

Pumpkins . . . generally round and deep orange in color • famed use is pumpkin pie and as Halloween jack-o-lanterns • primarily sold Oct.–Nov. • rich in vitamin A and fiber.

Quince . . . hard, greenish-yellow apple-like fruit; round or oblong in shape with a woolly surface • edible only after long cooking; used mainly for jams and jellies • available in the fall • rich in pectin, a digestible form of fiber.

Radish . . . valued for its pungent flavor and deep pink-red color • edible portion is commonly the root, but tops are edible and prized in other cultures • roots vary in shape from round to cylindrical and common varieties white through pink and red • available all year, peak Mar.–May • highest quality are firm, well colored, and crisp; large roots may have pithy centers. Varieties are: *Red,* round to cylindrical; popular salad variety • *White,* may be globular but often have narrow tapering roots like a carrot; somewhat milder than red • *Horseradish,* white variety noted for its pungency and used as a prepared condiment • *Daikon,* or Japanese radish; large, white tapered 8″-10″ long, somewhat hotter than red radish; frequently pickled.

Rapini . . . leaves and stems resemble broccoli • usually eaten cooked • available Dec.–Oct. • highest quality are rich green, tender, and free from wilting, yellow or brown leaves.

Raspberries . . . juicy, many seeded fruit prized for its distinctive flavor and rich color • highly perishable when fresh; enjoy immediately • available primarily in July • moderate in vitamin C and rich in fiber.

Rhubarb . . . characterized by a sharp sour taste • edible portion is the red-green leaf-stalk; the leaves are poisonous owing to their high concentration of oxalic acid • available Feb.–June • highest quality is firm, crisp, tender, red or pink, and unwilted; leaf appearance indicates freshness; avoid wilted flabby stalk • field grown rhubarb is rich dark red and usually sold with leaves; hothouse rhubarb is light pink, milder, and usually sold trimmed.

Shallots . . . often confused with green onions or scallions • bulbs closely resemble small garlic bulbs except that they have brown skins • bulbs consist of cloves but unlike garlic, each clove is not encased in a membrane • edible part includes the green leaves and the white elongated bulb; cured bulbs are the most common form available • milder and more aromatic than onion • peak season is Nov.–Apr.

Spinach . . . varieties may have deeply crinkled or rather smooth leaves; all are deep green in color • leaves are eaten raw and cooked • stems are edible but may be tough • available all year • highest quality leaves are well developed, deep green, unwilted and free from wet spots • rich source of vitamin A; moderate in iron and vitamin C.

Sprouts . . . the tender early shoots of a variety of seeds and legumes • most commonly, sprouts derive from mung beans (bean sprouts), alfalfa and radish seeds • usually eaten raw but may be cooked • available all year • sprouts are nutritionally important only when consumed in large amounts, e.g. 1 cup or more • small amounts provide fiber.

Squash . . . *Summer squash,* utilized when immature, have soft rind and seeds, white flesh, with all parts edible; may be roasted • available all year, peak June–Sept. • highest quality are shiny, firm, well colored, free from injury and bruises, and have tender rind and seeds; smaller sizes are more tender and delicately flavored. Major varieties are: *Crookneck,* generally bright yellow with pebbled or smooth surface and curved neck; most tender are 4″-6″ long • *Straightneck,* lemon yellow, smooth or lightly pebbled, and cylindrical or club shaped; most tender are 5″-6″ long • *Zucchini,* also called cocozelle or courgette; dark green or green and white striped, 5″-8″ long and straight or club shaped • *Winter squash,* utilized when ripe or mature, have hard inedible rind, and usually orange flesh • available all year; peak supply Sept.–Nov. • highest quality winter squash are heavy for size, have hard, dull, intact rinds • when sold, cut up flesh should be firm and deep orange • rich source of vitamin A and fiber; acorn squash is modest in vitamin C. Major varieties are: *Acorn,* or Iowa squash, oval, acorn shaped squash with pointed end; dark green rind and small amount of yellow-orange skin when mature; excess orange on the rind may indicate stringy texture • *Banana,* long, cylindrical, with pointed ends; smooth thick hard gray to pinkish rind; dry, fine, deep orange flesh • *Buttercup,* turban shaped squash with dark green rind with lighter stripes or flecks; flesh is golden yellow, fine, dry, and sweet • *Butternut,* thick neck and bulbous end; tan colored skin should be free of greenish color; flesh is deep orange and fine • *Chayote,* pear sized squash with green spiny rind and single seed which may be sprouted • *Hubbard,* mixed group of large squashes with hard rinds which may be yellow, green, or grayish-blue, and may be pebbled; generally round in the middle with tapered ends and orange flesh • *Spaghetti,* yellow rind with pale cream colored flesh which separates into spaghetti-like strands • *Turban,* distinctively shaped squash characterized by enlarged "cap" at the stem end; rind may be any color from grey to green to orange; flesh is golden yellow and fine, dry, and sweet.

Strawberries . . . available Jan.–Nov., peak Apr.–July • highest quality are firm, bright, solid red in color with very little white or green, have caps attached, and are free from bruises and mold • highly perishable and must be kept cold and humid; store unwashed with caps on to preserve freshness • high in vitamin C.

Swiss Chard . . . both leaves and leaf stems are eaten; leaves are used like spinach and stems like asparagus or celery • stems may be white or deep pink • seasonally available May–Oct. • highest quality leaves are fresh, crisp, free from yellowing, and of rich green color • rich source of vitamin A.

Tangelos . . . hybrids derived by crossing tangerines with grapefruit or pomelo, hence the name • thin orange rind with aromatic, juicy segments; sweet and much less acidic than grapefruit • seasonally available Oct.–Jan. • quality judged as for oranges • moderate in vitamin C.

Tangerines . . . one of the three major groups of mandarin oranges • resemble oranges but have puffy appearance; deep orange rind which peels easily • available Nov.–Apr. • highest quality are heavy for size, deep orange colored and free from

APPENDIX

soft spots • moderate in vitamin C.

Tomatoes . . . varieties differ chiefly in size, shape, and color • mature red "fruits" are eaten raw and cooked; immature green tomatoes may be cooked or pickled • harvested at the mature green or pink stage ("vine-ripened") in order to withstand transport, and are ripened at the point of market distribution • tomatoes raised in greenhouses are more likely to be picked at a later stage of development and usually have small stems attached • year round demand and transport needs have resulted in tomatoes with firmer skins • premium flavored tomatoes are available only at local harvest • highest quality are plump, firm, juicy, free from blemishes, and have good color • moderate source of vitamins A and C; rich in potassium.

Turnips/Rutabagas/Greens . . . turnips differ from rutabagas commercially but not botanically; turnips have white flesh and may have purple tops, and the plants have hairy, thin leaves; rutabagas have yellow flesh and bluish, thick fleshy leaves • available all year, peak Sept.–Mar. • edible portions are the root and leaves (turnip greens) • highest quality roots are smooth, firm, heavy for size, and are free from shrivelling • turnips may be waxed to preserve freshness • greens should be tender, unwilted, moist, and free from yellow leaves • roots have modest amounts of vitamin C and fiber; greens are a rich source of vitamins A and C; moderate in riboflavin, calcium, and fiber.

Watercress . . . succulent leafy plant that thrives in running water; sold for its leaves and stems • enjoyed for its mild pungency in salads, sandwiches, and soups and as a garnish • highest quality is bright green, unwilted, free from yellow leaves, and has crisp stems • generally available all year.

CONVERSION CHART

Oven temperatures

Fahrenheit	Gas mark	Centigrade	Heat of oven
225	¼	110	very cool
250	½	120–130	very cool
275	1	140	cool
300	2	150	cool
325	3	160–170	moderate
350	4	180	moderate
375	5	190	fairly hot
400	6	200	fairly hot
425	7	220	hot
450	8	230	very hot
475	9	240	very hot

Solids

Ounces	Pounds	Grams	Kilos
1		28 -	
2		56	
3½		100	
4	¼	112	
5		140	
6		168	
8	½	225	
9		250	¼
12	¾	340	
16	1	450	
18		500	½
20	1¼	560	
24	1½	675	
27		750	¾
28	1¾	780	
32	2	900	
36	2¼	1000	1
40	2½	1100	
48	3	1350	
54		1500	1½
64	4	1800	
72	4½	2000	2
80	5	2250	2¼
90		2500	2½
100	6	2800	2¾

Liquids

Fluid ounces	U.S. measures	British measures	Milli-litres	Handy metric measures
	1 tsp	1 tsp	5	
¼	2 tsp	1 dessert-spoon	7	
½	1 tbs	1 tbs	15	
1	2 tbs	2 tbs	28	¼ dl
2	¼ cup	4 tbs	56	½ dl
4	½ cup or ¼ pint		110	1 dl
5		¼ pint or 1 gill	140	1½ dl
6	¾ cup		170	1¾ dl
8	1 cup or ½ pint		225	2¼ dl
9			250	¼ litre
10	1¼ cups	½ pint	280	2¾ dl
12	1½ cups or ¾ pint		340	3½ dl
15		¾ pint	420	4¼ dl
16	2 cups or 1 pint		450	4½ dl
18	2¼ cups		500	½ litre
20	2½ cups	1 pint	560	5½ dl
24	3 cups or 1½ pints		675	
25		1¼ pints	700	7 dl
27	3½ cups		750	¾ litre
30	3¾ cups	1½ pints	840	8½ dl
32	4 cups or 2 pints or 1 quart		900	9 dl
35		1¾ pints	980	
36	4½ cups		1000	1 litre
40	5 cups or 2½ pints	2 pints or 1 quart	1120	
48	6 cups or 3 pints		1350	
50		2½ pints	1400	
60	7½ cups	3 pints	1680	
64	8 cups or 4 pints or 2 quarts		1800	
72	9 cups		2000	2 litres
80	10 cups or 5 pints	4 pints	2250	2¼ litres
96	12 cups or 3 quarts		2700	
100		5 pints	2800	

Butter, margarine, and solid shortening

Ounces	U.S. measures	Metric measures
½ ounce	1 tablespoon	15 grams
1 ounce	2 tablespoons	30 grams
2 ounces	4 tablespoons	60 grams
4 ounces	8 tablespoons (½ cup or 1 stick)	115 grams
8 ounces	16 tablespoons (1 cup or 2 sticks)	225 grams
16 ounces (1 lb.)	32 tablespoons (2 cups or 4 sticks)	450 grams

Flour

Ounces	U.S. measures	Metric measures
¼ ounce	1 tablespoon	8.75 grams
1¼ ounces	¼ cup (4 tablespoons)	35 grams
2½ ounces	½ cup	70 grams
5 ounces	1 cup	140 grams
16 ounces (1 lb.)	3½ cups	490 grams

Sugar

Ounces	U.S. measures	Metric measures
⅙ ounce	1 teaspoon	5 grams
½ ounce	1 tablespoon	15 grams
1¾ ounces	¼ cup (4 tablespoons)	60 grams
3½ ounces	½ cup	100 grams
6¾ ounces	1 cup	200 grams
16 ounces (1 lb.)	2⅓ cups	480 grams

Syrup temperatures (for candies, jams, and jellies)

Fahrenheit	Centigrade	Stage
220	108	jellying point for jams and jellies
234–240	112–115	soft-ball stage for candies
244–248	118–120	firm-ball stage for candies
250–265	121–130	hard-ball stage for candies
270–290	132–143	soft-crack stage for candies
300–310	149–154	hard-crack stage for candies

Index

INDEX